UNSOLVED MURDERS

Thanks for help and encouragement to: David Evans, Martin Godleman, James Marriott, Jenny Martin, Richard Parry, Kerri Sharp.

UNSOLVED MURDERS

Russell Gould

Virgin

First published in 2001 by

Virgin Publishing Ltd
Thames Wharf Studios
Rainville Road
London W6 9HA

Look for our other true crime titles at *www.virginbooks.com*

ISBN 0 7535 0478 2

Typeset by TW Typesetting, Plymouth, Devon

Printed and bound by Mackays of Chatham PLC

Contents

Introduction

The murders in this book include some of the most notorious unsolved cases – crimes that took place mainly in the United Kingdom and the USA during the latter part of the last century. The crimes fit into certain categories of murder, including murder for apparently political reasons (Hilda Murrell, Karen Silkwood, Mary Meyer), assassination of celebrities (Tupac Shakur & Biggie Smalls), serial killings (the Zodiac killer, Bible John), the murder of a police officer during the course of his duties (PC Keith Blakelock), and the mysterious death of a British national in a foreign country (Helen Smith). Then there are the murders that captured the public imagination because of the particular horror evoked by the murder of a child; in the case of Caroline Dickinson there was the added mystery of how this young girl had been raped and murdered in the same room as her sleeping school friends without them being woken up. The JonBenét Ramsey murder has generated as many if not more column inches and hours of mainly speculative television time in the United States than the murder of Nicole Brown and the resultant arrest and trial of OJ Simpson.

The majority of the cases in this book took place in either the United Kingdom or the USA. Available statistics show that USA's murder rate (6.8 homicides per 100,000 population in 1997) is approximately four times that of the UK's (1.4 homicides per 100,000 population in 1996).

The availability of firearms as well as the activities of organised crime and urban gangs are factors in the large numbers of murders in the USA.

Between the earliest case in this book – the murder of Elizabeth Short in 1946 – and the present day, there have been highly sophisticated developments in the means of crime detection. Fingerprint records have been computerised and databases built up that are accessible to police forces worldwide. During the past decade the rise of street crime in cities in the USA and Europe has resulted in the proliferation of surveillance cameras which have given investigators valuable sources of evidence. However, the major breakthrough in crime solving in recent years has been the increasing sophistication of DNA analysis. Before testing for DNA was possible, forensic scientists would analyse blood or semen left at the scene of a crime in order to determine the blood group of the murderer or rapist. The reading of DNA coding – so-called 'genetic fingerprinting' – was first used in criminal investigations in the 1980s, although the structure of DNA was first discovered in 1952.

Human cells contain chromosomes, within which is found DNA – deoxyribonucleic acid. DNA consists of chains of four different substances: adenine, thymine, cytosine and guanine. These chemicals are arranged in a string of DNA in a pattern that is unique to one person – identical twins, however, share the same DNA. The same pattern of DNA is found in cells from every part of a person's body. DNA evidence at the scene of a crime may be taken from tiny samples of saliva, blood, semen or other body fluid. Small particles of skin or hair, if discovered, may also be analysed to provide a 'genetic fingerprint' of a suspect. DNA can be used both to eliminate potential suspects (as in the Caroline Dickinson case) and to provide evidence of guilt.

There have been recent developments in the use of DNA evidence to solve crime. Using new forensic and computer techniques, scientists are now able to 'read' DNA from tiny particles of blood, skin, dandruff or even the smallest traces of perspiration, for example by a finger brushing a surface – even if no fingerprint has been left behind. It is estimated that this advanced method of DNA analysis will make the results even more accurate. Previous tests can identify DNA as belonging to one individual in 50 million; the new test increases that figure to one in one billion (one million million). Where evidence has been preserved, police will be able to reopen cases and re-examine forensic material – this has been reported to be in progress in the cases of Keith Blakelock, Rachel Nickell and Hilda Murrell. In the Bible John case, hopes were raised that DNA testing would solve the mystery when suspect John McInne's body was exhumed in 1996 – but inconclusive results meant that those murders remain unsolved.

In the UK and the USA there are national computer databases in which the details of the DNA of persons convicted of serious crimes are logged. The UK's national DNA database holds over 300,000 profiles and an additional 27,000 analyses of DNA found at the scene of crimes that have not been solved. It is hoped that as further profiles are added, some will match those of the unsolved crimes. In the United States there is a network of DNA profiles known as CODIS (the Combined DNA Index System), in which the genetic records of offenders convicted of serious crimes such as murder, rape and child molestation are kept. As DNA databases grow and scientists become able to identify DNA from the most minute samples of evidence, it is hoped that many hitherto unsolved crimes, including some of the murders I describe in this book, will be solved, and those responsible will be convicted.

Russell Gould
September 2000

1 Elizabeth Short – 'The Black Dahlia'

Elizabeth Short – a child of the Depression

Elizabeth Short was born on 29 July 1923 in the Hyde Park area of Boston. Her father, Cleo Alvin Short, who had formerly been the owner of a garage business, was now earning a living designing and installing miniature golf courses. Her mother, Phoebe, had given birth to two children before Elizabeth was born, and was to have two further children with Cleo – all were girls.

By the end of the 1920s the family had moved to Medford, Massachusetts, and the golf-course business had been flourishing, but the Depression and the Wall Street crash of 1929 had caused the family much hardship. Personal financial problems had affected Cleo particularly badly. He disappeared in 1930, leaving his car on the Charlestown Bridge – a well-known suicide spot. Although no body was found, it was presumed that he had jumped off the bridge and met his death in the water below. Many men with business problems had taken this way out.

Phoebe Short was left with five girls – the youngest only two years old – to bring up by herself. Money was tight and Phoebe had to accept welfare payouts. To make ends meet, the family were forced to move to cheaper and smaller rented accommodation.

Like many others with financial worries, Phoebe and her children were regular cinemagoers – going to the movies was a cheap escape from the hardships of everyday life. From an early age Elizabeth had dreamed of becoming a movie star. At home the radio was always on, the apartment echoing to the popular jazz and dance-band tunes of the day. Although the family was poor, the girls were always attired in clean clothes and were smartly dressed when they attended their local Baptist church on a Sunday morning. Elizabeth was an attractive child and as a teenager received a lot of attention from boys.

Elizabeth – also known at this time as Betty – was not a great success as a student and left Medford High School at sixteen. She suffered from asthma, a condition she had had since a child, which was getting more serious as she got older. She suffered from night-time attacks in which she would have difficulty breathing.

Elizabeth leaves Medford

By the time she finished her schooling, the bitter Massachusetts winters were too cold for her to endure. From the age of sixteen, for the next three winters, she would go to Miami, Florida, where she obtained some work and was a part-time model. When Elizabeth was eighteen, her mother was startled to receive a letter from her missing husband Cleo Short, who was alive and working in California. Seeking to return to the family he had abandoned over a decade ago, he claimed that his rationale for his disappearance was that his wife and children would have been provided for better by welfare agencies than by himself. Phoebe refused to let him return. She felt angry and betrayed by what he had done. As the older girls and their mother were in regular employment, they did not need any financial help either.

In early 1942 Elizabeth – now always known as Betty – returned to Medford and obtained work as a waitress and a cinema usherette. However, she felt a pull towards California – Cleo had been writing to Betty and urging her to go and stay with him in Vallejo, where he assured her that there was plentiful work. The other big appeal of California was the movie business in Hollywood.

Betty Short arrived in California and was disappointed. She and her father did not get on, and arguments ensued about her apparent lazy behaviour and the sailors from a local naval base with whom she was spending time. Betty moved out of Cleo Short's house and found work and board as a civilian cashier at Camp Cooke, an army training base.

Betty becomes Beth

Having moved away from her family, she decided that from now on she would be known as Beth. Her glamorous appearance won her many admirers; she even won the Camp Cook beauty contest. But she did not welcome the advances of the men at the camp. Although she had no regular boyfriend during that time, she was popular and made many friends. It was while out with a group of such friends in the coastal town of Santa Barbara that Beth was arrested by police and charged with underage drinking; she was sent back to Medford as a result. From Medford she went on to spend the winter in Florida; she ended up in Los Angeles via the promise of some modelling work in Indianapolis.

Finally, in the movie capital of the world, Beth shared a hotel room in downtown Los Angeles with a girl she met named Lucille. Through Lucille, Beth met actors looking for work, agents and others who, like her, were attempting to get into the motion-picture industry. Their regular hangout was the Hollywood Canteen, where Beth found work alongside a girl who was to become a close friend, Georgette Bauerdorf. Beth had a few dates with a pilot,

Lieutenant Gordan Fickling, and an encounter with the actor Franchot Tone, fully documented in John Gilmore's *Severed*, in which she failed to respond to the star's advances. And, once again, Beth's accommodation changed: she made an arrangement with an artist named Arthur James to model for him in return for free lodging in a tiny room with a view of the Hollywood Hills.

The murder of Georgette Bauerdorf

At around this time there came some tragic news. Georgette Bauerdorf, Beth's former co-worker at the Hollywood Canteen, was found dead in a bath in her apartment. Wearing only a pyjama top, the corpse lay in bloodied water. An autopsy revealed she had died from being strangled. The strip of towelling used to strangle her was found rammed down her throat; she had apparently been viciously raped after she had died. Bruises on her head and abdomen indicated she had been involved in a struggle before being killed.

Georgette was not a typical would-be starlet. She came from a very well-to-do family, her father being an associate of the powerful press baron William Randolph Hearst. The principal suspect in the Bauerdorf murder, a GI with whom she had been involved romantically, was never traced. Georgette's family also used their connection with Hearst to put a stop to any details of the story appearing in the press after the initial reports had been published. The murder remains unsolved.

Engagement to Major Matt Gordan

After an aborted trip to Tucson, Arizona, with the artist Arthur James and another girl – during which James was arrested under the Mann Act (a law relating to the transportation of minors across state lines) and received a sentence of two years in jail – Beth ended up in Chicago, then returned to Medford. By December, she had moved back to Miami Beach, where on New Year's Eve at the end of 1944 she met a pilot, Major Matt Gordan.

Not long after their meeting, Matt proposed to Beth and she accepted, writing back home to Phoebe in gushing terms about this 'wonderful' man she planned to spend the rest of her life with. Gordan presented Beth with an expensive gift of a gold and diamond watch. He was sent off to India and Beth returned to Medford, awaiting his return and their marriage. Several letters Beth sent to him survive; in one she repeatedly tells him that she loves him, although she does tell him that she is dating other men – 'but most of them disgusted me'.

Back in her home town, Beth continued a romance with an old boyfriend named Philip Jeffers; although they spent their time together giving each other massages, Beth remained a virgin. In May 1945 Beth took delivery of a telegram. It was from Matt Gordan's mother:

> Received word War Department. Matt killed in plane crash on way home from India. Our deepest sympathy is with you. Pray it isn't true.

Unsurprisingly, Beth was devastated. She spent her time continually rereading the letters he had sent her; she also developed a fantasy that she had in fact been married to Gordan before he died, and that she had had his child, which had died at birth. When talking about Matt, she now repeated this story as if it were true.

From Florida, to Los Angeles, to San Diego . . . and back to Los Angeles

It was around this time that Beth Short started wearing make-up that caused her face to appear ghostly and pale, and began wearing black clothes. She returned to Florida, and then went north to Chicago to get together with her old flame Gordan Fickling, the pilot she had dated in Hollywood. She was in love again, and followed Fickling back to his base in California, where things did not go well between them. When Fickling pressed Beth to sleep with him, she refused, claiming she wanted to wait until she was married. Further strain was put on their relationship by her unwillingness to give up going out with other men.

Beth's nickname, coined by servicemen in a Long Beach drugstore she used to frequent, dates from this period in Hollywood and is a variant of the title of the film *The Blue Dahlia*, which was released at the time. Written by Raymond Chandler, it tells the story of a war veteran who returns to America to find he is the suspect in his wife's murder. Because of her unusual appearance – long black hair, black clothes and white make-up – Beth Short was referred to as the Black Dahlia.

Following her break-up with Fickling, Beth, now living in Los Angeles with a friend from Boston named Marjorie Graham, continued her attempt to make contacts in the movie industry. Her flirtatious behaviour was unabated. A shoe-store owner, Martin Lewis, took pity on the impoverished girl by giving her a pair of shoes; she gave him a blow job in his car but physically their relationship went no further. Other men were courting Beth, including a salesman, Ray Kazarian, a seller of radio advertising, Hal McGuire, and a discharged soldier, Edwin Burns. None of these men had penetrative sexual intercourse with Beth Short.

No longer living with Marjorie, Beth moved to Cherokee Street, where she lived with three other women, but they were none too pleased with their new roommate's late hours, her habitual coughing during the night and the loans of money or cosmetics that were never repaid.

Beth moved to a rooming house and continued her networking attempts by meeting up with an acting coach,

Lauretta Ruiz, and also posing for some promotional photographs. Beth then moved again – this time to the house of a nightclub owner, Mark Hansen, where a number of other young women were staying. Hansen was apparently offering Beth the chance of some professional work: he wanted her to appear dressed as a stripper in the *Beautiful Girl Revue of 1947* at one of his nightclubs.

Then Beth Short left town. She was following her new boyfriend, a US naval officer named Lester Warren, to his base in San Diego – expecting that he would propose marriage to her. After arriving in San Diego, Beth went to the movies, where an usherette named Dorothy French found her asleep after the film had finished. Taking pity on the girl, who said she had nowhere to stay and no money, Dorothy took her back to her house, where Beth took over the living room, sleeping on the couch, keeping late hours. Furthermore, Lester Warren appears to have been forgotten, and Beth was again dating men.

Robert Manley, a hardware salesman, was one such man. One day in December 1946 Manley noticed the glamorous Beth on a street corner and offered her a lift in his car. Although he was married, he arranged a date with Beth Short, and took her out to dinner; she was unresponsive when he kissed her. Manley was to see Beth again on 8 January 1947, when he arrived at the Frenches' house to find her. Beth was on the move again – this time she wanted to return to Los Angeles. Manley offered to drive her there. That night they drove out for a meal and went dancing, and then stayed in a motel together, but nothing sexual occurred between them.

The next day he drove Beth Short to Los Angeles, where he helped her leave her luggage at the Greyhound bus station. He then dropped her off at the Biltmore Hotel, where she did not take a room, although she was seen to make several phone calls from a booth in the hotel lobby. She hung around the hotel lobby for several hours. A doorman saw her leaving the Biltmore at 10 p.m. She went out into the Los Angeles night, where she was to meet her death.

The discovery of the body

Mid-morning on 15 January 1947, five days after she was last seen leaving the Biltmore Hotel, the naked, mutilated body of Beth Short was found on Norton Avenue in the Leimert Park district of Los Angeles. A housewife, Betty Bersinger, 25 years old, accompanied by her small daughter Anne, was heading down Norton Avenue on a trip to get the little girl's shoes repaired. Anne was first to see the white form of a body lying on a piece of wasteland; she pointed the object out to her mother, who went ahead of the child and had a look. Betty's immediate thought was that this was a discarded department-store mannequin. A closer look revealed a far more disturbing sight – this was a naked woman's body, totally severed in two at the waist. Betty and her child went off; she had to find a telephone to report what she had seen.

Meanwhile, a local fireman, Bill Nash, accompanied by a neighbour named Bill Preston, was driving along Norton Avenue and thought what he saw was a statue amid the weeds and rubble. After stopping the vehicle, the two men got out. What they saw stunned them. The body was neatly severed in two; her face appeared to be smiling. Bizarrely, a bunch of leaves of grass protruded from her exposed vagina. Nash raced home and phoned the police while Preston stayed outside vomiting.

Betty Bersinger had made her call to the police. However, not wanting to get involved in any way with what looked like a particularly grisly murder, she reported that what she had seen was a man lying dead drunk in the weeds along Norton Avenue. Two police officers, Frank Perkins and Will Fitzgerald, arrived by car at the scene. It was not difficult for them to find the body. Examining it while they called on the police radio for assistance, they could see that the upper half was that of a black-haired, smiling, dead woman, her arms lifted up, lying on her back. The lower part of the body had its legs wide open. The corpse showed signs of having been attacked with a knife, and there were rope marks on her limbs and around the neck.

The radio call for more officers had been heard in the newsroom of the *Los Angeles Examiner*; these were the early days of police radios and it was common for local newspaper reporters to sit in their offices with their wireless sets tuned to the police frequencies. Reporters and photographers arrived before more police did. Detectives Harry Hansen and Finis Brown from the Homicide Division arrived and were angry at the presence of journalists, who had taken photographs of the severed body and may have contaminated or interfered with the scene of the crime. On examination of the body and the surrounding areas, detectives drew the conclusion that, as there were no pools of blood in the vicinity, the victim had been killed and the body cut into two at some other location and then dumped on Norton Avenue.

Detectives were puzzled as to why the body had been left at this particular spot. The mutilated corpse had been placed in full public view next to a much-used sidewalk – as if the killer wanted his handiwork to be seen from the street. If the killer had driven a vehicle to Norton Avenue in order to dispose of Beth's body, he ran an enormous risk of being seen. Possibly the killer had taken this risk: a few hours before little Anne Bersinger had sighted Beth's corpse, a paperboy had observed a black vehicle idling by the kerbside near to where Short's body was later found. The body having been examined and photographed *in situ*, the two halves of the as-yet-unidentified corpse were then driven to the LA County Morgue.

The autopsy

On the morning of 16 January, 'Jane Doe 1' was placed on an examination table. Blockages in the rectum and vagina were removed. From the rectum the pathologists pulled out lumps of skin and muscle that appeared to match tissue that had been savagely gouged from the thigh area. An apparent blockage of the vagina persisted, even though the grass had been removed. This puzzled investigators, as they could see no object inside the body.

The autopsy was then conducted by Dr Newbarr, the Chief Surgeon of Los Angeles. His report reads in part:

There are multiple lacerations to the midforehead, in the right forehead, and at the top of the head in the midline. There are multiple tiny abrasions and lacerations. The trunk is completely severed by an incision, which is almost straight through the abdomen ... There are multiple crisscross lacerations in the suprapubic area, which extend through the skin and soft tissues.

There are lacerations of the intestine and both kidneys. The uterus is small and no pregnancy is apparent. The tubes, ovaries, and cul-de-sac are intact ... Within the vagina and higher up there is lying loose a piece of skin with fat and subcutaneous tissue attached. On this piece of loose skin there are several crisscrossing lacerations. Smears for spermatozoa have been taken.

It appeared as though many of the lacerations, including the dilation of the anal opening, were done after the woman's death.

If the lacerations took place when Beth was alive, they may indicate that she put up a struggle before she died, or that she was cruelly tortured with a knife before being killed. If they took place after her death, then one has to ask why the killer chose to do this. The placing of the skin and the clump of grass inside the vagina is also puzzling. Additionally, torn-off pubic hair was found within the rectum, which had been violated:

> The anal opening is markedly dilated and the opening measures 1¼″ in diameter ... There are multiple abrasions ... Smear for spermatozoa has been taken ...
> The stomach is filled with greenish brown granular matter, mostly feces and other particles, which could not be identified. All smears for spermatozoa were negative.

If this assessment of the contents of Beth's stomach is accurate, one is led to speculate that the woman had, during a session of unendurable physical pain and torture, been forced to eat faeces. If the attack had been sexual and she had been raped either vaginally or anally, the man had left no trace of sperm on the corpse. The killer had gone to extraordinary lengths to ensure the body was clean – Beth's hair had apparently been shampooed after she was killed. Certainly the body was remarkably free of blood-stains and the skin had a waxy white sheen, indicating that the corpse had been cleaned before being dumped in the vacant lot – the autopsy documents confirm that Beth's body had been washed following her death. The body appeared very pale, as if drained of blood.

Newbarr made other assessments about the body: the skull was not fractured, although there was some bruising to the neck; there was no sign that death had been by suffocation or strangulation. The actual bisection of the corpse was described thus:

> The trunk is completely severed by an incision which is almost straight through the abdomen, severing the intestine at the duodenum.

Newbarr also noted additional lacerations along the sections of skin where Beth's corpse had been severed. The autopsy concluded that cause of death was haemorrhage of the brain.

Sexual and sadistic motives

However, Dr Newbarr made a remarkable disclosure. In Gilmore's *Severed*, the surgeon is quoted as telling detectives that it was not possible to tell whether Beth had been raped, both because of the absence of sperm on the body and because Short did not have 'fully developed genitals . . . the area is shallow indicating that she did not have a completed vaginal canal'.

This fact explains something about Beth's behaviour with men during her lifetime: she may well have known that she was physically incapable of having sexual intercourse and felt unable to explain this to the men with whom she flirted. Beth's medical history reveals that, by her late teens, she had not yet menstruated. A doctor consulted by the Short family told Phoebe that Beth was a late developer as regards her reproductive organs, although her breasts and pubic hair were normal for her age. One of Beth's 'dates' has observed that beneath her underclothes she wore a pinned-on sanitary napkin, even though she did not appear to be menstruating. It is possible that she habitually wore a napkin in order to avoid sexual intercourse.

Around the time of Beth's involvement with Gordan Fickling, she had apparently visited a doctor using the false name of B Fickel and had requested a vaginal examination; the doctor had found this physically impossible to do as there was either some kind of blockage or there was a congenitally shortened vagina. Beth was duly referred to a urologist – whom she did not consult.

Detectives considered that the killer may have raped Beth anally, having found that the vagina was not long enough to make sex possible. As regards the faeces in the stomach, there was no way of telling if they were Beth's or someone else's. (Modern DNA testing would have been able to provide an answer to this). Additionally, Beth's genitals had been cut and mutilated, with some parts missing altogether. None of these details about the unusual vagina or the faeces in the stomach were released to the press.

The body identified by fingerprints

Fingerprints were taken in the hope of identifying this mysterious corpse; when they were sent to the FBI for comparison with prints on their records a positive result came back – the victim was Elizabeth Short. As she had been a government employee when working at Camp Cooke in 1942, her fingerprints had been recorded and filed with the FBI in Washington. So now the corpse had a name and an identity.

Press fascination with the murder case

As soon as Beth Short's name was known, but before it was published, the *Los Angeles Examiner* rang up Phoebe Short in Medford and, without telling her that Beth was dead, extracted the details of Beth's life from her. The *Examiner* was a Hearst paper, and was determined to beat its rivals in getting the most information on this story.

The Los Angeles newspapers went into overdrive, and Beth Short was front-page news. The *Examiner* ran scoop stories, including interviews with the French family in San Diego. The newspaper even published Beth Short's police photograph, which had been taken as a consequence of the Santa Barbara underage-drinking charges. Short's nickname, Black Dahlia, was now appearing in banner headlines as different aspects of Beth's tragic life were exposed to the public gaze.

Following a leak to the *Herald-Express* newspaper that Beth Short had not had sexual intercourse with men, there was press speculation about whether she had been a lesbian. Reporters posing as police attempted to infiltrate Los Angeles lesbian bars, where they searched for anyone who might have known the Black Dahlia.

Identification of the body and the funeral

The body was identified, as was required by law, on 22 January. Phoebe Short and Beth's sister Ginnie were shown Beth's head. The rest of her was hidden by a sheet – the family being spared that most horrific of sights: a mutilated body apparently sliced in two. Beth's face was badly bruised and distorted and Ginnie was able to make a firm identification only after she had seen a mole below Beth's left shoulder.

Beth Short's remains were buried in the Mountain View Cemetery in Oakland, California, on 24 January 1947. Beth's mother, her four sisters and the husband of one of them attended her daughter's funeral – Cleo Short did not appear. With the crowd of news reporters being kept at a distance from the family by a throng of police, Beth was buried following a brief religious service.

The parcel

On 26 January police were present at the opening of a package addressed to the *Los Angeles Examiner* and bearing the words 'Here are Dahlia's belongings. Letter to follow' in pasted-on cut-out newsprint. The brown-paper parcel had a strong odour of petrol. Inside were more personal papers relating to Beth Short, including her social security ID, her birth certificate and the ticket she would need to obtain her baggage from the Los Angeles Greyhound station. Also in the package was a diary dated 1937 and embossed with the name Mark M Hansen on the cover; this had been used by Beth as an address book and was full of the names and telephone numbers of men she had been dating.

The contents of the package had been rinsed and wiped in petrol, evidently in an effort to rid it of any fingerprints. As the package contained personal effects that Beth Short had on her person when she left the Biltmore Hotel that fateful evening, it is to be assumed that it was posted by the man who tortured, killed and mutilated her. Detective Finis Brown was convinced that the parcel had been posted by the sadistic killer – the careful way in which prints had been wiped was similar to the 'psychopathic cleanliness' with which Beth's body had been handled. However, there is some doubt as to whether or not fingerprints were left on the package. When news of the package was first reported, it was claimed that, despite its having been flooded with petrol, there were still at least twelve very clear fingerprints on it. By the time these allegedly identifiable prints had been sent to the FBI in Washington for investigation, they had apparently become smudged and indecipherable.

Possible connection with the Georgette Bauerdorf murder

Following a claim by the Los Angeles Sheriff's Office that there may have been some connection between the Beth Short killing and the murder of the heiress Georgette Bauerdorf some two years earlier, the LAPD started investigating any possible links. They focused on the Hollywood Canteen, where both girls had worked. The actor Arthur Lake, nationally famous for playing the part of Dagwood Bumstead from the *Blondie* comic strip on both the screen and on radio, had been seen talking to both Beth and Georgette during the time they were working there in 1944. When he was questioned by detectives, he stated that his family had connections with William Randolph Hearst (Marion Davies, Hearst's mistress, was the aunt of Lake's wife), and that the press baron would not approve of any discussion of Georgette Bauerdorf's death. After further questioning, Lake admitted that he could have met the two girls at the Hollywood Canteen, but could remember nothing more than that.

Possibly due to the influence of Hearst, police drew a blank investigating any connection between the two murders. However, both killings involved the placing of foreign objects within the bodies, the use of water (Georgette killed in her bath; Beth's body was carefully washed of all blood). Both girls were in the same social environment, the wealthy Georgette 'slumming it' by working at the Hollywood Canteen. A journalist, Aggie Underwood, who worked for a Hearst paper, the *Los Angeles Herald*, had gone some way into investigating any possible links between the two killings when she was suddenly promoted and warned that even the publication of Georgette Bauerdorf's name was not allowed.

There may well have been some connection between the two murders.

The police investigation

Five days after Beth's body was found, the number of full-time investigators working on the Dahlia case was increased from twenty to fifty.

The diary gave detectives a link to Mark Hansen, who was then interviewed. He remembered Beth Short as a girl who had rented a room in his house, but could not help police further, apart from telling them that Beth had probably stolen the 1937 diary from him.

Martin Lewis, the shoe salesman, was also among those interviewed by detectives. In *Severed* he accuses the LAPD of badgering him into telling them everything he knew about Beth Short. Lewis was apparently given the third degree by detectives, despite a cast-iron alibi (he was in Oregon with his family during the time) that accounts fully for the time in which Beth disappeared.

Major Matt Gordan was also investigated – detectives wanted to ascertain that the man had in fact died in a plane crash. This proved to be correct, and some new information surfaced – Matt Gordan already had a wife when he was courting Beth. This makes Beth's claims that she and Matt were engaged even less likely to be true.

The LAPD investigation gathered momentum. Police were anxious to find whether anyone knew of a place where a young woman could be taken, tortured and cut in half – a basement or isolated workshop. Policemen worked in shifts, answering phone calls from the public, examining forensic reports and photographs, returning to Norton Avenue time after time and attempting to build up a picture of the killer or killers. Detectives interviewed Gordan Fickling, and traced the last man Beth was seen alive with, Robert Manley, who had driven her to the Biltmore Hotel in Los Angeles. Acting on information given to them by Dorothy French, police got hold of a trunk containing some of Beth's personal items, including her letters. Many were from men she had dated; these men had to be traced, investigated and interviewed. Robert Manley told police about the suitcases Beth had left at the Greyhound bus station; these were opened by detectives, who found more clothing, letters and photographs of Beth's family and friends. Manley was also able to identify a pair of shoes and a purse recovered from a rubbish dump as belonging to Beth. Sniffing the purse, he recognised the perfume the Black Dahlia had used. Manley's life was blighted by his encounter with Beth Short: after he was investigated by police he suffered a nervous breakdown and had to undergo electric-shock treatment.

The LAPD was swamped with sightings of the Black Dahlia and information about men who had been behaving suspiciously or who the callers believed were responsible for Beth's murder. To add to all this intelligence, unhinged and deluded men began confessing that they had committed the crime. At the last count there were some fifty men who told police they had killed Beth Short.

When questioned, none of these confessors were able to persuade interviewing detectives that they had committed the crime. None of these men could tell police what had been placed in Beth's vagina or rectum – information that only the pathologists, the police and Beth's killer knew. The confessions continued well into the 1950s; the would-be murderers included a Californian lesbian who claimed she had murdered Beth following an argument and a New York dishwasher who said that he had cut the body in two after a person he could not name had killed the girl. A man known as 'Confessing Tom', who had a history of regularly confessing to crimes he had not committed, could not resist claiming responsibility for the Dahlia murder. A man named Daniel Vorhees tried to make police believe he had killed Beth, but made a mistake in claiming he had met her in Los Angeles in 1941, but Beth had first visited there in 1943. A soldier named Joseph Dumais also claimed he had met Beth Short.

Long before these confessions, the trail leading to the killer of Beth Short had gone cold. As early as February 1947 newspapers were speculating, quite accurately, that police had made no headway in the investigation and that the killer would never be caught.

The trawl through Beth's address books and letters had netted many hundreds of suspects. All of these were traced and interviewed, and subsequently none were charged by police.

Profile of the killer – likely motives

What sort of person would be capable of such a crime, and why would they do this? There has been much speculation of who the killer might be. John Douglas, former Head of the FBI's Serial Crimes Division, has suggested that the Dahlia killer was a white male living alone, who may well have had a police record, with some experience of cutting meat, either working as a butcher or having a hobby such as hunting. Having met her killer, possibly in a bar, she flirted with him and then rejected him. The man then went into a murderous rage and beat Beth Short to death, attempting strangulation in the process. Having killed her in a basement or deserted area where her screams for help could not be heard, he then washed the body thoroughly, cleaning the blood off and washing her hair. The killer then cut the body in half, both for sadistic pleasure and in order to make the corpse fit into a bag or suitcase.

It is difficult to find a reason why the body was taken to that particular spot on Norton Avenue; perhaps subconsciously the killer wanted to be caught. The body was placed within view of the public and arranged in a grotesque manner, the arms raised above the head and the legs wide open in a mockery of a sexually inviting pose. The posting of Beth's diary and possessions to the press showed that the murderer enjoyed the publicity that ensued from his crime; the fact that he had rinsed everything in petrol showed he was obsessive about not being traced.

1949 – the Grand Jury report

The failure of police to find the killer led to demands for an inquiry. A Grand Jury met to investigate police procedure generally; its report included comments on the Black Dahlia case and concluded that 'something is radically wrong with the present system for apprehending the guilty'. After the Grand Jury investigation, the LAPD underwent radical reorganisation and reform, with senior police officers transferred to other divisions and the early retirement of its head, Police Chief Horall.

Leslie Dillon and Jeff Connors – wrongly accused

In 1948 a Miami hotel worker, Leslie Dillon, wrote to Dr Paul de River, an expert in sex offences employed by the LAPD (although his credentials are now believed to be of doubtful authenticity). In his letter Dillon wrote that he had a friend in San Francisco who had met Beth Short in early 1947. De River arranged to meet Dillon in Las Vegas in January 1949, ostensibly to offer him work collaborating on a book. The meeting was in fact being monitored by the LAPD – de River believed Dillon was a possible suspect. De River and four detectives detained Dillon in a motel room and subjected him to some tough questioning. The questioning became more vicious as Dillon was moved to other motels, where he was stripped naked and chained to radiators. Dillon was eventually charged with murder, but then released. Dillon's friend in San Francisco, Jeff Connors, was also arrested and charged with murder. He too was eventually freed.

Both men were victims of the overzealous de River and a police department that was allegedly under his spell. It is certain that neither Dillon nor Connors murdered Beth Short.

The suspects

Since the murder of Beth Short, the names of several suspects, of varying credibility, have been linked to the killing.

George Knowlton

Born in Massachusetts in January 1937, Janice Knowlton had worked as a singer, been employed as a secretary by the Walt Disney Corporation and by the mid-1980s was running her own successful public-relations business. She began to suffer from depression in 1981; in 1985 her womb and ovaries were removed in an operation that she later was told had been unnecessary. Her depression became even more severe and began to be accompanied by thoughts of suicide. She was eventually hospitalised in late 1986 in a California mental institution. During therapy, Janice 'remembered' her father George Knowlton's serious sexual and physical abuse of her from an early age, and alleges that he was a member of a Los Angeles devil-worshipping cult. In her book *Daddy Was the Black Dahlia Killer*, she recalls George putting his erection in her face shortly after she was born; his attempt to penetrate her vagina when she was eighteen months old was stopped only by the intervention of her mother. In addition she recalls seeing her father committing at least eight sadistic murders, including the murder of Beth Short.

Janice alleges that her father, who died in 1962, was a lifelong paedophile. She also recalls seeing her father murder Beth Short and cut the girl's body in two in the garage attached to their house. In her book Knowlton claims that her father had a relationship with Beth. She recalls meeting Beth when she was nine years old. Knowlton alleges that Beth Short left the Biltmore Hotel and went to George Knowlton's house, and that at the time of her murder she was pregnant with George's child. Knowlton recalls seeing Beth tied up with ropes, remembers her father slashing at Beth's face and then killing her by hitting her head with a hammer. In her book she gives a graphic description of George sawing the body in two.

The LAPD discounted Janice Knowlton's allegations, claiming that George Knowlton was not, nor ever had been, a suspect in the Dahlia murder case. Given the nature of false-memory syndrome and taking into account Janice Knowlton's admission of psychiatric illness, her account of events, although certainly compelling, horrifying and thorough in its detail, lacks credibility.

Arnold Smith, a.k.a. Jack Anderson Wilson

'He's the boy . . . I'm going to nail this sonovabitch and close this goddamn case so help me God'
– *Detective John St John of the LAPD, to John Gilmore*

John Gilmore in *Severed* relates details of an account given to police via an informant. The account comes from a man named Arnold Smith, who was not willing to talk directly to police. Smith claimed he had known Beth Short, and had shown the informant a photograph of himself, the Black Dahlia and a man named as Al Morrison. Smith recalls taking Beth back to a hotel room he shared with Morrison and initiating sexual contact with the girl – to which she did not reciprocate, pushing him away. Smith claims that Morrison killed Beth Short in a house on East 31st Street, Los Angeles, after he had tortured her by cutting her body with a knife. After she was dead, following a vicious stab wound to the head, the body was carefully rinsed with water and then cut in two using a butcher's knife, then taken away in a car and disposed of.

The unnamed informant was interviewed by detectives. He could not lead them directly to the elusive Smith. Detectives believed his account, however, but maintained that 'Morrison' was a decoy, and that Smith himself was the killer.

Smith was also known as Jack Anderson Wilson, a man with a history of convictions for sex crimes, notably sodomy with males. Wilson had been known as Grover Loving Jr until 1942. He had been named as a suspect in the Georgette Bauerdorf murder. Wilson, as 'Smith', appeared to have known intimate details about Beth Short – in *Severed*, Gilmore quotes a forensic expert, Paul Cassinelli, who examined transcripts of Smith's confessions via the informant: 'Smith knew about Short's problem. He said "She couldn't be fucked" and that there was "nothing there".'

Gilmore himself met Wilson for the first time in the early 1970s in a Los Angeles bar, the 555 Club, which had been frequented by Beth Short in the 1940s. Wilson showed the writer a photograph of himself and Beth taken in the same bar. The story Wilson had to tell implicated a third party, but contained details that only the killer would know. Gilmore reported his meetings with 'Smith' to the LAPD's John St John; but the more Gilmore pressed Wilson for more details, the more the name of Morrison came up. Detective St John asked Gilmore to entrap Wilson so that the LAPD could finally get their hands on him. On 4 February 1982, days before he was due to have been arrested, Smith/Wilson died in a fire in Room 202 of the Holland Hotel in Los Angeles. He had been staying there for four years, a heavy-drinking alcoholic living on social security.

Gilmore's account is extremely convincing; additionally the LAPD's interest and involvement make Wilson an extremely credible suspect.

Dr Walter Bayley

A *Los Angeles Times* reporter, Larry Harnisch, has his own theory as to who killed Beth Short, which entirely contradicts both Gilmore's findings and Knowlton's 'recovered' memories. Harnisch had discovered a link between the area where Beth Short's body was found and a witness at the marriage of Beth Short's older sister Virginia

Short to Adrian West. The witness who signed the marriage register at the Los Angeles wedding on 26 February 1945 was one Barbara Lindgren. Harnisch has established that Lindgren's father was Dr Walter Alonzo Bayley, a surgeon whose work and home addresses were in close proximity to two places central to the Black Dahlia story:

- Bayley and his wife lived at 3959 South Norton Avenue, very close to the spot where Beth's body was found

- Bayley's office was at 1052 West 6th Street, a few blocks from the Biltmore Hotel where Beth was last seen alive

From these facts – and the additional details that Dr Bayley knew the Short family (an assumption that has not been proved), that he was suffering from Alzheimer's disease, and that in early 1946 his marriage was under strain – Harnisch concludes that Bayley killed Beth Short. Dr Bayley died in 1948.

Harnisch's analysis is based on pure speculation and the evidence he presents is circumstantial; he is reported to be writing a book that promises to provide further evidence of Bayley's motives and involvement in the murder.

Some myths and rumours about Elizabeth Short

She met and/or had an affair with Marilyn Monroe

There is absolutely no reason to believe that Beth Short ever *met* Monroe, let alone had the lesbian affair with her that has been rumoured. There are no first-hand accounts of their ever meeting – only speculation or claims by unnamed 'sources'.

She was a prostitute

Beth Short may well have 'used' men in that she went on dates with them and at certain times may well have depended on her 'dates' financially in order to stay alive, but this does not make her a prostitute. Her abnormally formed genitals and apparent reticence to get involved in any sexual activity would not have made it easy for her to be a prostitute, either.

She acted in 'stag' films

Certainly Beth Short was in the right place (Los Angeles) at the right time (the 1940s) to be involved in the nascent but highly profitable pornographic-film business. However, no pornographic films or pictures featuring Beth Short have come to light. Nor is there any evidence of her being involved in 'straight' acting. No audition, test footage or identifiable 'extra' footage exists of her, although she is often described as a would-be starlet.

Case not closed

The Black Dahlia case remains, technically, still open. All the documentation is kept in a filing cabinet in the LAPD's Robbery-Homicide HQ at the Parker Center at 150 North Los Angeles Street.

2 Mary Pinchot Meyer

Early life

Mary Pinchot was born in October 1920 to a wealthy family with homes in Pennsylvania and New York. Her father, Amos Pinchot, was a Yale-educated lawyer with liberal political views who practised in New York City. Amos's grandfather, Cyrille Pinchot, had emigrated to the US from France; he accrued wealth from buying land. Amos's father, James, had become a millionaire from his wallpaper business and had a reputation for philanthropy.

Amos Pinchot married twice; with his first wife, Gertude Minturn, he had two children named Rosamund and Gifford. After nineteen years of marriage, the couple divorced; the ending of their union filled the gossip columns of the New York tabloids. Shortly after the divorce Amos married Ruth Pickering. Ruth worked as an editor and journalist; she came from a middle-class but financially insecure background. A year later their first child was born and named Mary Eno Pinchot; when Mary was four, Ruth gave birth to a second girl, Antoinette, known as Tony.

Mary Pinchot was educated at the exclusive Brearley School in New York, where she excelled in athletic activities and was popular with her classmates. Girls at Brearley were encouraged by their parents to meet boys from a similar background; at one such social function Mary first met the young John Fitzgerald Kennedy.

Graduating from Brearley in 1938 she 'came out' as a debutante, attending dinners, balls and parties. A familiar face at such events was John F Kennedy, who became acquainted with Mary. The group of debutantes that included Mary were much-photographed for the society pages of the newspapers. That year, however, tragedy struck the Pinchot family for the first time: Rosamund Pinchot, who had been an aspiring actress, committed suicide by inhaling car exhaust fumes in her garage.

Following his daughter's death, Amos became clinically depressed and began drinking heavily. His political views veered rightwards, and he heavily opposed United States' involvement in World War Two. After the Japanese attack on Pearl Harbor his mental state deteriorated; his suicide attempt in 1942 was reported in the newspapers, after which Amos Pinchot withdrew completely from society, spending the rest of his life in hospital. He died in 1944.

Mary Pinchot attended the women-only Vassar College in New York State, where she moved in the familiar social circles that she had grown up in, although this changed drastically when the United States became involved in the war; the young men Mary had been meeting at dances and balls entered military service.

On graduation, Mary returned to New York and began duties as a journalist, working for the United Press. She became involved in leftist politics and at one point was a member of the American Labor Party. She also had her first serious boyfriend, when she lived with a navy newspaper reporter, Bob Schwartz, at a New York hotel. Despite the intensity of their relationship – they were together for three years – the couple drifted apart.

Marriage to Cord Meyer

Mary Pinchot met Cord Meyer in late 1944. He had returned to New York from military service in the US

Marines following serious injuries – his body had been damaged by shrapnel from a grenade and he had lost an eye. He was from a similar background to Mary, from a well-off and upper-class family, with wealth from sugar refining, real estate and coal. Cord Meyer had attended a private Episcopalian school in New England, and then gone on to Yale University, where he graduated with honours. In 1942 he had joined the Marines, and following training was sent to the South Pacific to fight the Japanese on the Pacific islands. His injuries were received at Guam in July 1944 during a night attack on his platoon; the man next to Meyer was killed. He was rewarded for his bravery with a Bronze Star and a Purple Heart.

Mary and Cord had similar literary interests and political views. As a consequence of his injuries and because of what he had experienced during the war, including the death of his twin brother, Quentin, at Okinawa, Meyer became a pacifist.

Mary Pinchot and Cord Meyer were married at Ruth Pinchot's New York City apartment on 19 April 1945. Their nuptials were reported in the New York press. Their honeymoon was spent at the initial convention of the United Nations in San Francisco, Mary attending as a reporter, Cord as a decorated veteran. John F Kennedy was there, too, as a member of the press corps; he and Mary greeted each other warmly, but Cord Meyer turned down Kennedy's request for an interview.

After the American bombing of Hiroshima and Nagasaki that ended the war, Cord became disillusioned with the ideals of the UN convention. In late 1945 the couple moved to Cambridge, Massachusetts, where Mary worked at the *Atlantic Monthly* and Cord began writing a book, *Peace or Anarchy*, about the future role of nuclear weapons in global security.

In the first years of their marriage Mary give birth to two sons: Quentin, named after Cord's dead twin, was born in early 1946 and Michael was born late 1947. Cord became President of the United World Federalists, propagating the idea of world government as a means of ensuring peace, a cause that Mary supported. He also became a fervent anti-Communist and in 1946 was active in preventing what he perceived as a left-wing takeover of the American Veterans' Committee.

In 1949, Cord, no longer believing that the ideals of world government could ever come to fruition, began teaching as a fellow at Harvard. In 1950 Mary gave birth to a third son named Mark.

Cord Meyer joins the CIA – Mary and Cord move to Virginia

In 1951 Cord Meyer was offered a job at the Central Intelligence Agency by its director, Allen Dulles. Mary, Cord and the children moved to McLean, Virginia, to be close to Cord's work at CIA headquarters in nearby Langley. They bought a large house known as Langley Common. Mary brought up the children, and took art classes and began painting in a part of the house that she turned into a studio.

One of Cord's early CIA assignments was to go to France with Mary and with another couple, posing as American tourists but on a secret mission to meet with trade union officials and offer them money to oppose Communist activists within their ranks. During the 1950s, this was to become Cord Meyer's forte. He was a part of CIA operations to oppose Communists in trade unions and political parties in Europe, Central America and Asia. He was involved in setting up the anti-Communist National Student Association and the Council for Cultural Freedom, which covertly funded the publication of the intellectual journal *Encounter*. In the 1960s his activities involved him in countering perceived Communist influence in the student and antiwar movements.

However, this distinguished career in anti-Communism had a rocky start. In 1953 Cord Meyer had been the subject of a whispering campaign within the CIA suggesting that he had close personal connections to left-wingers. One of the accusations made was that his wife had been a member of the American Labor Party. Following investigations and a written defence by Cord Meyer that went into explicit detail in answering the allegations, he was decisively cleared.

During their time together in Virginia, Mary and Cord socialised with other CIA couples partly out of duty; Mary preferred being with her former Vassar classmates. One of Cord's closest friends was James Jesus Angleton, the CIA's counterintelligence chief, whose job it was to discover Communist infiltration within the US intelligence services. Mary and Cord would often socialise with 'Jim' Angleton and his wife Cecily. Another couple who were very close to the Meyers were James and Anne Truitt. James was a journalist who reported for *Newsweek*; Anne, like Mary, was an artist.

Cord Meyer rose through the ranks of the CIA, becoming head of the International Organisations Division in 1954. In the summer of that year Mary went on holiday to Europe with her sister Tony; during that trip Mary had an affair with a middle-aged Italian artist. Tony began a relationship with a journalist called Ben Bradlee; the next year Tony and Ben married. The Meyers holidayed in Italy, where Mary met up again with her artist lover; Cord returned to the USA and Mary stayed on, ostensibly to visit her sister and Bradlee in Paris. Instead she spent time with the Italian painter.

Also in 1955 John F Kennedy, now a Democratic senator and married to Jacqueline Bouvier, moved into the residence next door to Langley Common. Jackie Kennedy and Mary became friends.

In December 1956 Mary's son Michael was killed when he was hit by a car while attempting to cross the road outside their home.

In May 1957 Cord and Mary and the two boys moved to Georgetown, a genteel Washington suburb where many of the politically powerful had homes. Mary was not to stay there for long: the following year she moved out, and petitioned Cord Meyer for a divorce.

Mary now having left Cord, her Italian lover was unwilling to continue seeing her. The identity of this Italian is not known; however in an interview in *Steamshovel Press* #6, a Washington writer, Deborah Davis, alleges that Mary's lover was an Italian Count who was also an intelligence agent. An embarrassing situation for Cord Meyer, who was involved in CIA activities in Europe. She then began a relationship, which was to continue until late 1959, with Kenneth Noland, a struggling artist who achieved success in the mid-1960s as an abstract painter. Noland was one of the founders of what became known as the Washington Color School.

Reichian therapy and drugs

Noland introduced Mary to his psychotherapist, Dr Charles Oller, and underwent therapy with him. Oller was a disciple of Wilhelm Reich, the controversial therapist and researcher whose central theory was that emotional problems could be helped by allowing sexual energy to be channelled through a person's body. Reich invented such concepts as the orgone (a type of 'good' energy), emotional plague (which Reich believed was responsible for political phenomena such as Nazism) and body armouring, which was a muscular rigidity that, according to Reich, was a parallel to emotional blockages. Mary had been seeing a non-Reichian psychoanalyst for some years; her experience with Dr Oller was beneficial.

In early 1962 Mary met Dr Timothy Leary, at the time a psychology professor at Harvard who was well known for his experiments on LSD, using himself and others as subjects. They took a dose of hallucinogenic mushrooms together, and Mary informed him that she had already taken LSD, which was not yet illegal. (LSD was outlawed in the USA in 1966.) This is not unlikely, as LSD, mescaline and marijuana were popular in the artistic circles that she moved in. She met with Leary frequently, and, according to his account in *Flashbacks*, gave him information on the liberal-left front organisations that the CIA had been secretly funding, including the American Veterans' Committee, which Leary himself had joined.

Following Kennedy's death, according to Leary, Mary alleged that the president had been killed by right-wing factions in the CIA. The murder of the president had been motivated because of his drug use. Leary says that Mary told him that the CIA believed that the result of Kennedy's being 'turned on' to LSD was that he would become an appeaser of Communism and more likely to end the war in Vietnam.

Relationship with JFK

Mary's first meeting with President Kennedy at the White House in October 1961 was recorded, like all other visits, by the Secret Service on their logs. This was to be the first of some fifteen visits, all taking place in the evening, that occurred until Kennedy was killed in November 1963. All of the visits but one occurred when Jackie Kennedy was absent from the White House. Mary and the President also met on many occasions outside the White House.

The two had been aware of each other for many years before. They had known each other through school and college social events; while Mary had attended Vassar, Kennedy had been studying at Harvard. They had met again during Mary and Cord Meyer's working honeymoon at the UN meeting in San Francisco, and had met again in Washington after Kennedy had been elected to the

Senate. A close connection between Kennedy and Mary was Tony Bradlee, whose husband Ben was one of the president's close confidants.

James Truitt was interviewed by the popular scandal and gossip magazine *National Enquirer* in 1976. He gave an account of their relationship and of the closeness between Mary and the president. Mary and the president would often dine together with Kennedy's friends; it is certain that many of the conversations were on topics of national security.

Kennedy's many sexual liaisons during his time as president were common knowledge in press and political circles; no one dared print a word of the scandal at the time. The director of the FBI, J Edgar Hoover, took a particular interest in the Kennedy family's private lives and that of JFK in particular.

Kennedy and Mary were sexually intimate, but were also both intellectuals with an interest in political and cultural matters, which they enjoyed discussing. They also had something else in common – an interest in and experience of drug use.

Kennedy suffered from Addison's disease, a condition in which the adrenal glands fail to function; to counter this he was given heavy doses of steroids. He suffered from constant back pain due to a congenital spinal condition. Additionally, he suffered from persisting venereal disease. He used a variety of drugs, including marijuana, procaine and cocaine, to cope with his back pain. He also took amphetamines to stay awake. Mary and the president frequently smoked marijuana together. It is not known whether JFK and Mary ever took LSD together; however, according to some sources there is an entry in Mary's diary in which she records that she and the president did take the drug prior to having sex.

Certainly Mary was in contact with Timothy Leary during the time she has involved with the president; in

Leary's autobiography *Flashbacks*, he recalls that Mary *wanted* to give LSD to someone she did not name but described as 'a friend who's a very important man'. Following the summer of 1962 when the affair between Mary and the president was at its peak, Jackie Kennedy and Mary were on extremely friendly terms, with Mary invited to several White House dinner parties. Nineteen sixty-two had been a difficult year for Kennedy: the death of his one-time mistress Marilyn Monroe, whom he and his brother Bobby had frequently gang-banged, had hit the headlines, and the Cuban missile crisis had almost caused a nuclear war between the world's two largest super-powers.

By the end of 1962 Mary and the president had ended their affair, but remained friends. A possible factor in this may have been the Washington rumour mill, which became active after the drunken publisher of the *Washington Post*, Phil Graham, told a group of newspaper editors at their annual convention in Arizona that the president was having an affair with Mary Pinchot Meyer. Graham, who knew both Mary and Kennedy, committed suicide by shotgun a year later.

During 1963 the couple remained in contact and Mary was on friendly terms with Jackie Kennedy. After Kennedy was assassinated, Mary and her sister Tony went to the funeral in Washington.

Questions persist about Mary's relationship with Kennedy. What, if anything, did he tell her that may have been confidential or related to national security? Moreover, what did the CIA know of their friendship?

The death of Mary Meyer
The twelfth of October 1964 was a cold but very sunny and bright day in Georgetown. Mary had just finished one of her abstract paintings, which she had produced on a

round canvas, and felt in need of some fresh air. She dressed up in warm clothes including winter gloves and a sweater, and headed down towards the Potomac river, continuing her walk along the towpath. An air force lieutenant, William Mitchell, who had gone for his daily run along the towpath, passed Mary and noticed that she was being followed by a lone black man.

A car mechanic, Henry Wiggins, accompanied by his colleague, William Branch, who worked at the nearby M Street Esso petrol station, had driven their truck over to Canal Road, having been called there by a driver to replace a dead battery in his car. As he was working on the vehicle, from behind the wall between Canal Road and the towpath he heard the screams of a woman calling for help, followed by a loud gunshot. Wiggins ran towards the wall to see what had happened. He heard a second gunshot, then managed to look over the wall. He saw a black man standing next to the body of a woman put an object into an inside pocket of his jacket and then run off towards a wooded area.

Mary Meyer had been shot twice. The first bullet had gone into her head and had caused a heavily bleeding wound; after this Mary had grabbed on to a tree, then staggered across to the water's edge; her assailant had then shot her again, this time in her back, severing the blood vessels in her heart. Contrary to some subsequent reports, Mary had not been raped; she had not been carrying a bag or purse so there appears to have been no motive of robbery.

Wiggins approached the body, which was lying on the ground. William Branch went off to phone police, who were quick to reach the scene and sealed off the surrounding towpaths. Detective Bernard Crooke examined the prone body; he realised that the corpse was that of an attractive woman. Other officers who arrived began searching the area. Police Officer John Warner found a black man hiding in a clearing. He was wearing a wet pair of trousers and a T-shirt, and was dripping with water and weeds, as if he had been swimming in the river; one hand had been cut and was bleeding. The man explained that he had fallen asleep while he had been fishing and had fallen into the Potomac. He told police his name was Raymond Crump, and that he was 25 years of age. Crump's jacket was later found floating in the river. When police searched his house, they found his fishing rod.

Crump was put in a prison cell. He was told by police of what they had found, but stuck to the story that he had been fishing. Detective Crooke arrived at Crump's cell bearing the jacket that had been retrieved from the river. When Crump put it on, it was a perfect fit.

Aftermath of Mary's murder – differing accounts of the search for the diary

On the evening of 12 October, Ben Bradlee identified the body as that of Mary Pinchot Meyer. The news spread throughout Washington, and the newspapers the following morning gave details of her life. Cord Meyer's employment by the CIA was not mentioned. According to Ben Bradlee, he and Tony Bradlee were contacted by James Truitt's wife Anne, who at the time was in Japan. Anne then said that Mary had asked her to take possession of her diary if anything were to happen to her, and that James Angleton was the person to give the diary to if Anne were not in Washington. Bradlee has denied that Anne sought Angleton's involvement. On the day after Mary's death, Bradlee went to Mary's house to find the diary, only to find Angleton inside – having broken in using his lock-picking skills – already searching.

The CIA boss's search was fruitless, despite his experience and CIA training – the Bradlees later found the diary in Mary's studio.

James Angleton's wife Cicely and Truitt's wife Anne give a different account of the way the diary was dealt with – they claim that, once the diary was found, Tony Bradlee gave it to Angleton and asked him to destroy it. Cicely Angleton and Anne Truitt also claimed that both papers and a diary were found, but that Angleton initially burned only the papers, keeping the diary and then handing it to Tony Bradlee, who destroyed it.

Angleton's own account of events is that he read the diary and the accompanying bundle of letters, noting the references to President Kennedy and others. He then offered to return the letters to those of Mary's correspondents that he could identify. It is also claimed that Angleton then gave the diary to Tony, who burned it.

Another version of events, given by Ron Rosenbaum in an article in *New Times*, additionally involves Cord Meyer in the search for the diaries. The bundle of correspondence has become 'hundreds' of letters, and either Angleton burned both the letters and the diary, or they were sent to the Pinchot family residence in Pennsylvania.

The search for the murder weapon

Police conducted a thorough search of the area by the river where Mary's body had been found and where Ray Crump had been hiding. Using scuba divers, dredgers and large magnets, they went down to the river bed to try to find the murder weapon, a .38 calibre pistol.

No weapon could be found.

Ray Crump

Raymond Crump Jr was born in Norwood, North Carolina, in 1939. He was descended from slaves who had 'belonged' to the cottonfield-owning Crump family during the early eighteenth century. Ray Crump's parents had moved to Washington in the 1950s. A high-school dropout, at the time of Mary's murder working as a labourer, Ray had a police record and had been given spells in prison for theft and public drunkenness. In 1962 he had been the victim of a robbery and had been badly beaten about the head. Since that attack, he had suffered from blackouts and chronic headaches.

The trial of Ray Crump

When Ray Crump's defence attorney, Dovey Roundtree, visited him in jail for the first time, the prisoner was in a very depressed and unhappy state. Roundtree attempted to get a ruling that Crump be declared legally insane and therefore unable to stand trial; after several months of psychiatric examination it was decided that Crump was fit to be tried.

The twentieth of July 1965 was the first day of Crump's trial, presided over by Judge Howard Corcoran. The prosecuting attorney, Alfred Hantman, like his opponent Dovey Roundtree, made no mention of the private life of Mary Meyer; Judge Corcoran, possibly acting on government instructions, ruled that such matters could not be discussed in court. Dovey Roundtree has since stated that at the time of the trial she was told by a source she does not name that Mary Meyer had been cleared for security by the White House and that her diary had been burned.

The twelve-strong jury were selected; two members were white.

The prosecution described how Mary Meyer's dying screams had been heard by a witness who had then seen a black man identified as Crump standing over her body. Police testimony was read out describing how Crump had been found hiding on the river bank and the jury were told that Crump's clothes, matching those of the man standing over Mary Meyer earlier, had been found in the vicinity.

Hantman admitted early in the trial that the evidence was largely circumstantial.

Ben Bradlee was questioned by Hantman, but was not forthcoming with any useful information. He did not mention that Mary had kept a detailed diary; at no time was the possible existence of a diary mentioned in court. The Washington DC pathologist then described the gun-shot wounds: she had been shot twice at very close range, in the rear of her head and through her back, the second bullet severing her aorta. Efforts by the prosecution to show jurors a map that showed a limited number of exits to the towpath were stymied by Dovey Roundtree: there were a number of paths and routes out of the area, through which an assailant could have escaped, that did not appear on the official map.

On 21 July Henry Wiggins gave his testimony, the key part of which was his identification of the man seen standing over Mary Meyer. The man Wiggins described was dressed in clothes similar to those found in the vicinity of the murder, but was several inches taller and much heavier than the defendant, who was five foot three and weighed between 130 and 145 pounds.

Police who arrived on the scene then gave their account of events. The jury were told that Crump had said he had been fishing, but that no abandoned fishing equipment was found by the Potomac. Next to testify in court were the FBI, who had gathered forensic evidence. No trace of gunpowder had been found on Crump's hands, although the FBI said, and Roundtree contested, that the river water may have washed away the evidence. Judge Corcoran ruled that the prosecution would not be permitted to bring into court the tree on to which Mary Meyer had been clinging after she had been shot for the first time.

The defence then presented their case. Three witnesses were called by Roundtree, all of them members of Crump's mother's Baptist church, all of whom attested that Ray Crump was not a violent man. Following some cursory questions by Hantman, Dovey Roundtree then told the astonished courtroom that she had now rested her case.

In her closing statement, Roundtree emphasised that no gun had been found and that Wiggins had described a man who was much taller and heavier than the defendant. Prosecutor Hantman showed the jury Crump's shoes, which he claimed would have made him appear several inches taller than he actually was. He claimed that the facts that Crump had removed his clothing and that no fishing equipment was found nearby was a sign of the defendant's guilt. He also hinted that the motive for the attack on Mary had been rape and that Crump had intended to drag her into the bushes and assault her; when she had repelled him, he had decided that his only way out of this was to murder her.

Before the jury were sent off to decide Crump's fate, Judge Corcoran instructed them. The options were to find Crump innocent, or to make a decision of murder in the first degree or murder in the second degree. If Crump was guilty of first-degree murder, the jury would have to make a decision of whether he would face the death penalty or life imprisonment.

The verdict – and beyond

On the following day, 30 July 1965, the jury gave their verdict. Raymond Crump was not guilty of killing Mary Meyer.

Following his acquittal, Raymond Crump was employed as a labourer. He also became involved in crime and was arrested 22 times after the murder trial, for offences including the use of firearms, assault, theft and arson. He spent some time in jail following convictions for these crimes, the latest known conviction being for arson in 1989.

Since his acquittal, Ray Crump has refused to discuss the Mary Meyer case. Neither the Washington, DC, police force nor the FBI questioned any further suspects; after Crump's acquittal the case file was closed. Detective Crooke is reported to believe that Crump was guilty; Dovey Roundtree is certain that another man committed the crime, possibly a jealous lover of Mary's, and that Crump had been framed. Roundtree is convinced there was some government involvement in her death.

Some unanswered questions

The key question raised by the murder of Mary Meyer is whether her death was, as Morrow suggested, the result of a decision taken by the CIA on the grounds that Mary Meyer knew too much classified information – information that she may have learned during her marriage to Cord Meyer or during her affair with John F Kennedy. The contents of the diary are also the subject of much speculation. Why did she explicitly request that, if anything happened to her, her diary should be handed to Anne Truitt or James Angleton? Does the diary, or do copies of the entries in it, still exist? Was the diary really burned, and, if so, why? Why are there so many conflicting stories about what has happened to the diaries and letters, and indeed if there were letters found at all? It also seems extraordinary that Mary would wish to have her diary given to, of all people, James Angleton. In giving the diary to Angleton, she would have entrusted the details of her private life to the CIA; as a committed liberal, she would be unlikely to have taken this course.

There are also many questions about Ray Crump and his behaviour on the day of the murder. Why did he lie about having been fishing? Why exactly had his clothes been removed? As regards the trial, was there a racial factor in Crump's acquittal? Most mysterious of all was, what happened to the murder weapon and why was it not found?

Questions about Dr Timothy Leary

Everything that Leary has written about his relationship with Mary Meyer and what she said to him about Kennedy's use of psychedelic drugs is anecdotal; another damning fact is that Leary did not mention the alleged Kennedy–Meyer–LSD connection until the publication of his autobiography *Flashbacks* in 1983. Surely Dr Leary, a vocal proponent of, and publicist for, the use of LSD, would not have been able to remain silent about the president's drug taking for *twenty years*!

Leary hints that Mary Meyer was involved in giving LSD to other women connected to intelligence agency and government men with the hope that they might persuade those men to take LSD and therefore convert them to the ideals of the 1960s counterculture. That this idea was ever put into action is extremely unlikely; like Mary's acid trip with JFK, it would seem to be a product of Leary's imagination.

It has been been a matter of speculation, and speculation only, as to whether Dr Leary himself was employed by the CIA. It is an accepted fact that the CIA had a programme known as MK-ULTRA, which involved the use of LSD and other substances for the purposes of mind control. Experiments with LSD were carried out on some CIA staff during the 1950s. It is also alleged that the CIA funded the research into pyschedelic drugs on the campuses of Harvard – where Leary was employed – and at Berkeley.

Conspiracy?

For many years afterwards, there was a wall of silence about the death of Mary Meyer. This was ended by the revelations in the *National Enquirer* in 1976, which published the interview with James Truitt in which he claimed that Mary and President Kennedy had a sexual relationship, that they took drugs together and that Mary's diary had been handed over to James Angleton. Truitt was heavily criticised by Mary's friends for selling his story to the *Enquirer*. In 1981 James Truitt, who had moved to Mexico, blew his brains out with a shotgun.

In 1992 Robert Morrow, in his book *First Hand Knowledge – How I Participated In the CIA–Mafia Murder of President Kennedy*, published details of his own involvement in the assassination of the president. Claiming to have been employed by a consortium of Mafia and intelligence agencies to buy rifles and plan the killing of Kennedy, Morrow also gave information about the killing of Mary Meyer. Morrow claimed that the CIA were alarmed by Mary's apparent knowledge of its operations regarding Cuba and the Kennedy assassination, and that information had been passed to the leader of the Cuban exiles in the USA, Robert Kohly, who had arranged for Mary to be silenced. Morrow provides no evidence that any of the events that he described took place.

It seems unlikely that Mary Meyer was killed as part of a cover-up over the assassination of President Kennedy. After all, before Mary's death, according to conspiracy theorists, one of the most questionable publications that in itself amounted to a cover-up, the Warren Commission Report, had been released, and accepted by the mainstream press and by middle America as an authentic investigation into the tragedy of 22 November 1963. Also, one has to ask the obvious question: as Mary's lover, what would the president have been able to tell her about his own assassination?

Motiveless murder?

An alternative possibility to those of the conspiracy theorists is that Mary was a victim of a random urban attack – that there was no motive for it, and that Mary

44

Meyer just happened to be at the wrong place at the wrong time. If Crump was innocent (the absence of a murder weapon might indicate that), and if Mary did in fact *not* have any knowledge of any secret so dangerous that she had to be silenced by being killed, then this is the most likely circumstance in which she was murdered.

3 The Bible John Murders

Bible John – 'a perfect gentleman'
The notorious killer known only as 'Bible John' committed three murders in Glasgow between February 1968 and October 1969. All his victims were female, attractive and were menstruating at the time of their deaths. All three were killed near their homes by being strangled with their own tights, having been brutally assaulted.

The man – described as very well dressed and with the demeanour of a perfect gentleman – found his female victims at the Barrowland Ballroom in the city centre. This was a strange place for a killer to go for the purposes of finding his prey: witnesses would see what was going on and who left the ballroom with whom, and a man who regularly attended the dances there, as 'Bible John' is alleged to have done, would surely have been recognised. Police were indeed able to construct several artists' impressions of the man – but to no avail. The man most frequently named as a suspect responsible for the three murders died in 1980; DNA tests with the aim of either proving or disproving the man's guilt were carried out and came to a negative conclusion when samples of the dead man's DNA were found not to match a semen stain found on a pair of tights belonging to one of his victims.

Had the murders taken place thirty years later Bible John would almost certainly have been caught, either by the closed-circuit TV cameras that are inescapable in most British cities, or by the advances in DNA testing that are now commonplace in modern crime solving.

The murder of Pat Docker

Twenty-five-year-old Pat Docker worked as an auxiliary nurse at the Mearnskirk Hospital in Glasgow. She had married a corporal in the RAF some five years previously, but the marriage had failed and, while her husband – the couple were not yet divorced – was serving at an RAF base in Lincolnshire, Pat and her four-year-old son Sandy were living at her parents' flat in Langside Place in the Battlefield district in the south of the city. An attractive woman, she enjoyed going out dancing on her free evenings in the city's ballrooms. Thursday, 22 February, was one such evening and Pat, wearing a yellow dress and grey coat with brown shoes and handbag, said goodbye to her parents, telling them she would be going to the Majestic Ballroom in Hope Street.

However, Pat did not go dancing there – instead she went to the Barrowland Ballroom in the Gallowgate area in the east end of Glasgow. 'Barraland' had been a popular place for a night out since it had been built in the 1930s. During World War Two and the golden era of the dance bands, it had been popular with foreign servicemen stationed near-by, who were eager to chat up the local women, many of whose husbands were on military service either hundreds of miles away or abroad. In the 1950s and early 1960s Barrowland became a rock 'n' roll venue where nationally and internationally famous stars and groups would perform. By the late 1960s, traditionally a Thursday night in the Barrowland was the night when men and women who were married – but not to each other – would meet.

According to eyewitnesses, Pat Docker met a smiling and presentable man on the dance floor with whom she spent the evening dancing – the man who killed her after she had left Barrowland. Her naked corpse was found the following morning by Maurice Goodman, a joiner, by the lock-up garage in Carmichael Place – near Pat Docker's parents' flat – where he kept his car. Her head had been viciously kicked and punched. She had been lying there for some time, and overnight temperatures had been cold; there had been a deep frost.

Goodman immediately called police, and detectives who arrived first at the scene were uncertain, before they moved the body, whether what they had been called to investigate was male or female: Pat Docker was unusually slim. A police surgeon, James Imrie, made a preliminary examination of the body at the garage and found markings on the neck that indicated strangling by a cord or belt; the facial and head injuries were gruesome but in themselves were ruled out as the cause of death.

The police did not ascertain who the victim was until the following evening, when Pat's father had read about the murder in the local newspapers; he rang police and was called in to positively identify the body. A search of the area revealed no trace of Pat's handbag or clothing. A postmortem was conducted by a forensic medical expert, Professor Gilbert Forbes, which confirmed Dr Imrie's initial judgement that Pat Docker had died from strangulation. Professor Forbes also revealed that Pat had been menstruating at the time of her murder and that there was no definite evidence of sexual assault.

The police investigate . . . and draw a blank

A prime suspect was Pat's husband, who had been on leave from the RAF on the night of the murder and had been staying with his parents in East Lothian. Arriving in Glasgow, he was questioned by police, and convinced them of the truth, that he had not seen his estranged wife for some months. The police investigation accelerated:

posters were put up requesting any information and potential eyewitnesses were interviewed. Pat's mother and father were extensively questioned, and they revealed what Pat had told them: that she had planned to spend Thursday evening at the Majestic Ballroom.

For some weeks police believed that Pat Docker had been at the Majestic, and concentrated their enquiries in that area until reliable witnesses concurred that Pat had in fact been at the Barrowland that night. Having wasted much time and effort interviewing dancers at the wrong ballroom, investigators had to start again at the dancehall that Pat had indeed been at. Police faced reluctance among the Thursday-night regulars to answer questions or indeed to admit they had been at the Barrowland that night, as many of them were married people conducting illicit liaisons there. To aid the investigation and hopefully jog people's memories, posters of the dead woman were put up all over Glasgow. Taxi drivers were systematically interviewed, as it was not known how Pat had gone back to Carmichael Place from the ballroom, or who had accompanied her. A trawl of the River Cart brought up Pat's handbag and part of her watch; but these items weren't much use as forensic evidence. But – apart from a single anonymous letter from someone claiming to know who was responsible, which may have been a hoax – no one came forward to identify the killer.

Drivers of various vehicles seen late at night near where the body was discovered were tracked down and suspicions about them were proved negative. Months passed, and police literally had no clue as to who had committed this brutal crime or why. Someone, somewhere, against all the odds, was getting away with murder.

The murder of Jemima 'Mima' McDonald

Like Pat Docker, Jemima McDonald, known as Mima, was separated from her husband. A mother of three children, two boys of seven and nine and a girl aged twelve, Mima had lived in a tenement building in Mac-Keith Street in the Bridgeton area of Glasgow. In the late 1960s this area typified the urban decay of the slums and was known for its overcrowded conditions and high crime rate. MacKeith Street was made up of buildings that were still judged capable of being lived in and those, although still standing, that were in ruins.

On the hot evening of Saturday, 16 August 1969, 32-year-old brunette Mima had gone out dancing at the Barrowland. She was a regular at the dancehall, and often went there on Thursdays as well as at the weekend – as her sister Margaret O'Brien lived in a flat in the same block it was easy to find someone to look after the children. She was dressed in a brown coat over a black dress and white blouse, and was carrying a handbag. Mima was seen dancing with a smartly dressed man with whom she remained until the end of the evening; after the last waltz she left the Barrowland with him, walking along Bain Street and towards Bridgeton Cross in the direction of Mima's tenement flat. The couple stopped in an empty disused building near MacKeith Street; possibly Mima and the unknown man went in there together to have sex. But, once she was off the street and alone with the man, he raped her and strangled her with her tights.

The next day Margaret O'Brien began to worry about what might have happened to her sister. It was not unusual for Mima to spend a night away from home, particularly after having been out dancing, but as the day went on, and Mima had still not appeared, Margaret's concern grew. When she heard some children talking about 'a body' they had found in a nearby building – a not unusual occurrence, because alcoholics and vagrants would often be found intoxicated or sleeping inside such places – she headed straight there, only to find her sister's beaten and raped body in a derelict room.

Police investigate ...

After examining the facts in both cases, police made a link between Mima's death and the murder of Pat Docker some eighteen months earlier. Both had been savagely murdered by strangulation after a visit to the Barrowland Ballroom, where each had been seen dancing with a well-presented stranger whom no one could identify. In each case, the woman's handbag could not be found. Also, both women had been menstruating at the time of their deaths. This last coincidence alarmed police: was there some sort of perverse sadist in the Glasgow area who could achieve satisfaction only by murdering menstruating women? And, if there was, when would he strike again?

As in the case of Pat Docker, the police investigation centred around the Barrowland; there were witnesses who had seen Mima leave the dancehall with a man, and from their descriptions of that man, believed to be Mima McDonald's killer, police were able to issue some sort of description. The suspect was between mid-twenties and mid-thirties in age, slim, with short reddish hair, wearing a suit and tie with a white shirt. But, as in the Docker investigation, some witnesses felt unable to co-operate with police, as they had been at the dancehall having told their spouses that they were somewhere else.

An artist's impression of the man was drawn, based on the most detailed description, which was given by a man and a woman who had seen Mima sit down with a red-haired man in a pub. Apparently the woman who had seen Mima's companion thought the man looked like a film star; the man, when questioned, appeared to be jealous of the suspect's good looks! The artist's impression was being used instead of the Identikit picture that Scottish police had been using at the time, because the descriptions by witnesses were considered too vague for the Indentikit picture to be of much use. The publication of this image on billboards and in newspapers created

Scottish legal history, because it was the first occasion that a picture of a suspect had been allowed to be used in this way.

Police at this stage were not admitting any link between the murders of Pat Docker and Mima McDonald, only speculating among themselves that this appeared extremely likely. Meanwhile, gossip and rumour spread among the public. The first murder of a dancer at the Barrowlands was enough to cause the women who went there to be more cautious about whom they went home with; the second murder caused a small degree of panic. Girls at dances made arrangements among themselves not to go home unaccompanied. Was the next man they were to accept a dance from a murderer? And when would the killer next strike?

The murder of Helen Puttock

Twenty-nine-year-old Helen Puttock, like Pat Docker, was married to a serviceman. George, however, was a serving army soldier, and the marriage, although it had its rocky moments, was still intact. Particularly hard for Helen had been her time as an army wife in Germany when George was sent to serve with the British Army of the Rhine. She had found it hard to make friends there, and returned to Britain with the children after a year. Helen now lived with her two young sons, David and Michael (and with George when he was home on leave), in Earl Street in the Scotstoun district of Glasgow. On Thursday, 30 October 1969, George was with his family on only a few days' leave, but he didn't have any problem with Helen going out dancing with her friends that night – even though Thursday nights at the Barrowland were reputed to be the night when married people had flings with other married people; he was happy to stay in and look after their two boys. Helen's sister, Jeannie Williams, arrived to pick her up; both girls were dressed in their finest winter clothes, including, for Helen, a fake ocelot-fur coat. The two girls planned to meet friends at the Barrowland; they were both aware of the murders of Pat Docker and Mima McDonald, and when they went dancing took the precaution of making sure they stayed part of a group.

At around 8 p.m. the sisters left the house on Earl Street, looking forward to their night out, catching a bus to Glasgow Cross. Arriving in town at around 9 p.m., they decided to go for a drink in a bar where they were joined by several friends. After an hour's drinking, during which Jeannie and Helen drank several whiskies each, the group joined the queue outside the Barrowland, and eventually were admitted, Helen checking in her trendy new coat at the cloakroom.

The dancehall was packed with couples who were either dancing or entwined kissing in dark corners. Jeannie was invited to dance by a man who told her his name was John – not an unusual name for a married man to use on a Thursday night in the Barrowland. While dancing with 'John', Jeannie noticed an especially well-dressed man with red hair standing alone, presumably eyeing the talent on the dance floor. Catching sight of Helen Puttock, he went over to her and asked her for a dance. Jeannie and her 'John' joined Helen and her new dancing partner, who also called himself John, and introduced themselves.

Helen and John spent the rest of the evening together at Barrowland, and the two couples left together. Jeannie had noticed some extremely odd behaviour by Helen's new friend as they were collecting their coats from the cloakroom: when a cigarette machine kept Jeannie's two-shilling coin and failed to provide her with cigarettes the good-looking man became extremely agitated and started demanding loudly that the manager of the Barrowland should come and sort this out. A verbal altercation with the manager ensued, John failing to succeed in getting the refund he expected. Leaving the Barrowland, Jeannie's 'John' went off to catch a night bus home.

Having promised to see Helen safely home, Helen's John joined the sisters in a taxi heading to Scotstoun. At first the conversation was awkward; John obviously resented Jeannie's presence and made no attempt to hide this, but eventually he became more chatty and said that he disapproved of the Thursday-night clientele at Barrowland because of the number of 'adulterous women' there: he also said that on New Year's Eve he did not celebrate by drinking himself senseless, as many Glasgow men did, but that he prayed. He continued to quote extracts from the Bible. Jeannie thought the man's conversation bizarre and that he himself was weird. John wanted the taxi to drop off Jeannie at her house first; Jeannie said goodbye to the strange man and her sister. The taxi drove off towards Earl Street; Jeannie had just had the last glimpse of her sister alive.

Arriving at Earl Street, John paid the taxi driver and he and Helen were at last alone. They went together to the entrance of 95 Earl Street, where Helen was strangled to death. Bible John left the scene of the crime, and was seen in a dishevelled condition on a night bus by a witness who thought the man must have been involved in a fight.

At seven o'clock on Friday morning, Archie MacIntyre, who lived at 95 Earl Street, was taking his dog out for a walk, as he usually did at that hour. Having left his flat, at the bottom of the stairs he found Helen Puttock's body, still wearing her fake-ocelot coat. Police were called and arrived quickly. Forensic examination revealed that there had been a chase and a struggle, that Helen had run away from John and headed towards a nearby embankment. John had run after Helen, grabbed her and beaten her repeatedly around the head until she lost consciousness. He had then carried her to the entrance of 95 Earl Street, where he had ripped off her tights, raped her viciously and then killed her by strangling. When police examined Helen's body at the scene of the crime, they discovered marks that suggested she had been viciously bitten. A plaster cast of these teeth marks was taken by police. Bizarrely, they discovered a blood-soaked sanitary towel apparently placed under her armpit by the killer. Like the other two victims who had met their death after dancing with a stranger at the Barrowland, Helen Puttock had been menstruating. And for the first time the assailant had ejaculated and left a semen stain on his victim's clothing. This physical evidence was kept secure by police.

A picture emerges . . . investigation into Puttock

This time the killer had shown his face, and had been closely observed by witnesses, notably Jeannie Williams, who had spent quite some time observing the man and his demeanour. Also, police could count on the manager of the Barrowland, who had been involved in an argument with John over a cigarette machine, and lastly the taxi driver who had dropped Helen and John off at Earl Street.

Police were now aware there was a serial murderer in Glasgow. The killer's victims had all left the Barrowland with a similar-looking man who had picked them up that evening; they were all strangled with their tights and all three women had been having their period at the time of their death.

The police investigation was led by Detective Superintendent Joe Beattie. He had broken the news of Helen's death to Jeannie. In the subsequent investigation George Puttock was ruled out as a suspect, largely because of the full account Jeannie could give of the events of that fateful Thursday night and Friday morning. Appeals were printed in the press for further witnesses; as in the other two murders, the clientele at Barrowland were scrutinised and questioned by police. Jeannie provided police with an artist's impression of Bible John, which was printed on the front pages of Scottish newspapers. Under the picture was a description of the killer based on Jeannie Williams's account, which read,

> He is 25 to 30, 5ft 10 in to 6ft in height and of medium build. Light auburn, reddish hair, brushed to the right. He has blue-grey eyes and nice straight teeth. But one tooth on the right upper overlaps the left. He has fine features and is generally of a smart modern appearance. This man was known to have been dressed in a brownish, flecked, single breasted suit with high lapels. His brownish coat – tweed or gaberdine – was worn knee-length. His wrist watch has a military-style strap. He may smoke Embassy tipped cigarettes and goes to the Barrowland Ballroom. He is thought to be called by his Christian name of John. He may speak of having a strict upbringing and make references to the Bible. This man is quite well spoken, probably with a Glasgow accent. There may be marks on his face and hands.

The police were using their most valuable witness – Jeannie Williams – as effectively as they could. A gruelling 300 times she was called to examine groups of men at identity parades – and 300 times she had to admit that the religiously obsessed and smartly dressed man was not present. Perhaps her judgement was marred by the sheer volume of men she was asked to look at. Perhaps Jeannie had had a few drinks and had seen the man mainly in the dark, and her perception of the Bible-quoting killer was affected that way. Police were anxious to interview the other 'John' with whom Jeannie had been dancing, the man who disappeared to catch the last bus home – but he proved impossible to track down. In all likelihood this 'John' was a married man who had too much to lose by coming forward.

With further help from Jeannie, police now had an Identikit picture – which was similar to previous artists' impressions. Articles in local newspapers speculating on the identity of the murderer had given him the name of 'Bible John', and this is what the man was called on the wanted posters. Helen's widower George took part in a press conference appealing for Bible John to give himself up. Public response to the publicity was promising – with some 4,300 people claiming to have seen the killer. The hairdressers, tailors, dentists and doctors of Glasgow were systematically interviewed by police. Believing that the man's religious utterances may provide a clue, churches were visited and clergy interviewed. Allowing for the possibility that Bible John may be mentally ill, hospitals were checked. All drew a complete, frustrating blank.

Bible John had murdered three times, and vanished into the Glasgow night.

Subsequent events

In 1970 a Dutch clairvoyant, Gerard Croiset, arrived in Glasgow to try to help police solve the crimes. Croiset was based in Utrecht, and was best known for using his reputed psychic powers to help find people, especially children, who went missing. An object or piece of clothing belonging to the missing person would be handed to Croiset, who would then visualise where that person now was and whether they were dead or alive. Even without being handed a possession of a missing person, Croiset could be told just a few details about them and he would know whether they were still alive; if he believed they were dead he was frequently able to indicate where the body was. He was able to solve cases in other countries without leaving Holland, and sometimes was able to do this after one telephone call from a relative of a missing person.

Croiset had previously been brought to Britain by the family of Muriel McKay, the wife of a *News of the World* manager who had disappeared and was feared abducted. Croiset was able to advise the family and provide some answers to their questions. (Muriel McKay's body was never found, although two brothers named Hussain were eventually found guilty of her murder.) Visiting Glasgow and sitting in the offices of the *Daily Record*, a popular Scottish tabloid newspaper, Croiset was able to make some drawings of places frequented by the killer. He told reporters that he believed Bible John was still resident in Glasgow and he specified that the killer lived in or near the Govan area, south of the city. The clairvoyant described him as being under the age of 28 and with fair hair and assessed his personality as being authoritarian.

Later that year a BBC television programme, *Current Account*, examined the case. Presented by Hugh Cochrane, the broadcast included a reconstruction of the last known movements of Helen Puttock, with actors retracing the steps of Helen, her sister Jeannie and the two 'Johns' they had met at the Barrowland Ballroom. Bizarrely, the programme also featured three men who looked like the Identikit picture of Bible John, all of whom had been interviewed, investigated and finally cleared by police. The final item on the broadcast was an interview with Detective Chief Superintendent James Binnie, who warned the killer that investigations were continuing and that he would be caught. After the transmission Glasgow police and the BBC received several hundred phone calls and thousands of letters offering information. But none of these contained the vital clues necessary for the investigation to proceed any further.

By the 1990s, advances in genetic profiling made it possible for the killer to be found – or for suspects to be ruled out – by examining the DNA in the semen left behind by the man who attacked and killed Helen Puttock and comparing it with DNA of a suspect. Most importantly as regards the Bible John case, the suspect need no longer be alive in order to be investigated – DNA could be taken from a dead body no matter how long that body had been buried. The investigation was reopened, and by 1995 four officers based in Glasgow, led by Chief Inspector Jim McEwan, were assigned to the task of finding suspects. With the aid of computers to analyse their data, the team re-examined statements and evidence gathered at the time of the murders and came up with a short list of twelve men. The chief suspect was a man named John Irvine McInnes, whose name kept reappearing on the files.

The life and death John McInnes

John Irvine McInnes was born in Stonehouse on 10 September 1938. His parents ran a drapery business. After leaving school he had a succession of jobs and then ran a sweet shop. Aged nineteen, he went on to do his compulsory national service in the Scots Guards, and then became a salesman in a Sauchiehall Street department store. In 1964 he married Helen Crockett McQueen Russell, and with his wife ran Innesfield, a private home for the elderly in Ayr. At the time McInnes's weird habit of getting into bed with patients when they were distressed was seen as an eccentricity.

The couple separated in early 1968, shortly after which their son Kenneth was born. They were finally divorced in 1972. At the time of the three murders, McInnes abandoned the job he had at the time, working for a stamp trading company. His whereabouts were not known for some time; he later lived in Newarthhill, Lanarkshire, returning occasionally to Stonehouse to see his family. By the end of the 1970s, for whatever reason – the breakdown of his marriage, his disillusionment with the Brethren religious sect, of which his parents were members, his problems with employment, or maybe even guilt he felt over the Bible John killings – John McInnes was severely depressed, making several attempts at suicide.

On the evening of 29 April 1980, he appeared in the Old Ship Inn in Stonehouse looking very unhappy, and rapidly drank a large quantity of beer and whisky before leaving. He then went to his mother's home and went up to the attic, where he cut deep into his armpit with a razor blade. He bled to death, and his body was discovered the following morning. He was buried in the nearby St Ninians Cemetery.

Was McInnes Bible John?

At the time of the Bible John killings, John McInnes was an habitué of the Barrowland and a man whose appearance fitted perfectly the descriptions of the murderer. McInnes had come to the attention of the police; he had appeared on four separate identity parades but had not been picked out on any of them. Subsequently McInnes referred to himself as 'Bible John' and boasted of the fact that he had been a suspect. Aged 28 at the time of the murder of Pat Docker, McInnes had always been a fastidiously dressed man. Furthermore, he had been raised by parents who were members of the Brethren religious sect, fundamentalist Christians whose adherents never drank or gambled and had a strict attitude towards sexual morality.

McInnes frequented the Old Ship Inn, always making sure that his mother did not see him enter the place, because she would have disapproved. Once there, he broke Brethren rules not only by drinking – although never excessively – but also by gambling. McInnes would play dominoes, for money, with the old men in the pub. He frequently won. Dressed in smart suits and wearing his regimental Scots Guards tie, he must have been a strange sight at the village pub full of aged men.

Constantly quoting the Bible, he enjoyed telling them of his dealings with the police as a Bible John suspect. According to Alan Crow and Peter Samson, in *Bible John – Hunt for a Killer*, one villager, George Golder, remembers McInnes laughing when he arrived at the pub after his fourth attendance at an identity parade. Until the exhumation, McInnes was a strong suspect. He physically resembled the Bible John Identikit, he was from a religious background and given to quoting the Bible, he was familiar with Glasgow and in particular the Barrowland. Also, he had split up with his wife Helen at around the time of the murder of Pat Docker. If he was enraged with Helen, could the motive for the murder have been a savage hatred of women that he felt able to express only by an act of frenzied killing? His Brethren upbringing involved sexual repression and he may have believed that women, especially those attending places such as the Barrowland in search of male company, were unclean, or even so evil that they deserved to die.

Other murders

There are five additional unsolved murders of women in Scotland. All the women were attacked and killed late at night after they had been out drinking or dancing. All the killings took place between August and December 1977.

On 5 August 1977, twenty-year-old Anna Kenny from the Gorbals area of Glasgow went missing; having spent the evening in a pub with a girlfriend and two men they had met there, she was last seen getting a taxi in the centre of Glasgow. Her remains were found some nineteen months later in a shallow grave in Kintyre, Argyll.

On 1 October 1977, a mother of two, Hilda McAulay from Mayhill, Glasgow, was killed after she left the Plaza Dance Hall. Examination of the body, which was found in Renfrewshire, showed that Hilda had been beaten about the head, raped and strangled to death.

On 16 October 1977, two friends, Christine Eadie and Helen Scott, both aged seventeen, were strangled, beaten and sexually assaulted in Edinburgh after the pubs had closed.

On 3 December 1977, a 23-year-old nurse, Agnes Cooney from Coatbridge, Lanarkshire, was killed; her body, violently mutilated by stab wounds, was found the following day by a farmer in a country field.

Newspapers speculated on the reasons for these killings and what sort of person might be responsible for them. Had Bible John resurfaced? It seems unlikely that there would be a seven-year gap before a compulsive killer started murdering again. Was there another serial killer on the loose? If so, had something stopped him committing further crimes? It may well be that these murders are unconnected to each other and to the Bible John murders.

The exhumation and its results

As we have seen, DNA profiling had revolutionised forensic investigation by the early 1990s, and by the end of 1995 the Bible John case was fully reopened and four police officers were assigned to the task. Led by Chief Inspector Jim McEwan, they re-examined the copious amount of information held on files in Glasgow. Detective Constables William Lindsay and Brian Hughes and a crime analyst, Susan McHarg, read all the statements given to police from 1968 onwards and interviewed the police officers who had worked on the case. John McInnes kept reappearing in the pages of reports and in interviews as a prime suspect.

Strathclyde Police prepared a report on their findings, together with a request for the exhumation of McInnes, which was necessary to compare DNA samples. There had been a preliminary comparison between DNA in the sperm left on Helen Puttock's clothing and the DNA, taken from a mouth swab, of McInnes's sister Netta Mackay, who was still alive. This was considered a close enough match for police to have a good case for proceeding with the exhumation.

When his body was dug up, police also planned to take a plaster cast of his teeth to compare with a bite mark found on Helen Puttock's wrist. Permission for exhumation was granted, and on 1 February 1996 the body of John McInnes was taken from where it had been laid to rest in 1980. Two leading forensic pathologists, Dr Marie Cassidy and Professor Anthony Bassutil, stood at the graveside at St Ninians Cemetery in Stonehill, while press and TV crews thronged the gates of the cemetery, anxious for photographs of the exhumation. It was a freezing cold morning and police had to use a drill to open the hard ground. The body of Elizabeth McInnes, John's mother, had to be removed from the grave so that police could reach McInnes's remains. Both bodies were placed in large coffins and taken away to be tested.

For the next six months, and at a cost to Scottish taxpayers of some £100,000, the forensic team worked on samples of McInnes's remains. Those involved included not only Scottish forensic experts, but also members of the Department of Biological Anthropology at Cambridge University and the Institute of Forensic Medicine in Berlin.

On 15 May McInnes's remains, along with those of his mother, were reburied in the cemetery at St Ninians. A floral tribute from his family was put on top of the fresh grave.

During the months leading up to the forensic tests being made public, Joe Beattie, now retired, was critical of the decision to exhume McInnes, claiming that ten witnesses had failed to identify him as being Bible John, and that therefore any examination of McInnes's DNA would be fruitless.

Then came an announcement of the outcome of their findings. The Lord Advocate of Scotland, Lord McKay of

Drumadoon, announced that there was not sufficient evidence to link John McInnes with the murder of Helen Puttock. He stated, 'The Procurator Fiscal considers that it is reasonable to infer that John Irvine McInnes was not the author of the semen stain ... Crown counsel have instructed that no further investigation is necessary in respect of John Irvine McInnes and have concluded that, on the evidence available, criminal proceedings would not have been justified against Mr McInnes. As in the case of any unsolved murder, the file on Mrs Puttock's death will remain open.'

Forensic tests showed no more than the possibility that the bite marks on Puttock's body had been caused by McInnes.

Following the Lord Advocate's announcement, Jeannie Williams spoke publicly about the man she believed killed her sister and explained that she was certain that John McInnes was not that man. The *Daily Mail* of 6 July 1996 reported her as saying, 'There was a resemblance in height and build but there were also differences, especially the jug ears of the man in the photograph. I will never forget the face of the man I saw the night my sister died.'

By 'photograph' it is presumed she refers to the Identikit picture made by police during the hunt for the killer.

Strathclyde Police apologised to relatives of McInnes for the distress the exhumation and the considerable publicity surrounding it had caused. The inconclusive result of the exhumation had been a great disappointment to Strathclyde Police, and there was some public outcry about the amount of money spent. The result the police were looking for may have been difficult to obtain because of the problems in testing DNA from a dead body. McInnes's family were reported to be relieved at the outcome. On 26 July 1996, the police file on John Irvine McInnes was officially closed. He could no longer be considered a suspect.

Conclusions

Superintendent Joe Beattie remained convinced during the course of his handling of the investigation that the killer had not been among any of the suspects who had been interviewed and attended identity parades – which of course would have ruled out McInnes, who had been questioned by police several times. He reasoned that Jeannie Williams would have been able to make a positive identification, as she had spent several hours with the man. Beattie was of the opinion that one lead among many had not been sufficiently followed up during the early stages of the investigation, and that this had allowed Bible John to remain a free man. But Jeannie Williams's judgement about what the killer looked like may well have been affected by the fact that she had seen Bible John only at night, that the Barrowland was not a brightly lit place and, more importantly, she had been drinking that evening. However, Jeannie has always maintained that if she were to see the killer again she would recognise him, and there is no reason not to believe her.

Bible John may have escaped detection in a number of ways. Somebody close to him may have protected him or harboured him; either a relative or a friend. He may have been committed to a mental institution far away from Glasgow; he may have been a member of a religious order or joined one subsequent to the killings. Charles Stoddart (*see* Bibliography) indicates that one of the early suspects had been arrested and convicted for gross indecency in 1970, and was committed to a mental institution; there were some coincidences between him and the profile of the killer (for example, police found a bible in his car and his teeth were of a pattern similar to that of the killer), but police investigating the Bible John murders, for whatso-ever reason, did not pursue this man.

The killings also raised questions that could not be answered by any forensic means, and if the killer was no longer alive could never be answered. Was the biblical commandment not to commit adultery the reason that Bible John sought out married women? And, most puzzling of all, did the killer know that his victims were all menstruating – and, if so, how? Why was the sanitary towel of one woman removed and placed under her armpit? The man responsible was undoubtedly a psychopath, but he was clever or lucky enough never to have been seen committing the murders, all of which took place in urban areas where passers-by could easily have witnessed them. It is also possible that more than one man was involved in the killings, or that McInnes had indeed been the killer and that the semen stain on Puttock's tights had come from another man. A multitude of questions remain unanswered.

2000 – a new suspect reported to police

In October 2000 British newspapers reported that well-known criminal psychologist Ian Stephen had been contacted by the American relatives of a man in his 60s living in England. These relatives claim that the married man was a close match of the photofit picture of Bible John and that he lived in the Coatbridge area of Lanarkshire in the 1960s. The man, whose identity has not been made public, is reported to have been brought up by his religious aunt. For reasons unknown the man and his family suddenly left Scotland in 1970. Strathclyde Police were reported to be examining this new lead.

4 The Zodiac Killer

A sadistic serial murderer

Running up a tally of a definite six and a maximum of 37 bodies, the Zodiac killer terrorised the Bay Area of San Francisco, California, for at least six years from his first known attack in late 1966. Using both knives and guns on his victims, this serial killer had a penchant for killing courting couples as they sat in their parked cars. Occasionally he would commit his crime wearing a black hood decorated with Zodiac symbols.

The Zodiac killer (or 'the Zodiac', as he called himself) appears to have been highly intelligent but careless in the way he took risks and publicised his own crimes: he left a number of clues as to his identity; he was seen by witnesses and survivors of his attacks, who described him to police; and he issued a series of taunting communications, usually by mail but occasionally by telephone. His handwritten letters sent to local newspapers and police were packed with misspellings and strange ciphers but had obviously been written by an educated man – they featured quotes from Gilbert and Sullivan operettas and some quaint spellings.

Newspapers and TV rushed to publicise these letters, in which he bragged about what he had done, and also threatened further deaths. A widespread fear over where he might strike next added to a climate of paranoia. His killings were thought to have stopped after a letter to the San Francisco police department in 1974; a final letter sent in 1978 may or may not be a hoax. Despite intense publicity and sophisticated police work, the Zodiac has never been caught, and, if he is still alive, may conceivably kill again.

David Faraday and Betty Lou Jensen

20 December 1968 – Vallejo, California

Vallejo, California – situated halfway between Berkeley and the Napa wine-growing area in Northern California – had become a boom town during World War Two. By the late 1960s the town was in decline.

David Arthur Faraday (17) was a student attending Vallejo High School. On the evening of 20 December he was preparing to go on a first date with a girl he had met earlier that month, sixteen-year-old Betty Lou Jensen, who studied at Hogan High School. They were both known to be hard-working, 'clean-cut' young people with spotless reputations. David was one of the top students in his class and was considered one of the school's outstanding athletes.

That evening, David said goodbye to his parents and drove off from his home in suburban Sereno Drive, Vallejo. He was driving his mother's vehicle, a 1961 Rambler station wagon. He took the car across the interstate highway and shortly afterwards, at around 8 p.m., arrived at Betty Lou's house at 123 Ridgewood. David came into the house and chatted with Betty Lou's father, Verne Jensen.

Betty Lou had told her parents that she and David would be going to a Christmas carol concert at Betty's school. However they did not drive there – instead, they visited a friend of Betty Lou's named Sharon, who lived on Brentwood. At 9 p.m. they left the friend's house, not telling her where they were heading. David drove the Rambler to a drive-in restaurant, where he and Betty Lou drank Cokes.

They then continued outside Vallejo city limits to Lake Herman Road, driving east to Water Way, a remote lovers' lane. David stopped the vehicle in front of the Lake Herman pumping station. He locked the car doors and reclined the front seats. Between 10.15 and 11 p.m. that night, the car and its occupants were seen by three sets of witnesses who drove past: a sailor and his girlfriend, a local ranch owner, Stella Borges, and a pumping-station contractor, Homer Your, and his wife Peggie. These drivers in turn had been seen by two racoon hunters whose pick-up truck was parked in a nearby field. At 11.05 p.m., another car came down a bend on the road and caught Betty Lou and David in its headlights. The driver drove forward and parked his car ten feet away to the right of the Rambler. At 11.10, both cars and their occupants – the new arrival being a stocky white man, wearing a wind-cheater and glasses – were witnessed by an oil worker driving home. From the available evidence it may be surmised that events then occurred as follows.

The man in the car pulled down his window and asked David and Betty Lou to leave their car. When they refused, he pulled out a gun. He then fired shots at the car, with the aim of forcing the terrified youngsters to leave the vehicle. When they got out of the passenger side, the assailant ran to their side of the car. Betty Lou was at this point outside the vehicle. The man instantaneously fired his gun at point-blank range at the side of David's head. His skull exploded with the impact of the bullet, but he was not dead, continuing breathing and making a raspy sound. A horrified Betty Lou ran away towards the roadside, pursued by the gunman who, from ten feet away, shot her in the back with five bullets, killing her. The assailant then drove his sedan away.

At 11.15 Mrs Borges drove past the scene where David Faraday had parked the car – she was on her way to pick up her son in nearby Benicia. Witnessing the bodies, she raced towards Benicia to inform police of what she had seen. Stella Borges informed two officers in a patrol car, who arrived at Lake Herman Road. David Faraday was found to be still alive, and an ambulance was called for. Inside the car they discovered a used bullet casing. Police put a blanket over Betty Lou's body, which was now lying in a pool of blood. Betty Lou was pronounced dead on the scene. At 12.05 a.m., David Faraday, arriving at Vallejo General Hospital on his way to the intensive-care unit, was declared dead on arrival.

Evidence left behind by the killer included nine more used .22-calibre bullet casings and several footprints. There was no evidence of any type of sexual assault or sexual motive for the crimes. Bullet slugs were also found, and these were examined forensically by Criminal Investigation and Identification in Sacramento. That police department's conclusion was that 'considerable difficulty will be encountered in positively identifying the responsible weapon . . . a conclusive identification of the responsible weapon will be extremely difficult, if not impossible'.

David Faraday and Betty Lou Jensen had had no enemies – police could not come up with any motive for the slayings. No one apart from their killer had witnessed the shootings, and there were no suspects.

Darlene Ferrin and Mike Mageau

5 July 1969 – Vallejo, California

On the day following the Faraday/Jensen murders, a shocked waitress, Darlene Ferrin, told a co-worker at Terry's Restaurant in Vallejo that she knew the two victims, and that she would never go near Lake Herman

Road again. Darlene had attended Hogan High School, where Betty Lou had been a student. Although aged 22, Darlene had braces on her teeth and looked and acted like a teenager. She was also seen by some as somewhat overfriendly – she would talk to strangers. Twice married, she lived in an apartment building with her husband Dean, a cook, and their baby girl Dena. Several suspicious events connected to Darlene were later reported to have taken place in the months following the Faraday/Jensen murders.

1. On 26 February 1969, Darlene's babysitter observed a stocky man in a white sedan car watching the Ferrins' apartment; when the babysitter discussed this the next day with Darlene she told her that the man was 'checking up' on her and that she had witnessed this man murdering someone.
2. On 15 March 1969, Darlene's sister, Pam Suennen, took delivery of a mysterious package at the Ferrins' home from a man wearing horn-rimmed glasses who had a white car and warned Pam not to look inside the package.
3. On 24 May 1969, Darlene held a painting party at the home she and Dean had bought at 1300 Virginia Street, next door to the local sheriff's office. Friends at the party noticed Darlene appearing nervous and ill. The 'guests', who were there to paint the newly purchased house, included men who Darlene's babysitter believed had been having affairs with Darlene. Dean was not present, and when a stocky man arrived, Linda Del Buono, a sister of Darlene, claims a now terrified Darlene was in such a state of fear that she begged Linda to leave the house and not to talk to the stocky man.
4. On 22 June 1969, Linda saw the stocky man sitting at a table for two and a half hours at Terry's Restaurant and watching an increasingly nervous Darlene at work.

5. Darlene told her fifteen-year-old sister Christina that 'something big' was going to happen within the next few days.

However, Dean Ferrin has claimed since that he noticed no unusual behaviour or any fears expressed by his wife in the months prior to her death. Their relationship, however, was deteriorating, and during the latter part of their marriage she had been dating other men and was often out in San Francisco until the early hours of the morning.

On the evening of 4 July 1969, while Dean was out working, Darlene had arranged a date with her friend Mike Mageau. They would go to San Francisco and see a movie. Darlene had told Dean that she would be home by 10 p.m., as Dean had plans to bring some of his restaurant colleagues home later for some Fourth of July celebrations. However, Darlene's plans changed – instead, she spent the evening at nearby Mare Island with her sister Christina, watching a firework display. At 10.30 p.m., the fireworks being over, Darlene drove to Terry's car park with Christina. She got out of the car and talked to an older man in a white car. Christina was then dropped off at her home, and Darlene went to the new house on Virginia where her babysitter told her that a man had been calling for her on the phone all evening.

Darlene changed her clothes and went out again to pick up Mike Mageau. As she pulled away from Mike's house, they noticed they were being followed by a car, a light-coloured '58 or '59 Falcon, which they could not shake off. Darlene drove into the empty car park of the Blue Rock Springs Golf Club. Hoping to lose the pursuing car, she quickly turned off the car lights. The other car entered the car park and its driver parked it a few feet away from Darlene's vehicle. It, too, also now had its lights off. Then the driver switched on the ignition and drove off at speed. The couple in the other car breathed a sigh of relief.

However, the same car returned some five minutes later, and was positioned with its lights on behind Darlene's vehicle. The occupant left the vehicle, carrying a glaringly bright torch. Mike thought this was a police check, and he and Darlene reached for their identification. The blinding torchlight came close, and simultaneously a shot was fired at Mike's face through the closed car window. Further gunfire ensued. Mageau was also shot in the knee, and Ferrin received nine bullets: two in each arm and then, like Betty Lou Jensen, five in her back.

The gunshots, followed by the speedy exit of the attacker's car, had been heard by 22-year-old George Bryant, whose father was the caretaker of the Blue Rock Springs golf course. However, the bodies were found by some teenagers who were driving around the area in search of one of their friends. They called the police. Detectives apparently took their time arriving at the scene because they thought the reported shootings were in fact the explosions of Fourth of July fireworks. Officer Hoffman and Sergeant Conway were already at the scene of the crime, another phone call to police having been made, in all probability by Bryant. They were talking to Mike, who was severely wounded and in great pain.

When Detectives Lynch and Rust arrived, they noticed that, strangely, Mike was wearing three pairs of trousers and three sweaters and other clothing – on a very hot July evening. They also recognised Darlene from Terry's Restaurant. Ambulances arrived for the injured pair. Darlene, still alive, was driven to hospital, only to be pronounced dead on arrival at 12.38.

At 12.40, a man telephoned the Vallejo Police Department and said he wanted to report a double murder. He gave directions to the golf course car park, claimed the weapon used was a 9mm Luger, and declared, 'I also killed those kids last year.' That call was traced to a phone box in front of the sheriff's office and within sight of

Darlene and Dean's new home. A witness noticed a stocky white man using the phone booth at that time who, seeing he had been observed, swiftly opened the booth door, automatically switching off the light inside it.

The first letters – the Zodiac's cryptograms

On 31 July 1969, letters were received by the San Francisco *Examiner*, the San Francisco *Chronicle* and the Vallejo *Times-Herald*. In each letter was a claim that the writer of the letter was the Vallejo murderer. In each letter was one-third of a series of cryptic symbols, and a demand that the three newspapers publish these codes on their front pages simultaneously. If this were not done, further murders would occur. The text of the letter to the *Times-Herald* was as follows:

Dear Editor

I am the killer of the 2 teenagers last Christmas at Lake Herman and the Girl last 4th of July. To Prove this I shall state some facts which only I + the police know.

Christmas

1. Brand of Ammo Super X
2. 10 shots fired
3. Boy was lying feet to car
4. Girl was lyeing on right side feet to west

4th of July

1. Girl was wearing patterned pants
2. Boy was also shot in knee
3. Brand name of ammo was Western

Here is a cyipher or that is part of one. The other 2 parts of this cipher have been mailed to the S.F. Examiner + the S.F. Chronicle.

I want you to print this cipher on your front page by Fry Afternoon Aug 1-69. If you do not do this I will go on a kill rampage Fry night that will last the whole weekend. I will cruse around and pick off stray people that are alone then move on to kill some more untill I have killed over a dozen people over the weekend.

At the end of the ciphered text was an enigmatic chain of letters forming the word

EBEORIETEMETHHPITI

The newspapers duly published the three sections of the cryptogram; only the *Times-Herald* published in full the non-encoded part of the letter it had received. Readers who guessed that the curious string of letters at the end of the message was an anagram of the killer's real name added various letters to come up with such suggestions as Emmet O Wright, Robert Hemphill, Leo Blackman, Timothie E Pheiberte and Robert Emmet the Hippie.

Meanwhile, a high school teacher and his wife solved the code within a week, and US Naval code-breakers verified their findings. The translated message was published on 12 August. In it the writer claimed,

I like killing people because it is so much fun it is more fun than killing wild game ... because man is the most dangerous animal of all to kill ... it is even better than getting your rocks off with a girl the best part is when I die I will be reborn in Paradice and all I have killed will become my slaves ...

Shortly after the three cipher blocks had been printed, the Vallejo chief of police requested another letter containing more facts about the killings in order to prove that the writer was in fact the killer. A second letter was then mailed to the *Examiner*, posted on 7 August. For the first time the writer commenced with the words 'This is the Zodiac speaking', and continued,

In answer to your asking for more details about the good times I had in Vallejo, I shall be very happy to supply them with even more material. By the way, are the police having a good time with the code? If not, tell them to cheer up, when they do crack it they will have me . . .

The letter went on to give further details about the 4 July shootings, and described in detail the use of a 'pencil flashlight' attached to his gun during the December murders, explaining that this was how he was able to hit his targets accurately and speedily without using gun sights. The writer concluded, 'I was not happy to see that I did not get front page coverage'.

Cecilia Shepard and Bryan Hartnell

27 September 1969 – Napa County, California

Zodiac next attacked in a region north of Vallejo, at Lake Beryessa in Napa County. Cecilia Ann Shepard had finished two years as a student at Pacific Union College in Napa County; on this day she was picking up her belongings at the college and preparing to move to University College in Riverside, where she planned to continue her studies in music. Helping her pack her belongings that morning was a former boyfriend, Bryan Hartnell, with whom Cecilia had remained on good terms.

They spent the afternoon of 27 September driving around Napa and visiting friends.

Around mid-afternoon, they decided to drive to Lake Beryessa, arriving there at 4 p.m. They walked out into a clearing to have a picnic, and sat on a rug they had brought with them. Apparently, Cecilia noticed a man some distance away. Then the man suddenly disappeared. A short period of time passed. After a while there was the sound of movement nearby, and the man appeared again. This time he emerged from behind a tree, holding a gun. The stranger's face was obscured by a weird black hood. On a bib below the hood the man had stitched on the symbol of a cross superimposed over a circle, the symbol that had appeared in the three-part cryptogram and would become known as the killer's 'signature' ciphers. The man had cut holes in the hood through which to see and breathe. Over his eyes he wore a pair of sunglasses, and around his waist were several lengths of clothesline.

The hooded man pointed his pistol at the couple and demanded cash and their car key, claiming, 'I want your car to go to Mexico.' The man explained he was an escaped convict who had killed a prison guard in Montana. He then told Cecilia to tie up Bryan with the clothesline. Then he retied Bryan, this time with painfully tight knots. He tied up Cecilia, and told the pair, 'I'm going to have to stab you people.' Hartnell begged the man to stab him first, and the man took out a foot-long sheath knife and stabbed Bryan repeatedly in the back, although he remained alive. He then turned to Cecilia and stabbed her ten times in the back, breasts, genitals and abdomen. While Cecilia was whimpering for the man to stop, Hartnell decided to play dead. When the man had finished stabbing the girl, although she, too, was still alive, he walked to Hartnell's car, where he wrote on the inside of the vehicle in a black marker:

Vallejo
12-20-68
5-4-69
Sept- 27-69-6.30
by knife

The murderer then drove to a pay phone, told police he wanted to report a double murder and gave the location of the bodies, claiming at the end of the call, 'I'm the one that did it.' The phone call was traced, and a set of fingerprints were recovered from the phone handset. These did not match with any known prints in any database.

Hartnell was to survive the attack and was able to give police a description of the hooded man as being, among other attributes, 'really fat'. Two days after the attack Cecilia Shepard died of her injuries in hospital.

Paul Stine

11 October 1969 – San Francisco, California

At around 9.30 on the evening of Saturday 11 October 1969 Paul Stine, a taxi driver, picked up a passenger who had hailed his cab on the corner of Mason and Geary Streets in San Francisco. According to the handwritten log of destinations that Stine kept in his cab, the passenger had asked to be driven to the intersection of Washington and Maple Streets in the Presidio Heights district. The passenger was taken to his destination, travelling along to the west of the city, but on arrival requested that Stine drive him one block further.

When the taxi was at the corner of Washington and Cherry, the passenger shot Stine in the right side of his head. The shooting was audible outside the cab. The passenger was seen by several witnesses – the first a fourteen-year-old girl in a building opposite where the taxi had stopped. Witnesses who saw the passenger searching Stine's clothing and taking his wallet and keys described him as a stocky figure. The killer also tore off a section of Stine's shirt, which he rubbed in his victim's blood. He wiped the interior of the cab with a cloth, presumably to remove fingerprints, and then fled.

The teenage girl and her friends, having heard the gunshot and become suspicious of the man's behaviour, called police, their call being logged at 9.58 p.m. A grievous error was then made: police mistakenly broadcast a description of the wanted man to patrolmen in which they stated he was a NMA – Negro Male Adult. Patrolmen Donald Foulkes and Eric Zelms were on their way to the scene of the crime when they noticed a stocky white man walking up Cherry Street. According to one account they questioned him as to whether he had seen any suspicious events in the vicinity and he replied he had seen a man with a gun on Washington Street; this account has never been corroborated by either of the officers involved. Minutes later, the police radio then corrected their erroneous description: the suspect was now white. At 10.55 p.m. Officers Armand Pelissetti and Frank Peda and Homicide Inspector Walter Kracke arrived at the scene and saw the body of Paul Stine in the seat of his cab. An ambulance arrived and Stine was pronounced dead. The cab, its interior awash with blood, was carefully examined. A 9mm bullet casing was discovered on the floor. Fingerprints, including some made in blood, were discovered within the vehicle. Partial prints were found that were neither Stine's nor those of other passengers Stine was known to have picked up that day. Eight fingerprint fragments were discovered – none of them giving the amount of detail to be of any use to investigators.

On Monday, 13 October, the San Francisco *Chronicle* duly received a letter from the Zodiac. Inside the envelope was the torn-off and bloodied portion of Paul Stine's shirt, and a missive which began, 'This is the Zodiac speaking. I am the murderer of the taxi driver over by Washington St. + Maple St.', and went on to taunt the police that they could have caught him on the Saturday if they hadn't been 'holding road races with their motorcicles seeing who could make the most noise'. The letter also threatened future terror: 'School children make nice targets. I think I shall wipe out a school bus some morning . . .'

When parts of the letter were published later that week, the public reacted with panic. Extra security was provided for school buses in the Napa region. Meanwhile, the killer had been seen. Patrolmen Foukes and Zelms helped police put together a composite picture of the wanted man.

Two hours after midnight on Wednesday, 22 October 1969, a phone caller made contact with the Oakland Police Department. He claimed to be the Zodiac and requested that either F Lee Bailey or Melvin Belli, two of the best-known defence attorneys in the USA, appear on a talk show on Channel 7 TV. The caller promised to make a phone call to the show, which went out daily at 7 a.m. Belli was contacted and duly appeared on the programme. At 7.20, the caller spoke to Belli. Asking to be called 'Sam', the caller, speaking to Belli in segments amounting to 35 calls in the space of two hours – of which twelve went out live on air – arranged to meet the attorney at the Fairmont Hotel, claimed he had medical problems and said he didn't want to go to the gas chamber. During the course of the call the meeting place was rearranged – Belli would meet the caller in front of a thrift shop in the Mission district of San Francisco.

Meanwhile police, listening in, decided that the caller had a much younger-sounding voice than previous callers. When TV crews gathered at the meeting place at the appointed time, there was no sign of the caller. It was later discovered that the calls were a hoax: the 'Zodiac' turned out to be a mental patient at Napa State Hospital.

The San Francisco *Chronicle* received two further envelopes containing communications from the Zodiac. This time, however, no hoax was involved. A further piece of Paul Stine's ripped shirt was enclosed with one of the letters. The first letter, posted on 8 November, was written on the back of a humorous greeting card decorated with a picture of a wet ink pen hanging up to dry and the caption 'Sorry I haven't written, but I've just washed my pen and I can't do a thing with it'. The card contained a new message in cipher form – some 340 symbols. The Zodiac asked the newspaper to print the new cipher, threatening, 'I get awfully lonely when I'm ignored, so lonely I could do my Thing!!!!!' Also were written the words 'Des July Aug Sept Oct = 7', which was interpreted as meaning that the killer had committed two murders more than the five he had previously claimed.

Detectives seized upon the unsolved murders, in San Jose in August 1969, of two teenage girls, Deborah Furlong and Kathy Snoozy. The pair had been violently stabbed to death with over 300 wounds between them. Release of information that the Zodiac may have been their killer caused fresh panic among parents in San Jose. On examination of the evidence, it seemed to police unlikely that the Zodiac was responsible, as he had not bragged about the crime shortly after the event – a delay of three months in informing police was not his style. (In the event, police guesswork was correct: in 1971 the killer of the two girls was found; he was not the Zodiac.)

The second letter, posted on 9 November, was seven pages long. In it the Zodiac again claimed to have murdered seven people. He said his future slayings would be arranged to 'look like routine robberies ... fake accidents'. He said he committed his crimes appearing in 'descise' and had covered his fingertips in glue so as not to leave prints, that he had bought his weapons by mail order and he had left 'false clews' in Paul Stine's cab. He then described a bomb he might construct, listing ingredients to produce home-made explosives. This was accompanied by a drawing of the bomb mechanism, which he said was 'stored in my basement for future use'. This new threat to use a bomb was not made public at the time.

Just over a month later, the lawyer Melvin Belli, having received attention from a fake Zodiac, was about to get a letter from the real one. To prove it, attached to the correspondence was another piece of Paul Stine's shirt. It had been posted on 20 December 1969, but took another week to reach Belli's office, where it was opened by his secretary. Belli, who was attending a conference in Munich, West Germany, was sent a photocopy of the letter and envelope. The letter wished Belli a 'happy Christmas' (this precise wording being unusual in the USA led detectives to wonder whether Zodiac had been born or brought up in England) and asked him for help – telling the attorney in the now familiar misspelled fashion, 'I am afraid I will loose control again and take my nineth and posibly tenth victom'. He wrote that there had been a delay in making the threatened bomb because 'the triger mech requires much work'. Once again, two further murders, unaccounted for as far as police were aware, had been added to the list.

Belli, writing in the pages of the San Francisco *Chronicle*, offered to help the killer in any way he wished. No reply came from the Zodiac.

Kathleen Johns

22 March 1970 – San Joaquin County, California

On the late evening of 22 March 1970 Kathleen Johns, a resident of Vallejo, was driving with her ten-month-old daughter Jennifer along Highway 132 in San Joaquin County when behind her appeared a light-coloured Chevrolet driven by a man who kept flashing his lights and sounding his horn at her. The stranger drove alongside her and shouted at her that one of her wheels was wobbling. Kathleen Johns was unwilling to trust this man, but he was now in front of her. Although very suspicious, but now having driven on to a road with more traffic on it, Johns stopped her vehicle and the man, who had parked behind her, got out and started using a wrench on the nuts on Johns's right rear wheel, pretending to tighten them when he was in fact removing them.

The man, whom Johns recalls as clean-shaven, of smart appearance and speaking in a bizarre monotone voice, then asked her to try driving her car. When she did, the wheel spun off. The man then offered to drive her to a service station. He drove her and her baby Jennifer around in a seemingly aimless fashion, not wanting to stop at any of the service stations that an increasingly frightened Kathleen Johns pointed out to him. When she eventually asked the man if he always helped people in this way, he replied, 'By the time I get through with them, they won't need my help.' Another thirty minutes passed before the man threatened to kill her and throw the baby out of the vehicle. After a period of 'two to three hours', according to Johns, she grabbed her child and jumped out of the car when it stopped. After running across a field, she hid in the shadows of an embankment. After a short while the man was seen to drive away.

Arriving at a nearby police station to tell police she had been abducted and threatened, Johns noticed the composite drawing of the Zodiac, and immediately realised this was the man she had just escaped from. When police were sent to find Johns's car, it had been set on fire. It is believed the Zodiac returned to her vehicle and torched it.

If this man was indeed the Zodiac, police now had an excellent witness. She had seen his face, apparently undisguised, and heard his voice at very close quarters; she had also seen the type of car he drove. Amazingly, Kathleen Johns and her child had escaped from the Zodiac without being physically harmed.

For several months now the Zodiac had not sent any letters to the media. Then, within the space of eight days, two letters were received, again sent to the San Francisco *Chronicle*. The first, posted on 20 April 1970 and arriving the following day, contained a series of symbols, for the first time combined with a numeral, the encircled figure 8, that the sender claimed would spell out his real name. Various attempts failed to come up with anything resembling a likely-sounding name. The letter claimed that he had attempted to attack a bus but the bomb had been 'a dud' because of rain. The writer now boasted of having killed 'ten people to date'. There was yet another drawing of the innards of a bomb, followed by the Zodiac symbol and the tally of those murdered so far:

Zodiac – 10 SFPD – 0

The second envelope arrived at the newspaper's offices on 29 April. It had been posted the previous day. Within it was a second humorous greetings card, and a demand from the Zodiac to tell the public about his threats to bomb a school bus. (Since the November 1969 letters, news about the bomb threats had been withheld by the media at the request of the police in order to avoid mass panic.) He also requested 'some nice Zodiac buttons [badges]' be made. Chief Al Nelder of the San Francisco Police Department held a press conference in which he warned of the possibility of a bomb being used to blow up a school bus.

No Zodiac buttons had been made. Zodiac's eleventh letter arrived, yet again at the *Chronicle*, on 29 June 1970. In it he wrote that he was 'very upset' that people were not wearing the buttons, and that he had 'punished' the people of San Francisco, not by bombing a bus but killing a man in a parked car with 'a .38'. According to the Zodiac, the murder tally was now twelve. Yet another bomb was threatened. This time its location was indicated by an enclosed service-station road map and a series of 32 ciphers.

Another letter received by the *Chronicle* on 24 July continued his complaint about the buttons. If people did not wear them he would 'torture all 13 of my slaves that I have waiting for me in Paradice'. The notion that those he killed would become his slaves after the Zodiac's death was not a new one and had appeared in several previous letters; but the figure of thirteen was a new claim. The writer confessed to abducting Johns and her child – 'that woeman and her baby that I gave a rather interesting ride for a coupple howers one evening'.

Two days later another letter arrived. This continued the theme of torturing 'all 13' slaves and described the means of doing this, followed by a stanza that twisted the words of Gilbert and Sullivan's 'Let the Punishment Fit the Crime' from *The Mikado* and a further parody of the song 'I've Got a Little List' from the same operetta. He also added a line about the map and its puzzling cipher that had been included in his letter of June 1970: 'P.S. The Mt. Diablo Code concerns Radians & #inches along the radians'.

A radian is an angular chunk of a circle – equal to 360 degrees, divided by $2 \times$ pi. Whoever was writing these letters was making the police aware that not only was this person a Gilbert and Sullivan aficionado, but he also had some knowledge of maths and maps.

Letters to San Francisco *Chronicle* reporter Paul Avery

Avery had written many of the *Chronicle*'s news stories about the Zodiac. The next letter to the *Chronicle* had his name on the envelope and arrived on 28 October 1970. Inside it was a children's Hallowe'en card on which was drawn a strange new cipher, thirteen eyes and the words 'Peek a boo, you are doomed'. It was signed with the Zodiac's customary Z and his cross-within-a-circle symbol. This letter was seen as a threat against Paul Avery's life, and Avery was given authority to carry a revolver and given training by police marksmen.

The Cheri Jo Bates connection?

A few days after getting the Zodiac's letter, Avery was sent an anonymous letter urging him to investigate the 'comparative similarities' between the killing of Cheri Jo Bates in October 1966 and the Zodiac murders.

An eighteen-year-old student and former high school cheerleader, Bates was murdered near a car park at Riverside City College. Her car had been disabled by interference with the electrical wiring, and Bates appears to have been stabbed in a dark doorway, twice in the chest and once in the back. Her throat had been violently cut, so viciously and deeply that her head was almost cut off. Police found a man's Timex watch with paint splashes over it, various footprints at the scene of the crime and skin traces under Cheri Jo's fingernails. A letter entitled 'A Confession' had been sent to a Riverside newspaper and to local police one month after the killing. The letter went into detail of how Cheri Jo's car had been interfered with and exactly how she had been strangled and stabbed. The writer also threatened to kill more women.

Six months after the killing, the local newspaper and police, and also Bates's father, were sent the carbon copies of the same letter, which claimed 'Bates had to die There will be more'.

In early 1967 a bizarre poem was discovered written on a desk at the Riverside City College Library, which appeared to refer to a murder. It included the words 'blood spurting dripping spilling all over her new dress' and concluded, 'just wait till next time'. Whether this was written by the killer, a student morbidly fascinated by Bates's death or by a hoaxer is not known.

As a result of the letter to Avery, Riverside police met with detectives from the other counties where the Zodiac had committed his murders, and agreed there was a 'definite link' between the Bates killing and the Zodiac. (Since then this theory has been discounted by Riverside police; as of 1998 they believe a local man was responsible for Cheri Jo's murder.)

On 15 March 1971 a letter from the Zodiac arrived at the *Los Angeles Times*. In it he claimed to be 'crack proof' and hinted at more killings, saying police 'are only finding the easy ones, there are a hell of a lot more down there'. The letter ended with the Zodiac symbol and the figures '$-17+$'. One week later, Paul Avery was sent a postcard with various words and photos cut from newspapers. The text included the words 'Sought victim 12' and 'Peek through the pines'. The writing of the address was consistent with previous Zodiac letters.

There was a gap of almost three years before the Zodiac wrote another letter to the press. On 30 January 1974 the San Francisco *Chronicle* received a letter: the writer said he had enjoyed seeing the film *The Exorcist*, which he called a 'saterical comedy', quoted further from Gilbert and Sullivan and threatened, 'If I do not see this note in your paper, I will do something nasty ...' There was a new 'score', 'Me-37 SFPD-0', and the writer signed off with a new bizarre symbol.

Two further letters in the Zodiac's unmistakable handwriting were sent to the *Chronicle* in May and July 1974. The first letter complained about the paper running an advert for the film *Badlands*; the second criticised the paper's columnist Count Marco Spinelli, and urged the paper to sack him. A frightened Spinelli left his job and relocated to Hawaii shortly after this letter was received. No other letter, however, made any threats or contained any boasting of the number of murder victims.

A final letter was sent to the *Chronicle* on 24 April 1978, nine and a half years after the last definite Zodiac victim, Paul Stine. Addressed to the editor, the letter claimed, 'I am back here with you' and criticised 'that city pig Toschi' (Detective Dave Toschi, who had led the investigations).

The profile of a killer

It is generally acknowledged that there were at least seven murders by the Zodiac killer during 1968–9. There are a number of other unsolved homicides in the regions of California that Zodiac operated in that could have been committed by this same killer, but no evidence to connect them other than that of location and the means of murder, victims being strangled or shot. The Zodiac outwitted the police time after time; he may have been clever, but he certainly was lucky, too. A psychological profile would indicate an individual who lived alone, had experienced rejection, harboured hostility to authority and had the ability to carry out his crimes rapidly, efficiently and without fear. Enjoying the limelight, he repeatedly sought publicity for what he had done, and any clues he claimed to provide through the use of cryptograms only led to dead ends.

Despite well-publicised composite pictures of the killer's appearance, no one came forward claiming to have recognised him. Was his 'descise' so thorough that no one could recognise him? And how was he disguised, if at all, when he drove Kathleen Johns around deserted roads for several hours in 1970? Many other questions to which there do not appear to be answers arise in this case. Why did the definite Zodiac killings take place during that particular eleven-month period? Did the killer die or get put in prison, or did he decide to stop murdering of his own volition? Did he continue to kill, but not to publicise his crimes? Were some letters subsequent to the murder of Paul Stine – obviously excluding those that contained the torn-off parts of the taxi driver's clothing – well-informed hoaxes?

There are several theories on the identity of the killer; some have surfaced recently that bear examination. The principal named suspects are as follows:

Bruce Davis – the Manson connection?

The Tate/LaBianca homicides took place in July 1969 in Los Angeles – during the middle of the Zodiac's murder spree. Both the Zodiac and the Manson 'family' were involved in the occult. There has been speculation linking the killings of Scientologists Doreen Gaul and James Sharp in November 1969 with the Manson family murders earlier that year – in both cases the victims were frenziedly and repeatedly stabbed to death. Methods employed in the Gaul/Sharp killings in turn have been identified as similar to those found in the murder of Cheri Jo Bates.

A Manson family member, Bruce Davis, who was not imprisoned at the time of the Sharp/Gaul murders, and who had lived in a commune with Doreen Gaul, is considered to be also a suspect in the Zodiac killings. It would appear unlikely that Davis, given his mental state and frequent use of drugs, would have been able to operate in the quick-witted way that the Zodiac was able to. Also, if Davis was the Zodiac, who then was the author of letters subsequent to the Stine murder? It would have been impossible for Davis to have sent these letters from prison.

Lawrence Kane – identified by victims

Positively identified by both Darlene Ferrin's sister Pam as a man who was stalking Darlene before her death and by Kathleen Johns as the man responsible for her abduction, Kane, aged 45 in 1969, had suffered head injuries in a car accident in 1962, and was said by his psychologist to be 'losing the ability to control self-gratification'.

At the time of the Stine murder, Kane lived in a building a few blocks away from where his taxi was found. K, A, N and E are four of the eight letters in the Zodiac cipher sent to police on 20 April 1969. Kane is still alive and lives in Nevada. The US television programme *America's Most Wanted* transmitted in 1988 named Kane as a credible Zodiac suspect. However, Lawrence Kane has not been charged with any crimes as a result of this televised investigation and it must be concluded that police do not consider him a suspect.

Arthur Leigh Allen

Prior to the Zodiac killings, Allen, born in 1933, had served in the US Navy, from which he was dishonourably discharged, and worked in an elementary school in Valley Springs, California. It is alleged that in January 1968 Allen told a friend that he intended to murder couples at random and to threaten to kill children in letters to the police – and that he would call himself the Zodiac. Having been sacked from his job as a petrol-station attendant in Vallejo in April 1969 – reasons for this were his drinking problem and an interest in small girls – he then worked as a janitor in an elementary school in Vallejo.

Allen was questioned by police following the Cecilia Shepard murder. Allen was one of many Zodiac suspects interviewed by police during 1971. He continued working in Vallejo until 1987, and died of 'natural causes' in 1992.

In an interview in the *San Francisco Examiner* published on 26 July 1991, Allen proclaimed his innocence and said that he had passed a lie-detector test on whether he was the Zodiac killer.

The Unabomber as Zodiac – Theodore 'Ted' Kaczynski

Using the name 'The Unabomber' in his communications with the media, and even having his book *The Unabomber Manifesto*, an explanation of his extreme ecological and anarchist views, published anonymously before his arrest, a former college professor, Theodore Kaczynski, born in 1942, was responsible for a seventeen-year campaign of terror from 1978 to 1995, which he conducted by sending parcel bombs through the mail. His targets were principally academics at universities and airline companies. He manufactured and sent a total of fifteen bombs, which caused many injuries. Kaczynski may well have had a grudge against universities, as his own career as a maths professor had ended when he resigned for unknown reasons from his job at the University of California at Berkeley in 1969.

During the time he sent out the bombs, Kaczynski was without employment and living as a hermit in Montana. During the last ten years of his activity, Kaczynski's packages killed three people:

- Hugh Scrutton, owner of a computer rental store in Sacramento, California, an advertising executive in New Jersey

- Thomas Mosser, New Jersey advertising executive

- Gilbert Murray, a lobbyist for the timber industry in Sacramento.

Kaczynski was arrested in April 1996 following a tip-off to police by his brother David Kaczynski, who had noticed similarities between the wording of the *Manifesto* and letters that Theodore had written to him. Following indictments, Kaczynski made a plea bargain with the US government based on his defence of mental illness; he was sentenced to imprisonment for life.

There are certain similarities between the police sketches of both the Unabomber and the Zodiac killer. Both men were highly intelligent, mathematically minded, skilled in the use of guns and used letters to communicate with the media about their crimes. Both killers appeared to revel in publicity and taunting the public about where they would strike next. During the time span between the Farady/Jensen killings and the murder of Paul Stine (December 1968 to October 1969), Kaczynski was teaching in Berkeley – close to where the killings took place. Many of the Zodiac's victims – including Stine – were full- or part-time students. Both the Zodiac and Kaczynski exhibited sociopathic tendencies and were able to repeatedly and systematically seek their victims and kill them.

Should Theodore Kaczynski, serving a life sentence, wish to further increase his notoriety and achieve more newspaper headlines, he might claim to be the Zodiac killer – which so far he has not done.

The case remains unsolved.

5 Helen Smith

About Helen Smith

Helen Linda Smith was born on 3 January 1956, the first child of Ron and Jeryl Smith. Ron Smith had been a police officer specialising in communications technology, who now had his own business repairing television sets. There was plenty of work, as sales of TV sets were escalating in Britain, so Ron's business flourished and the couple had three further children, Graham, David and Beverley.

Brought up in Leeds, Helen left school at the age of eighteen. Her first career choice was to serve in the police force, as her father and grandfather had done. However, the subjects she had studied did not make her eligible to apply to the police and she began training to become a nurse. In 1976, having passed her nursing exams, Helen began work at St George's Hospital, Tooting, in south London. At around this time Ron Smith sold his television-repair business to a larger company. Ron also found out that Jeryl had been unfaithful to him, and angrily demanded a divorce.

Helen Smith moved up north to work at St James's Hospital in Leeds. Having helped Helen move into accommodation for nurses, Ron, a man of old-fashioned morals, was not pleased when Helen started sharing a flat with a boyfriend. Having confronted Helen with his displeasure, Ron Smith and Helen quarrelled. In 1978, encouraged by her mother Jeryl, Helen applied for employment at the Bakhsh Hospital in Jeddah, Saudi Arabia. The advantages of working abroad were largely financial: pay would be much higher than that of state-employed nurses in the UK and the money would be tax-free, with accommodation provided by the hospital and better, less stressed working conditions.

Her application was successful. In early December 1978, Helen Smith flew out to Jeddah to start her new job. Helen was popular with her colleagues and became friendly with Dr Richard Arnot, a surgeon at the Bakhsh Hospital, who lived with his wife Penny and their two young children, eight-year-old William and six-year-old Lucy, in a sixth-floor apartment of a block of flats adjoining the hospital. Smith frequently babysat for the Arnots and was much liked by their children.

In the widely published photograph of Helen Smith in her nurse's uniform she appears younger than her age, looking more like a schoolgirl than an adult, giving the camera a broad and cheerful smile. According to an interview published in the *Daily Telegraph* on 28 April 1999, Smith was 'promiscuous' and went out with wealthy Arabs who would give her expensive gifts. An attractive girl, she was popular with the men she met, many of them expatriates earning large amounts of untaxed income in a country with strict Islamic laws on both the drinking of alcohol and sexual behaviour.

Saturday, 19 May 1979

It was Helen Smith who had proposed that Dr Arnot hold a party in his apartment that night. A few days earlier, approaching him at his desk in the hospital, Helen said she had met a young man named Tim Hayter, a professional diver from New Zealand, who was working for a salvage company and living on a barge in the harbour with a number of other men. She asked Arnot if he could hold a farewell party for Hayter, who was going off for a few weeks on leave; he could not have visitors in his own accommodation, as the barge was in an area that could be entered only by showing a security pass. Arnot agreed; he had wanted to learn how to scuba-dive, and thought Hayter sounded like a promising teacher.

The party started at around 8.30 p.m. on Saturday. Although alcohol was illegal, the means to manufacture it were readily available. In his book Richard Arnot describes his astonishment on first seeing plastic barrels, tubing, sugar and yeast openly on sale in Jeddah. As in any other 'dry' country with thirsty expatriates, there was a flourishing black market in imported spirits.

Those present that evening for varying amounts of time were

- Richard and Penelope Arnot; their two children had been put to bed in their own bedroom, which was situated at the end of the flat furthest from the living room where the party was held

- Helen Smith (Arnot asked several nurses to the party; Helen was the only one who was able to accept his invitation)

- Tim Hayter

- Dr Patrick Alan Kirwin, medical officer for the Lockheed Aircraft Corporation

- Johannes Otten, a Dutch tugboat captain working on marine salvage

- Harry Gutzeit, head of Harms Salvage

- Martin Fleischer, Klaus Ritter, Dieter Chapuis and Manfred Schlaeffer, German divers employed by Harms Salvage who were barge mates of Tim Hayter

- Jacques Texier, a French diver and marine biologist who worked with Hayter.

Also present for a short time were a Chinese friend of Texier's known only as Jimmy, who stayed for a couple of minutes, and another German called Peter, who was there during the first few hours of the party.

Flouting strict Saudi laws forbidding the consumption of alcohol even in private, the partygoers – all expatriates – were drinking bottles of black-market whisky. The alcohol had been provided by Kirwin, who regularly supplied the British community in Jeddah with bottles of Johnnie Walker at the considerable sum of £25 per bottle. The Arnots had bought a dozen bottles from him. Guests had also brought home-made gin, and the Arnots' wine was still also available. As the night went on, the illicit drink flowed freely, pop music was played, including records by Wings, Stevie Wonder, Fleetwood Mac and Captain and Tenille. Helen and Penny danced with several of the men. The party was without incident, and all those there apparently had a pleasant time. Dr Arnot left at 11.30 to attend his patients in the hospital ward; when he left his wife asked him if he could bring some more female guests back with him on his return. Arnot was unable to do this. He returned to the apartment at around 12.30 a.m. on his own, to find the party livelier than before. Helen Smith and Johannes Otten were dancing close together and appeared to be behaving affectionately towards each other. At 2 a.m., Dr Arnot, who was due to be in the operating theatre early that day, went to bed.

Shortly before 3 a.m., Penny Arnot recalls seeing Helen and Johannes going out on to the balcony that was directly outside the living room and assumed they had gone out there for some privacy and possibly to have sex. Just after that time, the four Germans – Fleischer, Ritter, Chapuis and Schlaeffer – left the apartment in order to drive back to the harbour, leaving Johannes Otten, who had accompanied them to the party, behind. They claim to have noticed nothing unusual outside the apartment building at the time they drove off. Penny Arnot appears not to have been concerned that she could not see where Helen or Johannes were and probably assumed that they had at some point – and unseen by her – left the Arnots' apartment to go back to Helen's flat. After the Germans' departure Jacques Texier and Tim Hayter made themselves comfortable on makeshift beds in the living room. Penny Arnot stayed up to tidy the apartment; at one point she woke Tim Hayter and had sex with him in the room while an embarrassed Jacques Texier feigned sleep.

Eight bottles of Johnnie Walker whisky had been drunk by the Arnots and their guests during the course of the party.

At 5.30 a.m. Penny Arnot took Hayter and Texier out on to the balcony to watch the sunrise. Penny was the first person to see anything out of the ordinary: the prostrate form of Helen Smith lying seventy feet below on the ground. At first sight she assumed that she had gone outside and, because of the alcohol she had consumed, fallen asleep. It was only after she looked across from where Smith lay and noticed Otten's corpse gruesomely impaled across the railings that Penny Arnot realised that a tragic event had taken place.

Penny's first action was to wake up her husband and tell him the horrifying news. Dr Arnot immediately dressed and rushed down the stairs of the flats to ascertain whether there was any chance that either Smith or Otten was alive. Impaled, Otten lay in a pool of his own blood, which was by now swarming with ants. Flies buzzed around the two, who showed no signs of life.

When Arnot, his wife and Hayter and Texier arrived on the scene it appeared that Smith and Otten had somehow fallen from the balcony. Otten's body had become impaled so deeply that it could be later removed from the spikes only by being hacked off; Smith lay still on her side on the ground. It appeared that the couple had been having sex just before they fell, and this seemed a likely reason for their having fallen: drunk and passionate, they had simply got carried away and fallen over the low wall outside the balcony.

Otten's shirt was hanging off him; his underpants were pulled down and his genitals were in a swollen state of arousal. Smith's dress was raised above her waist and her underwear was similarly pulled down. Otten's trousers were not at the scene; they were never found.

According to Arnot's account of events, when the surgeon felt for Helen's pulse he felt only cold skin. Like Otten, she had been dead for between one and two hours. It was curious, therefore, that the bodies had only just been noticed.

Aftermath of the discovery

Dr Arnot's first impulse was to call the police, but before he did that all signs of alcohol had to be removed from the apartment. The Arnots, Hayter and Texier were panicked into action, as the penalties for drinking were severe. First to be dealt with was a 60-litre bin of home-made wine, which had to be poured down the sink. Empty whisky bottles had to be concealed. In the midst of this the Arnots were disturbed by a knocking on the door. It was a Dr Rakhman, who lived on the ground floor, accompanied by the caretaker, who was there with the intention of informing the Arnots about the dead bodies outside.

After speaking to Rakhman, Arnot decided to go to the hospital next door and ring the police. But first he rang the hospital's owner, Dr Abdul Rahman Bakhsh, to inform him of the tragic events. When Bakhsh appeared not to understand, Arnot passed the phone to an Arabic-speaking colleague, who told Bakhsh the details again, and also asked him to call the police. This colleague, a surgeon named Dr Sukhtian, told Dr Arnot that he would do so immediately. Arnot then rang the British Embassy and informed the military attaché, Colonel Murray de Klee, of the deaths. Six Saudi police arrived by car at around 6.30; Arnot informed them that the deceased pair had been guests at a party he had given and confessed that during the evening alcohol had been drunk.

Meanwhile, a crowd had gathered who found the dead Johannes Otten's erect penis a source of amusement; his body was quickly covered up with sheets. Two men arrived from the British Embassy, which was located in Jeddah, not in the Saudi capital Riyadh, one of whom was Vice-Consul Gordon Kirby. A policeman took photographs of the corpses. Martin Fleischer, one of the party guests, arrived on the scene; police expressed an interest in him and began quizzing Arnot about exactly who had attended the party. The surgeon reeled off a list of those present, deliberately omitting the name of Kirwin, as he did not wish to get the illicit-alcohol trader into any trouble. In any case, reasoned Arnot, Kirwin had left the party early in the evening – an additional factor in not naming him at this point.

Police then went into the apartment building and examined the Arnots' apartment – which was immaculately tidy. They examined the balcony, and looked in each room, searching for clues.

Partygoers detained

Richard and Penny Arnot, their passports held by the British Embassy, were driven to the police headquarters in Jeddah, where they were placed in a cell; they were soon joined by Tim Hayter and Jacques Texier and then by the four German Harms employees and their boss Harry

Gutseit. They were then taken to the public hospital for blood tests; obviously the consumption of alcohol was a serious issue for the authorities. Following questioning of all the parties, Jacques Texier was released; the remaining expatriates were kept in the yard of the police building, surrounded by armed guards.

Ron Smith hears the news

News of Helen's death reached England in the early afternoon of Sunday, 20 May, when Helen's mother Jeryl, who lived near Leeds, was visited by a police officer who informed her that her daughter had died. Helen's sister Beverley rang Ron Smith and told him what she had heard. Ron Smith phoned the Foreign Office in London and asked for details; he was told that Helen had fallen from the sixth floor of the hospital where she was employed. Ron then rang the Bakhsh Hospital in Jeddah; the senior nurse who answered could not provide Ron with any further information. That evening Ron Smith rang the *Yorkshire Post* newspaper, which on the following day, Monday, 21 May, published the news that a nurse from Yorkshire had fallen to her death in Saudi Arabia.

Ron's son Graham had gone off to London to attempt to find out more. Graham met with a civil servant, Roger Davies, and was told that Helen had fallen from the sixth floor of an adjacent block of flats, not from the hospital, that a Dutchman had been found dead on the ground alongside Helen and that the police in Jeddah had made a number of arrests after the discovery of the bodies. Davies told Graham Smith that the arrests were to do with the drinking that had taken place at the party, and that no one was under suspicion of causing Helen's death.

Ron Smith then rang the Foreign Office again, curious as to why his son had been given information that no one, apparently, was willing to tell *him*. The Foreign Office man he spoke to, Brian Money, became angry with Ron Smith and told him that any information given out by Davies was classified. Following further national-newspaper coverage on Tuesday, Money rang Ron Smith and asked him not to talk to the media about his daughter's death as the Middle East was a sensitive area and the government was fearful that trade with Saudi Arabia could be affected by the negative publicity that could be caused by what Ron had to say. This further infuriated Ron Smith. Money then said that Helen's body would be flown back to the UK at the end of the week. Smith then angrily asked whether there had been a police investigation or a postmortem. Ron Smith decided he would have to go to Saudi Arabia to ascertain what had happened. The Saudi Arabian Embassy in London was happy to provide him with a visa. Ron Smith's flight left for Jeddah on the afternoon of Friday, 25 May.

The expats remain in police custody

The partygoers were kept in the police station yard and systematically interrogated. Texier was found by police and sent back to join the others under police guard. On Monday, 21 May, they were split into two groups and placed in hot, humid, cockroach-infested cells within the police headquarters; Penny Arnot was taken away to a local prison where there was a women's wing. After a number of days in the cells Dr Arnot was told that police investigating the case believed that there had been no foul play involved in the deaths of Smith and Otten. However, there remained the matter of the drinking of alcohol at the party and also the fact that, contrary to Saudi laws on social gatherings, there had been men and women who were not related to one another meeting at the Arnots' flat. The questioning continued, with the emphasis now on who had drunk what and at what time. And for the first time Richard Arnot heard that Tim Hayter had sex with Penny in the living room after the other partygoers had gone, and while Jacques Texier was asleep in the room with them.

Ron Smith in Jeddah

On the Saturday, 26 May, Ron Smith met with Francis Geere of the British Embassy, who drove him to the Bakhsh Hospital and showed him the block of flats outside which Helen Smith and Johannes Otten had been found dead. They then drove to the police station, where Smith met a heavily guarded and handcuffed Dr Arnot. Arnot expressed his sorrow at Helen's death and told Ron Smith that Helen had been a delightful girl and that the party had been 'super'.

Richard Arnot then explained that he had gone to bed before midnight and that the first he had known of the deaths was when he had been woken at around 5.30 in the morning to be told the news. Despite feeling some sympathy for the chained-up Arnot, Smith was not impressed with him; Smith felt it had not been right for Arnot to go to bed and leave his wife and Helen with so many drunk and single men. He also ridiculed Arnot's explanation that the bodies had been discovered only because the remaining guests chose to go on the balcony to watch the sunrise.

Ron Smith was taken to see Dr Abdul Bakhsh at his hospital. Bakhsh told him of how he had been informed of the deaths by Dr Arnot early on the Sunday morning, and that he had seen the dead bodies and recognised the woman as Helen Smith. Furthermore, the nurse had been in breach of her contract by being out after curfew hours and therefore the hospital was not liable for paying the cost of the return of the body to the United Kingdom. After an argument about this, Bakhsh gave in: he would pay the costs of repatriating the body after all.

On the way back to his hotel, Geere told Arnot that the British Embassy had arranged that a plane would fly him back to the UK the following morning; Ron replied that there was no way he was going home until he had seen his daughter's body. Geere arranged access to where Helen's body was kept, and that evening he and Smith arrived at the mortuary. Helen Smith's body was taken out of a refrigerated storage area. Lifting off the white sheet in which Helen was wrapped, Ron Smith saw her face, and became alarmed when he noticed an indentation on her forehead as if she had been struck by a blunt instrument. Despite having apparently fallen such a distance before hitting the ground, Ron noticed that her head also showed a remarkable lack of damage. Ron Smith now wanted to examine the rest of the body; the mortuary attendant's resistance to this melted when he was told by Francis Geere that Smith was a former British policeman. Ron Smith pulled the sheet back and saw that the right side of the body and Helen's thighs were severely bruised, but no bones appeared to have been broken. The body was intact – no postmortem had been performed on it. (Smith would later find out that Islamic law forbids the performing of postmortems unless express permission is given by the next of kin.) Seeing the condition his daughter's body was in, Ron Smith was certain that what he had been told – that Helen had died following a fall from the balcony on the sixth floor of the Arnots' apartment – was not true. Simply, the injuries to the body were not consistent with a fall from such a great height and at such a great speed – calculated to be approximately 45 miles per hour on impact with the ground.

Ron Smith was now determined to find out how his daughter had died. He did not catch the plane home to Britain the following morning. Later that day he went with Francis Geere to talk to Colonel Mussagh at the police station where the partygoers were being held. Police were now treating the deaths as suspicious; there would be a proper investigation. Ron Smith gave his written permission for a postmortem to be carried out. Satisfied with what he had been told, Smith told Geere that he would now be happy to return to Britain.

Smith was then summoned to the hospital by a worried Dr Bakhsh, who urged Smith not to talk to the media while investigations were taking place; if he agreed to this the funeral expenses would be paid for. Ron Smith agreed. On leaving Bakhsh's office, Smith was confronted by two nurses who had worked with Helen, who said they knew how she had been murdered. That evening Ron Smith met a number of staff at the hospital, some of whom had seen the dead bodies lying in the shadow of the block of flats. A colleague of Helen's, Sister Joan Arundale, told Ron Smith that she believed Helen had been raped before being killed and that her body had been taken out of the flats and placed on the ground. Smith also learned that there had been apparent inconsistencies between the account of events that Penny Arnot had given to the British Embassy and what others had said. When he asked to read Penny's statement, embassy staff refused.

Ron Smith stayed in Jeddah for a further week. He met with a pathologist, Dr Ali Kheir, and re-examined Helen's body. He also made frequent visits to the police station, hoping for further information.

The Foreign Office in London were sent telegrams from the British Embassy in Jeddah informing them that the police had stated both to diplomats in Jeddah and to Ron Smith that the deaths of Smith and Otten involved no foul play. Ron Smith denies that he was ever told this. On 6 June 1979, Ron Smith flew home from Saudi Arabia.

Partygoers still held

On 30 May, Richard Arnot, the four German divers, Tim Hayter, Jacques Texier and Harry Gutzeit were shackled together in pairs and moved to the Ruwais prison. This was a very unpleasant place: the cells were squalid, dark, overcrowded and smelling of human faeces. While incarcerated in the same cell, Hayter confessed to Richard Arnot that he had had sex with Penny in the early hours of the morning following the party. Arnot learned that Penny had confessed to police that she had slept with Hayter; adultery was a capital offence in Saudi Arabia, the method of execution being stoning to death.

Up to this point the expatriates had no idea of what charges they might face. Early in June, a few days after being taken to the Ruwais jail, the group of prisoners were shown statements in Arabic and English, and were asked to sign them. The statements concerned the attending of the party at which drink had been served and women had been present. Tim Hayter's and Penny Arnot's statements additionally contained the admission that they had been together at that party. The prisoners appeared in court on 6 June and the statements were presented, again there being no mention of the deaths of Helen Smith and Johannes Otten. Informed that their case was being taken to the governor of the region, Prince Fawaz, the expatriates awaited a decision on their future. Penny Arnot was released from prison on 9 August 1979. The men were allowed to leave prison on 24 October. The group were told that they would be awaiting sentence for the offences that they had admitted to in their statements; they would not be allowed to leave the country.

Court hearings and sentencing – expats freed

The eight accused were called to be tried in a court where they would be judged under Islamic sharia law, which is based on the teachings of the Koran. At their first court appearance on 9 January 1980, the judge acknowledged receiving their statements; at their second on 16 February, Hayter and Penny Arnot now denied that they had been sexually intimate. Chapuis, Ritter, the Arnots and Hayter also admitted drinking alcohol. On 24 March the judge pronounced sentence:

- Dieter Chapuis and Klaus Ritter – 30 lashes for drinking alcohol

- Penny Arnot and Tim Hayter – 80 lashes for drinking alcohol and for changing their statements about whether they had had sex

- Richard Arnot – a year in prison and 30 lashes for permitting the party to take place, drinking, serving and possessing alcohol and allowing Penny to be in the company of other men

The expatriates waited for news of when the sentences would be carried out. Eventually clemency was granted by the Saudi royal family, under pressure from the British government. Much to their relief the Arnots were permitted to fly out of Saudi Arabia on 8 August 1980; Tim Hayter, Jacques Texier and the Germans were also permitted to leave the country.

Ron Smith's second visit to Jeddah

In June 1980, Ron Smith returned to Saudi Arabia; as in his previous visit, he went on an intelligence-gathering operation, taping his conversations using concealed equipment. People, especially the staff at the Bakhsh Hospital, were this time less than willing to talk to him. He headed for the British Embassy and met again with Francis Geere. He also wrote a letter to the Jeddah Supreme Court requesting that he might bring a private prosecution against the partygoers for the death of his daughter. Smith also sought out the translator who had worked on statements taken during the trial of the expatriates, and learned from him that, contrary to previous accounts, the two bodies had been discovered not by Texier, Hayter and Penny Arnot when they went on to the balcony, but by Jacques Texier alone, who had left the party in the early hours of the morning, having arrived very late at the party in order to pay back Tim Hayter a sum of money that he owed him.

On 17 June, Helen Smith's body was flown back to Britain; Ron Smith returned home shortly after, having had his notebooks, films and cassette tapes confiscated by Saudi officials at Jeddah airport. (They were later given back to him.)

Proceedings in the UK

The body of Helen Smith arrived in England, was taken to Leeds and given to the local coroner, John Walker. Ron Smith met with Walker's deputy, Miles Coverdale, to ask for an inquest. Coverdale refused, and said he would order that Helen's body should be buried or cremated. After some argument, Coverdale conceded that an autopsy would be performed on the body by a Home Office pathologist.

On Friday, 27 June 1980, Dr Michael Green of Leeds University performed an autopsy on Helen Smith. On 16 July the press were issued with a statement by the deputy coroner. This gave details of the autopsy conclusions:

- the previous postmortem performed in Saudi Arabia had resulted in the removal of internal organs

- the right side of Helen's pelvis and the right shoulder had been fractured, and she had been alive when she sustained these injuries

- there were minor bruises and scratches on her face – consistent with slaps or blows from a fist, not with injuries from a fall

- 'The absence of external bleeding, fractures of the skull or of the long bones is not inconsistent with a fall from a height of 70 feet' – these injuries would be expected only if the body landed on the head or feet; Helen's body appears to have landed on her right side.

The press statement concluded that, having considered Ron Smith's evidence, Coverdale did not consider that opening an inquest would be justified.

Ron Smith was understandably unhappy with this conclusion. He had been given the complete text of Dr Green's autopsy report, having been warned, bizarrely, that its contents were covered by the Official Secrets Act. The report did not present any alternative scenario other than that Helen Smith had fallen from the balcony to her death, and had not asked any questions as to whether the various bruises on the body were consistent with a sexual assault or rape. However in an interview in the *Sunday People* published on 17 August 1980 Green stated, 'If I was to say Helen Smith's death was an accident, I would be a liar,' and said he had doubts as to how her death had been caused.

From the moment Ron Smith saw the battered state of Helen's face in the Jeddah mortuary, he was certain that she had been attacked and beaten shortly before her death – however that death may have been caused.

The *Private Eye* allegations

The satirical and investigative magazine *Private Eye* published allegations of a cover-up by the Foreign Office over the death of Helen Smith in its issue of 27 August 1980. The article, written by *Arab News* journalist, Jack Lundin, alleged that Helen was involved in an incident at the Arnots' flat, where she was beaten up and gang-raped, and her body was thrown over the balcony. Johannes

Otten had been murdered because he had witnessed the assault and rape. The article alleged that the Foreign Office had covered up the Smith death because it wanted to protect British interests in Saudi Arabia and mend the relationship with the oil-rich Saudis that had been threatened by the transmission in the UK of the television programme *Death of a Princess*. The programme had been broadcast in April 1980 on independent television, and had been a dramatised documentary on the execution of Saudi Princess Misha for adultery three years previously. After the programme went out, Saudi Arabia threatened to break off diplomatic and trade relations with Britain. Harmonious relations were restored only after fulsome apologies from the British government.

Shortly after publication of the *Private Eye* article, the Foreign and Commonwealth Office issued a statement countering Lundin's claims and boldly stating, 'There is no cover-up'.

The Arnots sell their story

The *Daily Mail* published Richard and Penny Arnot's account of events, for which they were paid £10,000, in September 1980. The article paints an innocent picture of the mood of the party, mentions Helen's penchant for Arab boyfriends, and describes 'a sexual buzz in the air' due to the chemistry between Helen and Johannes Otten. Penny describes the night as 'a lovely super evening' with a friendly atmosphere, and recalls telling Helen and Johannes to 'have fun' as they went out together on to the balcony. The sequence of events as the Arnots describe them are

- the discovery of the body and the awakening of Richard Arnot

- the remaining alcohol disposed of

- Dr Bakhsh, the police and the British Embassy were telephoned (in that order).

Arnot recalled finding Otten's passport quite some distance from the man's body and in the *Mail* article ruminates over where Otten's trousers had gone. The trousers were not in the flat, on the balcony or found outside – they had disappeared. Penny and Richard Arnot's conclusion is that the trousers had been stolen by a passer-by. Penny Arnot explained that she had not in fact had sex with Hayter that night, and that the story had been made up by her during arduous questioning to explain that she could not have murdered Helen and Johannes.

Ron Smith requests further autopsy

In October 1980 Ron Smith went to Denmark to speak to Professor Jorgen Dalgaard, a pathologist who held the Chair of Forensic Science at Aarhus University. Having reviewed evidence that had come from Dr Green's postmortem in the form of slides, photographs and documents, Dalgaard agreed to come to England to perform an autopsy on Helen Smith's body. Deputy Coroner Coverdale heard of this and asked Professor Alan Usher, a world-renowned forensic scientist from Sheffield University, to perform a postmortem alongside Professor Dalgaard. Dr Michael Green would also be present and would conduct yet another autopsy on the body.

On 16 December 1980 the three pathologists met in the mortuary in Leeds. The exterior of the body was cleaned, and the sawdust that had been placed where the internal organs had been was carefully removed. By the following day, their work was over. Samples had been removed by each man for testing.

Professor Dalgaard's findings

Dalgaard conducted a press conference on 17 December, in which he stated that Helen's injuries were consistent with a fall from 'a moderate height' – not from a height of seventy feet.

In March 1981 Dalgaard presented Ron Smith with his full report: the bruises on Helen Smith's face had been caused by her having been hit hard, probably by a punch or a slap; also, the blow to Helen's head, which had caused a four-by-five-inch lesion, had been forceful enough to have knocked her unconscious. Dalgaard also noted a wound to the neck and concluded that the bruising to the thigh could have been the result of a deliberate assault. He examined the damage to Helen's shoulder and concluded that this was not a fracture but an 'ablation', which may not have been caused by a fall. Dalgaard noted lesions in the genital area 'most likely due to forceful sexual activity'. On the distance Helen's body had fallen, Dalgaard's estimate was a conclusive one – 'something between a few and several feet, but not more than twenty to thirty and definitely not about seventy feet'. To summarise: a likely cause of death was bleeding in the brain caused by a blow to the head that *could not have been caused by a fall from the balcony in the Arnots' flat.*

Professor Usher's findings

Professor Alan Usher estimated that the injury to Helen's head may have been caused by slaps on the top of the head or from her head being forcefully banged into a wall or a solid piece of furniture. He raised as a 'possibility' the scenario that Helen had been knocked unconscious during a struggle in the flat, her body being thrown into the courtyard below from a distance of 'not more than thirty feet'. He posed the question, as Dalgaard had done, of whether Helen had been alive or dead when she fell on to the ground, and concluded that she was alive. On the subject of injury to the genitals and whether Helen Smith had been raped, Usher stated that the fresh bruising on the inside of the thighs appeared similar to that seen in victims of sexual assault or rape and was consistent with the legs being 'prised apart by an assailant's knee or knees'.

Both Dalgaard and Usher did not concur with Dr Green's earlier report to Deputy Coroner Coverdale as regards three major issues: whether damage to the shoulder was a fracture, how the bruising to the thighs had been caused and whether the major injury to the head that had resulted in a sizable lesion had been the cause of death.

Dr Kheir's findings

In December 1980, Ron Smith had been sent a translation of Dr Ali Kheir's autopsy report on Helen Smith. This document detailed bruises to the body, stating that the injuries could have been caused by a fall. Dr Kheir found semen present in the vagina and a level of alcohol present in the blood. Bizarrely, Kheir concluded that 'death was accidental' and due to fractures and internal bleeding in the brain, chest and abdomen. However, Smith had not been sent the full document – a full page was mysteriously missing. This 'missing' page was eventually found and translated; it contained further details on injuries to the head and brain, damage and internal bleeding in the abdomen, and the contents of the stomach, lower digestive tract and bladder.

Ron Smith's fight for an inquest

The speculation in the media regarding whether and when an inquest would take place continued following Dalgaard's and Usher's autopsies.

On 4 August 1981 the coroner for the reorganised Eastern District, Philip Gill, informed Ron Smith by letter, and simultaneously stated in a press release, that, as Helen Smith's death had 'occurred outside the jurisdiction of the English Courts', no inquest could take place. Ron Smith was horrified by this apparently irreversible decision.

Ten days after Gill's announcement, Ron Smith appeared in court for not paying his local council rates. He used his courtroom appearance to make a statement that could be fully reported in the press without the risk of a libel suit. In court, Ron Smith accused Richard Arnot of the murder of his daughter and said that members of the Conservative Cabinet, and the local coroner and police force had been involved in a cover-up over the death.

On 11 November 1981, Ron Smith was granted a hearing in which he could appeal against the coroner's decision. On the same day the Director of Public Prosecutions made a public statement that there would be no criminal charges arising from Helen's death. Smith's hearing took place during March and April 1982; his application to appeal was turned down. Ron Smith's appeal against this decision came to court on 28 July 1982. The Court of Appeal, on whose bench sat Lord Justice Donaldson, the Lord Chief Justice Lord Lane and Lord Justice Waller, ruled in Ron Smith's favour – a ground-breaking judgement that decided that a coroner's court would in future have the possibility of jurisdiction on the deaths of all British subjects abroad.

The inquest

Following a failed attempt during October and November 1982 by Ron Smith to remove Philip Gill as coroner (in Smith's eyes, Gill lacked the necessary impartiality), the inquest into the death of Helen Smith commenced at Court No. 1 at Leeds Town Hall on 18 November 1982, with evidence to be presented to a jury, who would give their verdict. Lawyers representing the Smith family were Geoffrey Robertson (for Ron Smith) and Stephen Sedley (for Helen's mother, now remarried and known as Jeryl Sheehy). Sir David Napley represented Dr Richard Arnot; David Eady acted for Gordon Kirby, the Vice-Consul at the British Embassy in Jeddah at the time of Helen's death; Harold Fowler represented the Germans present at the party. Two Foreign Office barristers were also present.

Evidence was presented at the inquest as follows:

The pathologists

Dr Michael Green

Dr Green presented the court with an account of his original autopsy of 27 June 1980. He mentioned the injury to Helen's right shoulder, admitting that he was 'mistaken' in describing it as a fracture. He defended his view that the body had fallen as much as seventy feet by presenting statistics on injuries caused by falls from varying heights. Examined by Robertson, Green was questioned on whether Helen was conscious at the time of the fall and on the possible reasons for her head injuries. Robertson pointed out that Green's statistics related to falls on to surfaces of varying hardness – had Helen fallen from the Arnots' balcony, she would have landed on hard marble – and with differing injuries to a person falling on grass or earth. Stephen Sedley questioned Green about the injuries to the genitals and the possible scenario of rape. Green admitted that the fact that Helen had her underwear on one leg only may have been indicative that she had not been consenting to intercourse; he went so far as to say that her body presented a picture of 'the typical victim of rape' and the circumstances were consistent with her legs having been forced open.

Dr Ali Kheir

Having been flown in from Jeddah, Dr Kheir described how he arrived at the Arnots' flat after the bodies had been removed from the ground below and examined the balcony – which he said was two feet six inches high. Like Dr Green, he described external bruising to the limbs and injury to the head, concluding that the damage to the brain was not indicative of 'criminal violence'. Kheir believed that the lack of genital injuries led him to conclude that Helen had *not* been raped. He confirmed the discovery of semen in Helen's vagina and admitted that no analysis of the sperm had taken place to indicate who had had sex with her.

Professor Jorgen Dalgaard

Dalgaard spoke of the lesion on the left side of Helen's head, which he believed had been caused by a violent blow. This was the lesion that Dr Green had believed had been caused by a reaction to a chemical in hair dye. He believed that the blood found in the base of the skull was caused by the blow that had caused the lesion – a blow that could have knocked Helen unconscious and even killed her, but a blow that was

'very definitely not due to a fall from a height'
(Dalgaard quoted in Wilson and Harrison, p. 36
– see bibliography).

Dalgaard cast doubt on how far the body had fallen, estimating that the small lesions to the abdomen could have been caused only by a fall no higher than the first floor of a building. He also told the inquest of bruises he found inside the thighs and around the genital area.

Professor Alan Usher
Giving evidence on Monday, 22 November, Professor Usher concurred with what Professor Dalgaard had said, but was willing to entertain the idea that the lesion that Dalgaard had concentrated on *had* been caused by a fall. A mysterious fracture to the sternum was also discussed during examination by Geoffrey Robertson; Robertson's own suggestion, that the injury could have been caused by an attempt to resuscitate Helen by pushing down hard on her chest, was met with some agreement by Usher.

Further witnesses
On 23 November Martin Fleischer, one of the Germans involved in salvage work in the harbour, took the witness box. He named the guests who arrived and described the layout of the Arnots' flat. He described how Helen and Johannes Otten were seen to be more and more affectionate towards each other, and denied there had been any trouble – the party had been a friendly occasion. Fleischer was followed by Dr Joe Deguara, a pathologist at the Bakhsh Hospital who was summoned to where the dead bodies had been found. Degaura told the inquest that he had noted the lack of serious injuries one would have expected as a result of a fall from a great height. Deguara's suspicion at the time and since has been that Helen Smith and Johannes Otten were murdered.

Next to give evidence was Dr Kirwin, who admitted supplying the Johnnie Walker whisky drunk at the party. He also claimed to have been at the party for about an hour, although his name was not mentioned to Saudi police by the other guests following the two deaths for fear of incriminating him for the supply of the alcohol. Two days after the deaths of Helen and Otten, the British Embassy advised him to return to Britain – he was never to return to Saudi Arabia.

On Wednesday, 24 November, the three other Germans – Manfred Schlaeffer, Klaus Ritter and Harry Gutzeit – gave their account of the party. The drinking, the dancing, the good mood of the partygoers were all emphasised in their evidence.

One widely reported incident took place during Schlaeffer's evidence. At one point Ron Smith was heard to mumble loudly, 'I am not accusing the German divers: I'm accusing Richard Arnot of murder and . . .' – the last word being largely unintelligible.

Members of the press who had tape recorders – which had been permitted in the court by the coroner – were able to hear what that last mumbled word was. It was reported as being 'Texier'.

On the following day, 25 November, the newspapers reported Ron Smith's outburst.

At the start of the inquest proceedings that day, Richard Arnot's solicitor, Sir David Napley, accused Smith of being in 'gross contempt of this court'. Later that day and following arguments from both sides, Ron Smith was fined £50 for contempt.

On 29 and 30 November evidence was presented by Gordon Kirby; the defence attaché at the British Embassy in Jeddah, Colonel Murray de Klee; Michael Weston, who had been the acting ambassador in Jeddah at the time of the deaths; and Francis Geere, the embassy official who had had his patience tried by Ron Smith during his visits to Jeddah in 1979.

The embassy staff's accounts were followed by those of the employees of the Bakhsh hospital, many giving evidence about what they had seen on the ground outside the Arnots' flat. Their evidence both raised and underlined several essential unanswered questions about the deaths:

• why were Otten's personal identity documents and passport found some distance away from his body? If his trousers had been stolen, why had the thief left the potentially far more valuable passport?

- Helen Smith's diary contained an entry detailing an appendectomy performed on her by Dr Arnot; apparently Helen had told her colleagues that she had indeed had such an operation. No sign of an appendectomy such as a scar was found on her body; there is the possibility that Arnot was performing an abortion on Helen Smith (which would have been illegal in Saudi Arabia) and that the appendix operation was a deliberate lie to avoid prosecution. It was also unfortunate that the internal organs had been removed in Jeddah as by this time it was impossible to ascertain whether Helen's appendix was intact.

- Dr Rakhman, the consultant who saw the bodies at 5.30 that morning and alerted the Arnots (who already knew) by knocking on their door, claims that when the door was opened he saw a short white man who had a beard standing behind Richard Arnot. Neither Texier nor Hayter matched that description. So who was this bearded man?

On 1 December Ron Smith went into the witness box. He gave an account of how he was received by the British Embassy staff and of his dealings with Dr Bakhsh, and described his examination of Helen's body in the mortuary in Jeddah. His feelings on seeing the state of the body were that, 'There was no way my daughter had fallen any considerable distance on to a solid marble floor.'

Dr Richard Arnot gave his evidence on 2 December. He recalled the whisky being brought to the flat – contradicting Dr Kirwin, who said he had brought it at midday. He said he was absent between 11.30 and 12.30 while doing the rounds of his patients at the hospital, and that he went to bed at 2.00 a.m. He described how he was awoken at 5.30 a.m. and went down to examine the dead bodies. He told of how he had felt Helen's pulse and estimated that she had been dead for several hours; he saw Otten's genitals as being 'in some state of sexual excitement' and appearing 'grotesque'.

Arnot told of how he had found Otten's watch, which had stopped, indicating that the time of the fall had been 3.10.

The Arnots' lawyers sought the opinion of another pathologist, Professor Keith Mant, who informed them that a penis erect due to sexual excitement would certainly subside during a violent fall; Otten's erection had most likely been caused by the injury to the spinal column when he had impacted with the ground – the same reason that hanged men have erections after death.

Arnot said that he believed that Penny Arnot and Tim Hayter *did* have sex that night; after all, Hayter himself had confessed this to him during the first night they shared a cell in the Jeddah prison.

Neither Penny Arnot nor Tim Hayter appeared in court. The jury were given the text of an interview she had given police in August 1980. A brief extract of a television interview with Hayter was also shown to them.

Jacques Texier was next to give evidence. He told the court that he had seen Helen and Johannes go out on to the balcony together at approximately 2 a.m. He claimed to have seen them embracing on the balcony *when he looked through a window in the kitchen*. A curious statement to make, as the Arnots' kitchen did not look out on to the balcony. Texier went on to say that the Arnots' living room was noisy due to its proximity to a poorly functioning air conditioner. However, he had gone to sleep and had been awoken by the sound of Penny Arnot and Hayter having sex in the same room. Texier described the three of them going on to the balcony, the sighting of the bodies and the awakening of Richard Arnot. Texier's account differed from Arnot's in that, according to the Frenchman, Dr Arnot's immediate action was to attempt to get rid of the alcohol by pouring it down the drain – *not* to dash down to the bodies to check them for signs of life.

Summing up

On the afternoon of 7 December Coroner Philip Gill began his summing up, continuing on the following day. Among other points, he emphasised the opinion that pathologists examining the body in the United Kingdom a long time after the death of Helen Smith may have been misled by some of the 'mirage of lesions' on her body. Gill's view was that these lesions may have been made after Helen's death: during transportation to the morgue in Saudi Arabia, on the journey of the body back to the UK or during storage of the body in the mortuary in Leeds. He explored whether Helen and Johannes had fallen together, with the possibility that she had been holding on to him as they fell – that his body may have cushioned her fall. Gill raised the likelihood of the trousers having been stolen by a passer-by. The jury were presented with three possible verdicts:

- unlawful killing – if the injuries to Helen's body had been caused by an act or acts of violence committed before her death

- accidental death – if Helen and Johannes fell from the balcony while having sex and the injuries to her body were due to that fall

- an open verdict – if the jury believe they had been presented with insufficient evidence to indicate either unlawful killing or accidental death.

The jury's verdict

On 9 December 1982, after deliberating for seven and a half hours, the jury returned an open verdict on the death of Helen Smith. Ron Smith told the press, 'I am delighted', and the Smith family's solicitor, Ruth Bundey, read out a statement on their behalf in which the jury were thanked. The statement concluded: 'An open verdict is vindication of what the family has fought for, and demonstrates to all that the suspicion of foul play remains unanswered.'

Subsequent events

Dr Richard Arnot was disappointed with the open verdict, having hoped the jury would decide that the death was accidental. He moved to Australia, where he works as a flying doctor. With his wife Margaret, a teacher, he has had three children. In 1999 Dr Arnot's book, *Arabian Nightmare*, was published. It is a straightforward account of events in Jeddah and of the inquest in Leeds. Dr Arnot remains firmly of the opinion that Helen Smith's death was accidental and that she fell off the balcony while having sex with Johannes Otten. Ron Smith's reaction to the publication of *Arabian Nightmare* was positive: he welcomed the book, as it would place the death of his daughter into the public spotlight once again.

Penny Arnot married John Close a few weeks after her divorce from Richard was finalised. Close was a journalist who had been working in Jeddah in 1979 and whose father, Raymond H Close, had been the head of the CIA in the Middle East. In 1979 Raymond Close, having left the CIA in 1977, was employed by the Saudi royal family as an intelligence adviser. There has been speculation that it was due to the intervention of Raymond Close that Penny and Tim Hayter were granted clemency and the other partygoers were freed from prison. Now known as

Penelope Thornton-Close, she does not speak of her marriage to Richard Arnot or her time in Saudi Arabia. Socialising within upper-class New York circles, Penny was paid well for her work as an interior decorator and together with her husband made a large amount of money from real estate. Newspapers in April 2000 reported on how the Closes' marriage had ended, allegedly due to her violent tempers and attacks on John Close, usually during arguments about money.

Tim Hayter is reported to be working in the oil industry in Borneo.

Jacques Texier is in his mid-seventies and has retired from diving. He now lives in Thailand.

Ron Smith still lives alone in Guiesely, Yorkshire. He has refused to allow his daughter's body to be buried or cremated until it is ascertained exactly how she met her death; the corpse is deep-frozen in the mortuary at Leeds General Infirmary. He is still hopeful that the Helen Smith case will be reopened, and in 1997 was reported to have written to the UK Home Secretary, Jack Straw, requesting this. In an interview given to the *Daily Mail* in April 1999 he appeared as determined as ever to find out the truth: 'People say to me "It happened all those years ago. Let the matter drop and get on with your life." But I'm going to continue with the life that I have lived. I will never give up until I get justice.'

6 Karen Silkwood

Who was Karen Silkwood?

Karen Gay Silkwood was born in 1946 in Longview, Texas. With her aptitude for studying science, Karen was an honour graduate from her high school and won a scholarship to Lamar College in Beaumont, Texas, to study medical technology. In 1965, a year after starting her college studies, Karen married Bill Meadows; in the next five years they had three children, Beverley, Michael and Dawn, whom Karen spent her time looking after in the family's home in Longview, while her husband went out to work.

But the marriage was not a happy one and did not last: by the summer of 1972 Bill's inability to manage finances and, far more hurtful to Karen, his infidelity resulted in Karen's walking out and leaving Bill to look after the children. Having left Longview without informing Bill where she was going, she called him a couple of days later to say she was in Oklahoma City. Bill Meadows divorced Karen; he went on to marry Kathy, the woman with whom he had been having an affair. Over the next couple of years before her death, Karen was to have her children visit her every couple of months.

After a brief time working as a clerk at Oklahoma City Hospital, Silkwood applied for the more highly paid and responsible job of laboratory analyst at the Kerr-McGee

Nuclear Corporation's plutonium fabrication plant, which had been built along the Cimarron River near Crescent, Oklahoma. Karen's application was successful, and on 5 August 1972, and at a rate of pay of $4 per hour, she started working in the metallography laboratory where the plutonium pellets manufactured by the plant for use in nuclear reactors were examined and tested for quality.

About the Kerr-McGee company – a poor safety record

Robert Kerr was a qualified lawyer whose money came from the Oklahoma oil business. Born in 1896 of humble origin, which he frequently boasted about, Kerr had started an oil-drilling company, Anderson & Kerr, with his brother-in-law in 1929. Profiting by deals made with local businesses, the Continental Oil Company and Philips Petroleum, Anderson & Kerr became highly profitable. On Anderson's retirement in 1937, Kerr joined forces with a longtime Philips Petroleum geologist, Dean McGee, to form the Kerr-McGee company, exploiting the oil and coal resources of the region.

In 1942, able to finance his own campaign, Kerr ran for the governorship of Oklahoma as a Democrat. He won, and once he was in office his political ambition grew. He won a Senate seat in 1948, and put himself in the presidential ring at the Democratic Convention in Chicago in July 1952, gaining a respectable 65 votes on the first ballot. The nomination was won by Adlai Stevenson, Governor of Illinois, who went on to be defeated in the presidential contest by Eisenhower.

Kerr continued to serve in the Senate, and the Kerr-McGee company went from strength to strength. McGee's involvement had successfully extended the company's search for oil to Louisiana. By the early 1950s Kerr-McGee owned its own oil refinery. In 1963 Robert Kerr died, leaving a personal fortune of $70 million. The company was now involved in the production of uranium for a US government body, the Atomic Energy Commission. By the 1970s Kerr-McGee owned uranium mining, milling and processing plants in New Mexico, Arizona, Colorado and Wyoming. The uranium plant at Crescent, Oklahoma, was built in 1968. A plutonium plant was added alongside it two years later.

These twin facilities were to process uranium – used mainly for nuclear power purposes – and plutonium, which was sent from Kerr-McGee's plant for use in an experimental fast breeder reactor owned by the Westinghouse Corporation. Plutonium is also used in the manufacture of nuclear weapons. Milled uranium – which Kerr-McGee mined from the Lukachukai Mountains in the Colorado Plateau in Arizona – was processed into yellow cake uranium hexafluoride, which is refined and made into small uranium pellets. These pellets are put inside fuel rods in nuclear reactors. Plutonium is a by-product of the nuclear fission process and is obtained from nuclear reactors. Kerr-McGee's plutonium was delivered from a reactor in Washington State as a solution of plutonium nitrate. At the plant, uranium and aluminium hydroxide were added to the plutonium. Heavy uranium and plutonium metals would emerge from this mixture as a greenish mud, which would then be baked and dried. The plutonium/uranium mix would be made into powder and then into pellets.

It was these pellets – intended for use inside steel rods known as 'fuel pins', used to power nuclear reactors – that Karen Silkwood would examine and test by placing X-ray film next to random samples. Once developed, the film would show any leakage of radiation. Karen would use the same procedure to test welds in the fuel rods. Working from samples from manufactured batches of pellets and fuel rods, Silkwood could then test further products from the same batch and make a decision to reject an entire run of pellets or rods.

Workers have described safety standards at Kerr-McGee as extremely low; training in how to protect oneself from ill effects of radiation was limited to one half-hour lecture. One reason for this may have been that Kerr-McGee had little experience of dealing with nuclear material – for a long time the corporation had earned its profit from the oil business – and its managers did not understand how dangerous small amounts of uranium and plutonium could be. Uranium and ammonia fumes filled the work areas, which were kept at unbearably high temperatures. At the time no one was alerted to the dangers of being contaminated with radioactive material. Because at no time were Kerr-McGee workers encouraged or trained in the use of respirators, their lungs breathed in dust and harmfully radioactive air. Additionally, workers whose skin and clothes were contaminated ran the risk of additionally contaminating their families when they went home.

The consolidation of uranium and plutonium processing at Crescent proved highly profitable for Kerr-McGee. As far as profits for shareholders were concerned, the company was doing exceptionally well. In 1974 Kerr-McGee was nominated as among the top twenty companies in the USA.

Silkwood at Kerr-McGee

Soon after starting work at the plant, Karen began a relationship with a co-worker named Drew Stephens, four years her junior, whose marriage had also ended. When his ex-wife left their former home in Oklahoma City, Karen moved in with him. They shared an interest in nuclear fuel technology and dirt-bike racing (they owned a pair of Suzuki bikes on which they sped around the countryside), and had similar tastes in music. Drew was a keen car racer and a member of the Sports Car Club of America; Karen bought a white Honda Civic car and Drew taught her how to control and manoeuvre it at high speed. Soon she was joining in car-racing activities, even winning a trophy for a women's race.

In November 1972, only a few months after Karen started working at the plutonium plant, members of the Oil, Chemical and Atomic Workers' Union (OCAW) began strike action at Kerr-McGee. The union was on strike for better wages, improved training and better health and safety procedures. Karen was involved in picketing the plant; the strike continued for some two and a half months and was not a success for OCAW. Kerr-McGee had no difficulty recruiting strike breakers, mainly local young men who were keen to work for the going rate of three dollars an hour. As the holiday season approached, more and more strikers caved in and crossed the picket line; Karen Silkwood was one of the last to put down her placard. Once the strike was over she was back in the plant, this time under a new contract with Kerr-McGee. The experience of participating in the strike had opened Karen's eyes to Kerr-McGee's attitude to its workforce and strengthened her commitment to OCAW and to what she saw as the rights of the workers.

Karen's life with Drew was not making her happy – he told her he did not feel sufficiently committed to her and now wanted to date other women. She moved out of their home in Oklahoma City shortly after the strike had finished and became extremely depressed. Karen took an overdose of pills in September 1973; a friend whom she called rushed over to her apartment and forced her to vomit, possibly saving her life. Towards the end of the year she moved back into Drew Stephens's home, but the reunion was short-lived and Karen moved out again. Despite this and the insecurity that she felt about Drew's wanting to be with other women, their relationship was to continue until Karen's death.

In the spring of 1974, in an effort to increase productivity, Kerr-McGee changed the shift patterns of its workers. Longer shifts were introduced; workers were expected to work both day and night shifts; and safety regulations continued to be ignored. A serious incident occurred: some plutonium waste in a plastic bag emitted smoke, contaminating the room and causing the seven workers on that shift to inhale an enormous amount of insoluble plutonium. The government- and industry-sponsored Atomic Energy Commission (AEC) reacted by criticising Kerr-McGee's safety standards; William Shelley, the company's director of regulation and control, replied that investigating the cause of such incidents ran contrary to 'the requirements of sound business judgement'.

Further contaminations followed. Two men called in to fix a faulty pump were covered by uranium particles; the men left the plant during their lunch break, causing potentially dangerous contamination of the restaurant where they had eaten. A woman in an on-site laboratory was poisoned by ammonia that had accumulated in the air. Karen herself was affected when an air filter used to gauge radioactivity indicated a leak from a glovebox (the enclosed container fitted with gloves inside a tube) where she examined the uranium pellets; Kerr-McGee were obliged to test her to see how much radiation had reached the tissues inside her body.

The changes in shift patterns and these incidents, together with Kerr-McGee's apparent nonchalance over health and safety, angered many of the workers. Drew Stephens was not being treated well: in early September 1974, for reasons that may well have included his relationship with Karen Silkwood and his support for the previous year's strike, he was transferred to the General Laboratory. On 12 September a disillusioned Stephens handed in a letter of resignation.

There were further developments at Kerr-McGee. OCAW activity at the plant was under threat: in a move that was seen by union activists as being a result of undue management influence, fifty workers had forced a vote on whether the union was to be decertificated at Kerr-McGee. Karen began discussing Kerr-McGee's poor safety record with her co-workers.

The pressure was clearly on the pro-union workers, and Silkwood felt particularly affected by this. As a consequence she became worried and depressed; her sleep had been affected by her having to work nights. Her doctor prescribed her methaqualone, a highly addictive and fast-acting sleeping pill also known by its proprietary name, Quaaludes. Karen began using the pills to get to sleep during the day; she also started to use them as a tranquilliser during the time she was awake.

In August 1974 Karen Silkwood stood for election to the union bargaining committee – three members of OCAW who would represent the workers during contract negotiations with Kerr-McGee management. Those elected were Jack Tice, an experienced activist, Jerry Brewer and Karen Silkwood. Karen's worry over conditions at the plant had been a major motivation to her standing for election; once appointed, she was given responsibility for health and safety. Tice had already been in contact with the leadership of OCAW in Washington on this very issue, and a meeting had been arranged between the bargaining committee members and the union's legal staff.

Tice, Silkwood and Brewer take the safety issue to OCAW in Washington DC

On 26 September 1974, the three committee members flew to Washington DC to discuss their fears about safety aspects of the plutonium plant. Meeting two OCAW officials, Anthony Mazzochi and Steve Wodka, Karen listed 39 safety violations by Kerr-McGee, including negligence in the use of respirators, use of a contaminated vacuum cleaner in a work area, faulty valves in pipes carrying radioactive liquid and lack of shower facilities in the event of a contamination.

Wodka asked Karen for more evidence. On her return to Oklahoma, Karen logged further incidents of workers inhaling or getting splashed with radioactive material and of seriously contaminated gloves being used instead of being destroyed. Just as seriously, Karen now included the accusation that X-ray photographs of the plutonium fuel rods were being falsified to make faulty rods appear intact. Using these faulty rods in a reactor ran the risk of at best radioactive contamination, at worst a potential nuclear explosion. OCAW wanted further proof of these allegations, so Karen now noted the batch numbers of fuel rods whose X-ray results she suspected were being tampered with.

In October 1974 Silkwood and Drew Stephens met with an off-duty police officer, Bill Byler, and discussed security at Kerr-McGee. They were joined by a police informant, Steve Campbell, and the conversation turned to Drew's interest in firearms and in particular a pair of M16 rifles that were in the car Drew had borrowed from a friend of his who served in the National Guard. Byler informed the Intelligence Unit of the Oklahoma City Police Department of what Stephens had said; there was a subsequent meeting between Byler and James Reading, an ex-cop now employed as Kerr-McGee's security boss. Reading then met a woman named Jaque Srouji, who was keen to talk to him, as she told him she was a journalist who was writing a book on the nuclear industry. This was only part of the truth: as well as being employed by the *Tennessean* newspaper based in Nashville, Srouji was also an FBI informant. Information that Reading passed to Srouji may well have resulted in FBI surveillance being placed on

Silkwood and Stephens. In a BBC television *Panorama* programme broadcast on 5 March 1979, Srouji claimed the pair were given 'blanket surveillance', which possibly included phone tapping, and that Kerr-McGee had joined law enforcement agencies in carrying out this surveillance.

Tension at the plant

Meanwhile, Silkwood had been separated from Brewer in the workplace under a newly discovered rule that forbade union members to meet during company time. On 10 October Dean Abrahamson and Robert Geesaman, both nuclear experts from the University of Minnesota, were invited by OCAW to speak to Kerr-McGee workers on the potential dangers of exposure to the nuclear material they were handling on a daily basis. The academics told their audience that contact with plutonium was a known cause of cancer and that exposure even to microscopic quantities could be lethal. They condemned the Atomic Energy Commission's safe limits for exposure. They explained that airborne plutonium can make its way to the lungs, blood, stomach, bones and liver.

At this time the management and OCAW members were still at loggerheads over the union decertification vote, the date of which was drawing closer. Voting took place after Abrahamson and Geesaman's visit. By some twenty votes, the result was a victory for OCAW, and they would continue to represent workers at the plant.

Karen Silkwood kept talking to her colleagues, gathering more evidence for Steve Wodka at OCAW in Washington. She was told that large amounts of plutonium were missing from the plant, enough to make several atomic bombs; security at the entrance to the plant had for years been virtually nonexistent, with workers apparently able to leave without being physically searched or passing through a radiation counter. Plutonium could easily have been smuggled out of Kerr-McGee in a pocket or bag.

The pressure on Karen was increasing and she was finding it difficult to cope; by the end of October she was taking Quaaludes more frequently than ever, and to her friends appeared distressed, worried and unhappy. On 17 October she phoned Steve Wodka to tell him that she had found evidence in the form of documents that could prove that faulty plutonium fuel rods were being passed by the X-ray department; Wodka said that he, accompanied by a *New York Times* reporter, would be travelling to Oklahoma to meet her and see what she had found. The date Silkwood and Wodka arranged for this meeting was 13 November.

5 November 1974 – Silkwood contaminated

Karen was at work as usual. She had been working on writing reports on fuel rods. At 3 p.m. she routinely tested herself with a radiation counter – she was uncontaminated. At 5.30 p.m. she went to her locker to eat a sandwich she had brought with her from home. As she returned to her desk the radiation alarm went off: a plutonium spillage had been detected. Karen was taken out of the room; her clothes were put in a bag to be taken away to where they could cause no further contamination; she herself went through the procedure of having several showers using detergent and potassium permanganate. She rubbed her skin raw to attempt to get any spillage of plutonium out of the pores in her skin. After getting dressed, Karen returned to work, finished her shift and went home. When she returned to the lab the next day, she used the alpha counter to detect her radiation levels – as she moved it across her body the alarm went off. Even after a further decontamination and scrubbing session, Silkwood had high levels of radioactivity around her hands, nose and mouth.

How had Karen become recontaminated since she had apparently scrubbed the spilled plutonium off herself the day before, and her clothing had been removed from the site?

Aftermath of the contaminations

On hearing of the repeated contamination, the company sent inspectors to check out Karen's apartment. Very high levels were found; everything Karen had touched made the alpha counters click away; radioactivity was highest in the kitchen, especially around the refrigerator and the bologna and cheese that were kept inside it. The radioactive contents of the apartment – including personal papers – were placed in drums by the inspectors and taken back to the plant.

Strangely, an AEC investigation into the contamination revealed that two urine samples given by Karen following these incidents had been tampered with: plutonium had been deliberately added to them. Further investigation revealed that the contamination came from plutonium to which Karen Silkwood had never had access – which ruled her out as deliberately contaminating her own samples in order to embarrass Kerr-McGee over radiation levels.

Karen, by this point, was very disturbed by these events. According to Drew Stephens she was 'hysterical ... completely out of control' and believed that the high levels of plutonium she had been exposed to would kill her.

Steve Wodka arrived in Oklahoma City to go with her to meet AEC inspectors who had arrived to investigate this extremely serious and apparently puzzling case of contamination. In talking to the AEC, Karen realised that she had apparently been contaminated each time after she had touched bologna sandwiches that she had made – and was even more frightened that she had in fact eaten heavily radioactive food. Steve Wodka, accompanied by Karen, had meetings with two consultant physicians, Dr Neil Wald of Kerr-McGee and Dr Sternhagen of the AEC. It was agreed that Kerr-McGee should be responsible for further medical investigation of the extent of the contamination and the future health risks for Karen.

The company paid for Karen, accompanied by Drew Stephens, to go to the AEC's laboratory in Los Alamos, New Mexico. On their arrival there on Sunday, 10 November, Stephens was tested and no trace of contamination was found. Then Karen was tested. Swabs from her nose and mouth showed that Karen was uncontaminated. She was put in a metal chamber and her lungs were scanned for traces of plutonium. Levels were low, but some americium (a product of decaying plutonium) was present. A full body test showed negative results. Further tests to ascertain exactly what the levels of americium were revealed that she had eight nanocuries of the substance in her lungs. In 1974, the AEC's highest permitted level of plutonium for a lifetime's exposure was sixteen nanocuries. Scientists working in atomic energy have since stated that the AEC's radiation limits at the time were between eight and one thousand times too high for safety.

Briefed on the results of these tests, Karen was reassured by an AEC physician, Dr George Voelz, that her exposure to plutonium was unlikely to cause any health problems. Karen and Drew were considerably relieved, and Karen no longer worried that she would rapidly develop cancer. They left Los Alamos and arrived at Oklahoma City late on a Tuesday night. Tomorrow was an important day – Karen would be meeting with Steve Wodka and a *New York Times* journalist, David Burnham, to hand over a dossier of documents proving, among other accusations, that the fuel-rod test results were being falsified.

13 November 1974
Karen was back at work for the first time since the contamination incidents. Along with Tice and Brewer, she

had a meeting with management at 5.30 p.m. to discuss contracts. She arranged that Drew Stephens would go to the airport to pick up Wodka and Burnham, and that she would make her own way to meet them at the Holiday Inn Northwest.

At the OCAW–Kerr-McGee meeting, management was represented by Morgan Moore, who had previously told AEC investigators that he was of the opinion that Karen had contaminated herself deliberately to make the company look bad. (Karen herself always denied she had done this.) At the end of the meeting, Karen was about to leave for the Holiday Inn. She spoke with another union member, Jean Jung, showed her a notebook and a manila folder containing documents and photographs and told her that what she had to tell the *New York Times* would be highly damaging to Kerr-McGee. Meanwhile, Wodka and Burnham had arrived in Oklahoma and been driven by Stephens to the Holiday Inn.

They were not particularly happy with their reception. Unusually, Wodka's reservation had been mislaid and there was no free room; Steve would have to stay in the same room as Burnham. The phone in Burnham's room was apparently not working. After a futile search for a pay phone, at around 7.30 p.m. Wodka returned to the room he was now sharing. The phone line was working, and Steve got through to Jack Tice, asking the union activist where Karen was. Tice had some bad news for Wodka, who, stunned, informed Burnham and Drew Stephens, who was in the room at the time, that Karen was dead.

The 'accident'

Half a mile away from the Kerr-McGee plant, Karen's Honda Civic had gone off the road, having been driven across the highway, continued along a grass shoulder and then gone over a wall and crashed into a concrete bank at

45 miles per hour. She was killed instantly. A passing truck driver noticed the wreckage, and the Oklahoma Highway Patrol were informed. Apparently by chance, two Kerr-McGee employees, Law Godwin and Fred Sullivan, were next to drive along the scene of the 'accident'. Godwin looked inside the car with a torch and saw a motionless woman, her face covered in blood, apparently crushed by a steering wheel. He recognised the woman as Karen Silkwood. Officer Rick Fagen of the Highway Patrol arrived with a Fire Department ambulance. The door of the Civic was cut open and Silkwood's body removed. The ambulance took Karen to the Logan Country Hospital, where she was pronounced dead on arrival. The wrecked car was taken to a local garage. Fagen searched the car and found, among other items, what he suspected were two marijuana cigarettes. He also discovered a pill and half a tablet. These items were sent to the police lab for analysis. Karen's folder and notebook, containing evidence of malpractice at Kerr-McGee, which Karen was seen to take with her with the intention of handing it over to Wodka and Burnham at the Holiday Inn, had mysteriously disappeared. While the car was at the garage, Kerr-McGee would have been able to remove anything they chose from it quite freely.

How had the accident happened?

Drew Stephens was devastated and outraged at Karen's death. He was certain that she had not died as the result of an accident, and that someone had deliberately forced her off the road. He knew that Karen was a good driver, experienced in driving fast and making complicated manoeuvres at high speed; she had been travelling in good weather conditions on a fairly empty road that she knew well.

The Oklahoma Highway Patrol believed otherwise. Officer Fagen's accident report, written on 15 November, claimed that the accident had been a result of Silkwood's drinking and drug use. The assumption was that a doped-up Karen had fallen into a stupor behind the wheel and lost control of the vehicle. The report claimed Karen had been under the influence of drugs at the time of the crash. This report was not based on any forensic information: it simply contained Fagen's assumptions of how the crash had been caused. At this time, the results from the lab on the cigarette and pills found in the car were not known (they were later found to be two joints, one Quaalude and half a pill too small for analysis), nor had an autopsy been conducted. Fagen also assumed that before her death Karen had been drinking alcohol at the Hub Café (she had not drunk that day).

What caused Karen Silkwood to crash her car?

OCAW's immediate reaction to Karen's death was one of shock and sorrow. Then the union rapidly became suspicious of how Karen had died, believing that her death had been no accident. They hired Adolphus O Pipkin, a highly renowned accident investigator with over twenty years' experience in the field. He had investigated more than two thousand car crashes. He examined the crash vehicle and then went out to the part of the highway where Karen had died. Pipkin's analysis concluded that:

- the dents in the rear bumper were concave and therefore could not have been made when the vehicle was being pulled out of the ditch

- the steering wheel's sides were bent forward, which indicated that Silkwood could not have been unconscious at the moment of impact, as she had been holding the wheel

- tyre patterns found at the crash scene also indicated that the car had been forced off the road – if Karen had not been pursued, there would have been signs of violent braking in an attempt to prevent the car crashing into the concrete wall.

Pipkin concluded that the car had been hit from behind by another vehicle and forced off the road, and Karen had crashed the car in an attempt to get away from her pursuer and back on the road. This report was leaked to the press; Pipkin later found out that he was under investigation by the Pinkerton detective agency, who were anxious to find out if he had a valid investigator's licence. Kerr-McGee and James Reading were interested in Pipkin and anxious to find some way of undermining his credibility.

On 21 November, facing pressure from the media, a local medical examiner, Dr AJ Chapman, issued a press release that ruled that Karen's death had been accidental. Included were the following assertions:

- Karen's death had been caused by the injuries she had received, which included multiple fractures and lacerations

- her body was free of radioactive material at the time of her death

- analysis revealed she had a blood level of methaqualone (Quaaludes) halfway between a therapeutic and a toxic dose; also in her blood was a trace of ethyl alcohol

- the dents in the rear bumper had been made while the car was being moved from the crash scene.

Pipkin brought in Dr BJ Harris, an engineer and accident-analysis expert. The report of their investigations concluded that, as Karen's car had gone off towards the left-hand side of the road, it was less likely that she had gone to sleep or become unconscious, as in these cases the car usually veers towards the right because of the camber of the road. Harris had carefully examined the dents in the rear bumper and believed that they could not have been caused by impact of any part of the Honda with the concrete wall nor by its removal from the ditch.

The Oklahoma Highway Patrol removed Fagen from the case and substituted Larry Owen, their own accident expert. The OHP held a press conference to argue that, as the dents were not smooth, the damage had been cause by friction against the wall. Since there were no tyre marks on the grass, the OHP concluded that Karen had not attempted to move her vehicle back on to the road. Finally they rubbished Pipkin's reasons for the car having moved left across the highway, claiming that Karen's wheels were not properly aligned. Pipkin was able to refute these claims, and had the bumper and fender examined by a metallurgist, Dr Gerald Greene, who found traces of a black material inside some of the scratches around the dents in the fender. When this material was analysed it was found to be rubber, indicating that the front bumper of a pursuing vehicle had hit Karen's car, and with some force.

What Kerr-McGee and the AEC did next

Kerr-McGee started clamping down on OCAW activity at the plant, forcing through their contract with the union and ignoring the requests for training and better safety that the union negotiators had wished to see included. Security and health and safety still appeared a low priority; uranium pellets were found outside the plant buildings, thrown on the ground. The management started what the union perceived to be intimidatory measures: staff were asked to take a lie-detector test while answering questions about employees' contacts with Steve Wodka and Karen Silkwood, and about antinuclear activities, affairs with other staff and drug use.

When the plant reopened after the enforced Christmas shutdown in January 1975, employees were warned about giving any information about Kerr-McGee activities or working practices to anyone outside the company. Seven OCAW members who had refused to take the lie-detector test were removed from the main buildings on the plant and forced to work in a warehouse while being watched over by security. Tice and Brewer were seemingly singled out for punishment: Brewer was sacked for having a poor attitude and Tice was sent to the most unpleasant and dirty part of the uranium plant.

Kerr-McGee and the Atomic Energy Commission conducted enquiries into how Karen Silkwood and her apartment had been contaminated and whether there was any truth in the accusations that faulty and dangerous fuel rods had had their X-ray images tampered with. They concluded that two urine samples had been deliberately spiked with plutonium, that they did not know how or by whom the food in her refrigerator had been contaminated, that Karen had swallowed plutonium as well as having been exposed to it by inhalation and that it was possible that Karen could have stolen plutonium, even if it was from a batch that she was not directly working on.

A lab technician named Scot Dotter was found to have been doctoring negatives with a felt-tip pen; he admitted doing this but claimed that his bosses at Kerr-McGee knew about this practice and that he had been covering up flaws in the negatives, not in the welds in the fuel rods. An AEC investigation confirmed that Dotter was telling the truth.

James Reading and Kerr-McGee attempt to trash Silkwood

Steven Campbell, an undercover informant and the associate of Police Officer Bill Byler, with whom Silkwood and Drew Stephens had had a meeting in October 1974, began to supply information about Karen directly to Kerr-McGee's security boss, James Reading. Stephens, unaware of Campbell's connections, asked him to take photographs of his diary and of his notes on the contamination and killing of Karen Silkwood, as Drew was concerned that Kerr-McGee would try to steal them; Campbell agreed and went on to pass copies of all of Stephens's documents to James Reading. Reading was attempting to dig up dirt on Karen and anxious to find any further information on her use of drugs and her sexual activities. Reading hired private detectives to investigate the accident investigator Adolphus Pipkin's private life and tax status.

The FBI were also involved in their own investigation into the whereabouts of the larger quantities of plutonium that had allegedly gone missing from the plant as 'material unaccounted for'. FBI Agent Larry Olson's enquiries centred around Karen Silkwood and whether she herself had deliberately removed plutonium from the plant. As far as the FBI, the police and the AEC were concerned, Karen's death was an accident and therefore not an issue; they were far more interested in finding out who had illegally removed plutonium from Kerr-McKee.

The campaign to find the truth escalates

Reporters for US National Public Radio came to Oklahoma to investigate the Silkwood case. Interviewing associates of Karen and those workers at the plant who were willing to talk to them, they learned that between 44 and 66 pounds of plutonium was unaccounted for at Kerr-McGee. In an NPR broadcast it was also questioned whether the level of methaqualone (from Quaaludes) in Karen's blood would have been anywhere near enough to impair her driving. The broadcasters criticised the Oklahoma Highway Patrol over their acceptance of Officer Fagen's accident report.

After the NPR broadcasts and an ABC TV *Reasoner Report* programme on Kerr-McGee and Silkwood, the story was now receiving national attention. The National Organization for Women (NOW) started campaigning against the Justice Department's closure of the Silkwood case and calling for a Congressional investigation into her death and the alleged cover-up. NOW contacted the liberal Democrat Senator Abe Ribicoff, who agreed to support the campaign by asking for the release of FBI and Justice Department files on Silkwood. However, Ribicoff's questions would be limited to the health-and-safety issues at the plant, not involving the contamination of Karen Silkwood or the question of exactly who may have forced her car off the highway. Ribicoff handed over the investigation to Senator Lee Metcalf, who set up a hearing into Karen's case, which was cancelled after Metcalf was warned that any investigation into Kerr-McGee would involve national security issues.

The case was passed to the Sub-Committee On Energy, which appointed Peter Stockton as investigator. His job was to find out why safety had been neglected for so long at Kerr-McGee and whether, before her death, Silkwood had been subject to surveillance and by whom. The Congressional hearings took place, but not before the FBI had pleaded that they *not* take place for reasons, again, of national security.

1976 – Congressional hearings conclude Kerr-McGee negligent

The Congressional hearings into the Silkwood case began on 26 April 1976. Witnesses criticised the frequent contamination with plutonium of Kerr-McGee workers and premises, the lack of security in the plant, the minimal safety training. Subpoenaed to testify, the 'journalist' and FBI informant Jacque Srouji admitted under questioning that FBI documents existed that suggested that Silkwood had been under surveillance up to the time of her death. She also claimed to have seen reports that Karen was a habitual marijuana smoker who had attempted suicide on several occasions. Srouji doubted that Silkwood had contaminated herself, nor did she believe that her death was a suicide. Srouji also stated that she herself had copies of papers that included FBI documents relating to Silkwood.

These hearings embarrassed Kerr-McGee because they brought into the open the facts about the appalling lack of safety in the plant. It was also apparent that the FBI were, thought Srouji, apparently still attempting to portray Karen Silkwood as a drug user and emotionally unstable. The Atomic Energy Commission also appeared negligent, as their inspectors had failed to report any problems with either safety or security at Kerr-McGee. After the hearings, Westinghouse did not renew the fuel-rod contract with Kerr-McGee and the plant was effectively closed down.

The Silkwood family bring their case

Karen's parents, Bill and Merle Silkwood, had wanted the hearings to include the question of who was responsible for Karen's death. Now they wanted to bring a criminal suit against Kerr-McGee and the FBI. Daniel Sheehan, an attorney, was highly sympathetic towards Karen's parents and was firm in his belief that Karen had been unlawfully killed, although he was aware that there was absolutely no concrete evidence with which he could prove this. Sheehan persuaded the Silkwoods to file a civil suit against Kerr-McGee: they would sue for damages for negligence and, if this could be proved, for violation of Karen's civil rights.

A private investigator, Bill Taylor, was to help Sheehan in attempting to find out more about Kerr-McGee's negligence at the plant, the FBI's interest in Karen Silkwood and whether the energy company and the Bureau had conspired in a cover-up; during the time of his investigations his house was burgled and he was the subject of an attempted assault in a motel room.

February 1977 – the civil suit

The first part of the court case *Karen Silkwood v the Kerr-McGee Corporation* involved depositions by witnesses, some of whom had to be subpoenaed, testimony by defendants and the gathering and sharing of evidence by both sides. By the time this civil suit came to court in February 1977 Bill Taylor still had no evidence of Kerr-McGee's illegal surveillance of Karen or of any collusion with the FBI in a cover-up. Sheehan subpoenaed Srouji to appear, hoping that the presiding judge in the case, Luther Eubanks, would order that she hand over the FBI documents she claimed to have photocopied. Under questioning by Sheehan, Srouji admitted copying some FBI documents, but denied having read FBI summaries on the Silkwood case, although she did admit she had been shown a pile of papers containing the summaries by the FBI. When questioned on the wire-tapping of Silkwood, her contacts with Kerr-McGee and her copying of FBI files, she did not answer, invoking the Fifth and First Amendments.

Sheehan eventually subpoenaed the FBI to produce their Silkwood documents. When the 2,000 photocopied pages arrived, most of the main details of names, dates and places had been deleted, although it was obvious that Srouji had been actively in contact with the FBI in relation to Karen Silkwood. The FBI material contained absolutely no reports of the fatal car crash or any speculation on how it may have happened. Srouji's main FBI contact, Larry Olson, was questioned in court and admitted that Srouji had been an informant during 1975–6. Kerr-McGee's head of security, James Reading, was also questioned by Sheehan; he claimed he had met Srouji, as she was a writer who was working on a pro-nuclear-power book. He denied bugging Karen's phone or harassing her before her death; indeed he claimed not to have known of Karen Silkwood until he had been informed that there had been contamination of her apartment.

On 27 October, unhappy with the Silkwood legal team's contacts with the media, Judge Eubanks stated that their case 'did not amount to a hill of beans'; while Sheehan was in the process of applying to have Eubanks taken off the Silkwood case because of this statement, he heard that Eubanks had resigned. Judge Luther Bohanon was now presiding over the courtroom. He was impatient with Sheehan's team, denying them an extension of time to find further witnesses. Examining Bohanon's background, Sheehan found out that Senator Bob Kerr had forced his appointment as a federal judge in 1961. Sheehan demanded that Bohanon be removed as presiding judge due to an apparent conflict of interest. Bohanon was replaced by Judge Frank Theis. The court hearings recommenced. The FBI's Agent Olson admitted possessing photographs of Drew Stephens's diary that had been passed to him by James Reading (who in turn had obtained them from Drew's photographer 'friend' Steve Campbell). Reading in turn admitted paying Campbell for documents and information. Sheehan subpoenaed Oklahoma police officers, who denied bugging Karen and claimed they had not heard of her until the car crash. They also denied any working relationship with Reading or Olson.

In September 1978 Judge Theis dropped the charges of conspiracy against Kerr-McGee and the FBI, on the grounds that, even if this was proved, the Silkwood family would not be able to claim damages. Sheehan was not happy with this, and appealed against Theis's judgement. In the meantime, the trial would go ahead, but the Silkwood lawyers would be trying Kerr-McGee only for the negligence within the plutonium plant that had led to the contamination of Karen Silkwood in her apartment.

The Silkwood estate were demanding $1.5 million to compensate for Karen's contamination and the stress this had caused her in her lifetime, and a further $10 million as a punitive sum. If the case was won, the money would go to Karen's three children. Both sides would put their cases in front of a jury. The Silkwood lawyers would try to prove that Kerr-McGee was negligent and that that negligence resulted in the injury of Karen Silkwood by contamination of plutonium. The Silkwood team did not know exactly who had contaminated Karen and could not prove that Kerr-McGee was responsible; but neither did Kerr-McGee know for certain that Karen had taken plutonium from the plant and contaminated herself deliberately.

The Silkwood team had a new member. An experienced personal-injury lawyer named Jerry Spence opened the trial by showing the jury Karen's children, who sat in the front row of seats. He then went on to interview nuclear and medical experts on how dangerous plutonium was, then examined former Kerr-McGee employees, who described the poor health and safety at the plant and the carelessness with which radioactive materials had been treated. OCAW's Steve Wodka was also questioned by Spence; he described Karen's state of mind and how this had been badly affected by the contamination incident.

After a month of examinations by the Silkwood team, the Kerr-McGee lawyers began to put their case before the jury. They aimed to prove that what happened to Karen Silkwood could not legally be defined as an injury, and that the contamination had been self-inflicted or that she had been contaminated during the course of her work. If the jury could be made to believe the latter point then Kerr-McGee would not be liable to be sued for personal injury.

Those responsible for the design of the plant and the safety and alarm systems it used were brought into court also, and faced fierce questioning by Spence. The final testimony was by Dr George Voelz – the AEC doctor who had examined Karen at Los Alamos after the contamination incident – and a cross-examination by Spence in which the physician was criticised for the way he had examined postmortem specimens from Karen's organs and bones. Both sides presented their closing arguments to the jury.

On 18 May 1979 the jury gave their verdict. Their view was that Karen had not taken plutonium from the plant to her apartment. Her estate was awarded $505,000 as compensation for Karen's suffering and Kerr-McGee were ordered to pay $10,000,000 damages. Silkwood's family, lawyers and supporters were jubilant.

In November 1980 Kerr-McGee appealed against this judgement, pleading that the sums of money awarded to the Silkwood estate were too large. They gave reasons why the trial had not been conducted fairly by Judge Theis, and requested it be declared a mistrial. The Federal Court of Appeals in Colorado upheld this appeal, awarding $5,000 for damage done to Silkwood's property as a result of the contamination. In 1986, the Silkwood family accepted $1.3 million from Kerr-McGee in an out-of-court settlement.

7 Hilda Murrell

Death of a rose grower

On Saturday, 24 March 1984, the body of Hilda Murrell, a world-renowned rose grower, was found in a wood in Hunkingdon, six miles from her home in Sutton Road, on the outskirts of Shrewsbury. The 78-year-old victim was mutilated by stab wounds and bruises. Her car, a white Renault 5, and a knife used in the murder had been abandoned near her body a few days earlier on Wednesday, 21 March – the last day Hilda Murrell was seen alive. West Mercia Police investigating her death concluded that Miss Murrell was the victim of a burglar whom she had interrupted in her home, where she lived alone – and, as their investigation deepened, changed key details regarding what they believed were the circumstances of her death.

In examining the case of Hilda Murrell, a series of facts, some seemingly unconnected, need to be taken into account. From a police point of view, the crime remains unsolved. Cumulative evidence, however, appears to point to a political motive for her unlawful killing, with the possible direct involvement of the state.

Who was Hilda Murrell? Her life and political connections

Born in Shrewsbury in 1906, Hilda won a scholarship to her local high school, where she became head girl. She attended Newnham College, Cambridge, and read English, Medieval Languages and French, graduating in 1928. For the next thirty years she worked for the family firm, Murrell's Roses, and had been a gold-award winner at major flower shows. In 1962 she opened a new business, Portland Nurseries, from which she retired in 1970. She then became active in local conservation work and opposition to nuclear war and nuclear power. By the 1980s she was active in opposing the Conservative government's plans to build a pressurised-water nuclear reactor at Sizewell, on the Suffolk coast.

Hilda Murrell's political activism involved membership of the Shrewsbury Peace Group, the Campaign for Nuclear Disarmament (CND), Greenpeace and END (European Disarmament Group). At the time of her death Hilda was preparing her Sizewell B paper with help from and via involvement in ECOROPA, the European Group for Ecological Action, an openly political organisation campaigning on a pro-environmental and anti-nuclear platform. ECOROPA and many of these other organisations were certainly a target of the security services during the 1980s. Moreover, Murrell was an active participant in these groups, and took her views into the public arena. She had letters published in national newspapers and even wrote directly to Prime Minister Thatcher criticising what she saw as 'the madness of nuclear power'.

These activities would certainly have been known by MI5 and possibly by local Special Branch officials, as monitoring of the press was an important means of gleaning intelligence on those the government thought of as 'subversive'.

This was not the only 'political' dimension of Hilda Murrell that would have been known to the British security services. Her nephew, Commander Rob Green, with whom she was in frequent contact, had served in the Royal Navy during the Falklands conflict. As a former fleet intelligence officer, Green was aware of secret details surrounding the sinking of the Argentine warship the *General Belgrano*, which was sunk by British forces on 2 May 1982 while outside the declared Total Exclusion Zone. Green would have known the exact details of the Prime Minister's orders to HMS *Conqueror*, the nuclear submarine that carried out the attack.

Rob Green had retired from the Royal Navy in 1982 to work as a thatcher in Dorset. At the time of Murrell's death, controversy was raging in both Parliament and the press over the sinking of the *Belgrano*.

It is estimated that the likelihood was that Murrell was part of an ongoing investigation by Special Branch at the time of her death.

What exactly happened?

Reports of the sequence of events between 21 March and the day Hilda's body was found were initially contradictory and sometimes vague. By a piecing together of various accounts, the following course of events seems most likely.

Wednesday, 21 March

This was a day on which Hilda had planned to visit her friends, Drs John and Alicia Symondson, who lived in nearby Wales, for lunch. At around 10 a.m. on the day of her murder, Hilda Murrell drove her Renault 5 into Shrewsbury. She visited her bank and withdrew £50. She was seen shopping in the Safeway supermarket, and returned home by midday, having briefly visited a neighbour to pay for a raffle ticket.

She then returned to her home, where she appears to have disturbed an intruder and become involved in a violent struggle. It is not known whether Murrell was dead or alive when she was put into her own car and driven away by her attacker. No fewer than 69 witnesses observed the Renault being driven fast and erratically away from Murrell's home. The driver appeared to be heading towards Shrewsbury and then surprisingly changed course by making for the Newport road. Hilda's abandoned car was seen by a local farmer, John Marsh, at around 1.20 p.m. – it was Marsh who rang the local police and reported the vehicle. A 'running man' was seen in the area at around the same time. As Hilda was late for her lunch appointment, Alicia Symondson rang her home – there was no reply and the phone was heard to ring normally. Dr Symondson called again later that afternoon – again, the phone was not answered.

On that morning two suspicious sightings were made near Hilda's home: in the morning a neighbour who did occasional gardening work for her, Brian George, had seen a man and a woman, who he claimed looked 'suspicious', walking along a road towards Murrell's home; also, a red Ford Escort car was seen being driven hear her home.

Thursday, 22 March

Hilda Murrell's vehicle remained in the ditch where it had apparently been abandoned. No further police enquiries were made about it. Later, police stated that a check with the Driver and Vehicle Licensing Centre (now the Driver and Vehicle Licensing Agency) had given them incorrect information about who was the owner of the vehicle. A local landowner, Ian Scott, visited the copse where Murrell's body would later be found. He saw no trace of her, despite a thorough examination of the area. 'I examined the place so thoroughly I would have seen a dead rabbit, let alone a person,' he later claimed. According to later reports in the *Shropshire Star*, a witness told police that a man was seen visiting the copse, driving there in a dark car. Meanwhile, at Hilda's house, the curtains remained shut and lights left on.

Friday, 23 March

By this time, Hilda's friends had begun to wonder where she was. When they rang her home, there was no reply. When they rang her bungalow in Wales, where they presumed that she had gone, again there was no answer. To callers, both phones sounded as if they were working normally – so they concluded that Murrell had gone elsewhere.

Her neighbour, Brian George, noticed that the kitchen door of the house was open – but did not regard this as suspicious. John Marsh, who had initially reported the abandoned Renault to police, reported it again. According to police, on this Friday a red Escort was again sighted – this time driving slowly past the wood in Hunkingdon.

On Friday evening, the police finally made the effort of tracing the correct owner of the Renault, and then called at Hilda's home – only to find no one there – and then left.

An extraordinary occurrence also took place that day. A Shrewsbury man, who specialised in the counselling of people with sexual problems, was visited by two senior police officers who asked him if he knew of anyone who might have a sexual fixation on elderly women, a man who would get kicks from breaking into such a woman's bedroom and handling her clothing. Moreover, the officers asked if such a person might be of a violent disposition. The counsellor, a credible witness of good reputation, who asked to remain anonymous because of the sensitive nature of his job, made a statement of events to Tam Dalyell MP in the presence of a journalist, Judith Cook, author of a book on the Murrell case.

It is the chronology of the visit that raises serious questions about the police investigation of Murrell's death. The Shrewsbury sex counsellor read reports of the discovery of Hilda's body the following evening and presumed that the officers who had visited him were referring to the Murrell murder; he was shocked and puzzled by why police had visited him on the Friday, when the body was not supposed to have been found until the following day.

Saturday, 24 March
Police returned to Hilda's house at 6.30 a.m. and went inside – later they claimed to have 'forced entry' which would be a strange thing to have done if the kitchen door was still left open at that time. They looked around the house but did not go into Hilda's bedroom – thinking she might be in there asleep. Brian George arrived at around 8.45, intending to do some gardening work. He found police still at the house, but found it odd that there was no confirmation at this time that Hilda was missing. The PC in attendance said he had obtained a spare key for Murrell's house from one of her relatives who lived nearby, and that he would be locking up the front door of the premises and returning to the police station. This he did. At 9 a.m. George was joined by a second gardener, David Williams. They found that the kitchen door was still open. When they went inside they saw that the kitchen was strewn with Hilda's handbags and papers relating to the Sizewell enquiry. They went into the house and saw that a systematic search had taken place in all rooms. George has maintained since that what he saw in the house was definitely not the aftermath of a burglary. When Brian George and David Williams entered Hilda's house, they found a pile of mail and newspapers behind the front door – the same door that the police had allegedly locked only a short time before. Alarmed, the two men then tried to use the phone to call Hilda at her bungalow in Wales, only to find no dial tone on the line. They went to Brian George's home to try again. On getting no reply, they called the police.

A large-scale search was then initiated, both in Hilda's home and around the area where her car had been abandoned. At 10.30 a.m. the partially clothed body was found lying face up. Injuries included stab wounds, scratch marks and bruising. Murrell had been sexually abused before her death.

'Investigations' commence

On the discovery of Hilda's body, Detective Chief Superintendent Cole, chief of West Mercia CID, was appointed as head of the investigation. Simultaneously, the West Mercia Special Branch began a seemingly independent enquiry into the death of Hilda Murrell. A postmortem took place at 6.15 p.m. on the day the body was found. A report by a Home Office pathologist, Dr Peter Ackland, described the injuries as having been inflicted by a knife, and indicated that it was unlikely that the body had been moved after death. He gave the cause of death as hypothermia. Rob Green, Hilda's next of kin, was not able to obtain a copy of the postmortem report. After the opening of the inquest, Green asked when his aunt's body could be released for burial – and was told this was not possible in the forseeable future, that perhaps it could happen when the murderer was caught, which could take months or years. Green was then astonished to be phoned by Shrewsbury police and told that a second autopsy had been performed and that he had to remove his aunt's body immediately. On 25 August 1984 Hilda Murrell was finally cremated, despite the murder still being officially unsolved.

What the local papers said

Police briefed the local press with conflicting stories. The news story first appeared in a local paper, the *Shropshire Star*, two days after the body was found. Police had told the paper's reporters that Murrell had been found brutally murdered and that her home in Shrewsbury had been 'ransacked'. Detective Chief Superintendent Cole also told the press that Murell had last been seen shopping at

11 a.m. on Wednesday (21 March), and that her car had been seen unoccupied and reported to police, who treated it as an abandoned vehicle. Only after the car had been abandoned for two days did police trace its owner and visit Murrell's house. There being no one at home, police returned the following day (Saturday, 24 March) and, according to Cole, 'forced entry'.

At another press conference Detective Chief Superintendent Barrie Mayne said the theory was now that Murrell had returned to her home 'to find a robbery in progress'. The press were not told if Hilda Murell had been stabbed in her car, at the spot where her body had been left or at home. By 28 March the police were claiming that the killer may well have been 'a local man', and released details of a man seen running near to where the body was found. On 29 March a crucial detail was given – police claimed Hilda's telephone had been 'torn out'. At further briefings the press were told that it was not known if anything had been stolen from the house. Fifty pounds, which Hilda had withdrawn from her bank on the day she died, was eventually found to be missing, and those investigating seized on this as a likely motive. On 30 March, the *Shropshire Star* reported that Hilda Murrell had been active in opposing the pressurised-water nuclear reactor being built at Sizewell.

It took some time for the details of the story to be explored by the national press. The *Times* on 26 March had reported the use of police helicopters to try to find Hilda's killer. On 18 August 1984 the *Guardian* ran a piece on Hilda's death, which mentioned her opposition to Sizewell.

Hilda's fears before her death – claims by Purser and Otter

Prior to her death, Hilda had shown some awareness that she was under surveillance. To her contacts involved in opposition to Sizewell, she seemed more uneasy generally. She sent her nephew Rob Green a copy of her Sizewell paper, asking him to read it at the hearing should anything happen to her.

Her friend, 85-year-old Constance Purser, was visited by Hilda on 19 March 1984. Hilda tried to leave some papers with Purser, who sensed there was some danger in taking them, and declined. Purser assumed these papers had some connection with Hilda's evidence to the Sizewell committee. According to Purser, since December Hilda had been worried about the security of her Shrewsbury home.

On the morning of Hilda's murder, she had telephoned her friend Laurens Otter in Wellington to ask him to come to Shrewsbury and collect some papers from her. During this conversation, she told Otter that she had received threatening phone calls and believed that her mail was being opened. She also informed Otter she was expecting an Inspector or Chief Inspector Davies, or Davy, who would be 'coming up from London' to visit – in connection with what she did not say. Otter was unable to meet Hilda that day.

The evidence of both Purser and Otter was not taken seriously by police, who failed to pursue these lines of enquiry. Purser made great efforts to contact police and be interviewed; on 16 April she was aggressively questioned by police about whether she was colluding with Hilda's nephew Rob Green in making her statement.

The picture of Hilda Murrell that may be gleaned from these accounts is that she was a frightened woman, well aware of the danger that her political and environmental concerns could place her in, and knowing that she was being systematically observed from close quarters. Subsequent investigation by Gary Murray (see bibliography) has revealed that the owners of an empty property facing Hilda Murrell's home were, at the time of her death, the

West Mercia police. The house was sold after Hilda's death. It seems almost certain that this house was owned and used for surveillance purposes.

The developing story hits the media and Parliament – Dalyell's claims

On 19 November 1984, with the police investigation into Hilda Murrell's death still apparently making no concrete progress, the *New Statesman* broke the details of the murder, Hilda's opposition to Sizewell and her connection with her nephew Rob Green, a Royal Naval commander during the Falklands War. On 20 December 1984 the Labour MP Tam Dalyell addressed the House of Commons on the murder of Hilda Murrell. Dalyell was a well-known critic of government over the conduct of the Falklands War and in particular the sinking of the *General Belgrano*. In his speech, Dalyell was heavily critical of the police investigation into Hilda's death, outlined Rob Green's connection with his aunt and with signals intelligence, and spoke of two large anomalies in police statements about the murder. One of these was that the police claimed that the break-in had been committed by an ordinary burglar, yet the house had been carefully searched and the phone cut off by the careful disconnection of one wire; after the disconnection callers ringing in would still hear a ringing tone. The other anomaly was that police at first claimed Hilda Murrell had been sexually assaulted; they then claimed that this was untrue. The truth was that she *had* been assaulted and semen had been ejaculated over her body.

It was also asked why Hilda's relatives had been denied a copy of the postmortem report.

Dalyell described Hilda's exact involvement in the Sizewell hearing, and then made the claim, based on his own security and intelligence contacts, that Commander

Robert Green was 'certainly under a cloud of suspicion' because he had left the navy and was thought to possess copies of documents and 'raw signals' that incriminated Prime Minister Thatcher over the *Belgrano* incident. Dalyell claimed that men acting on behalf of the intelligence services had been searching her home for *Belgrano*-related documents that Rob Green may have passed to his aunt for safekeeping. They were then disturbed by Murrell's arrival and then 'things went disastrously wrong' and during a struggle Murrell was 'severely injured'.

Replying for the government, a junior Home Office minister, Giles Shaw, said the allegations would be given 'full consideration and a proper, and I hope comprehensive, reply'. Perhaps contradictorily, he also told the Commons that the anti-nuclear background of Miss Murrell had been investigated and 'no evidence has been found to link those activities with her death'.

A month later West Mercia police issued an eleven-page statement rejecting Dalyell's claims. Although this statement denied involvement of British intelligence officers, it did not mention any use of civilian contractors or freelances.

Police try to pin the blame on Robert Higgins and David McKenzie

A local burglar, Robert James Higgins, was visited by police in January 1985 and taken to Hilda Murrell's house. When his own home was searched, an anti-nuclear pamphlet was found. Higgins informed the press that he thought police were trying to pin Murrell's murder on him. In addition another local petty criminal was arrested and grilled at length by police regarding Murrell's murder. In neither case were any charges made.

An unemployed hotel worker, David McKenzie, was convicted of the murder of two elderly women in 1990.

During his trial, prosecution lawyers intimated that he would also be charged with the Murrell murder. Formal charges regarding Murrell were never brought against McKenzie, who was judged to be mentally ill.

This appeared to be the conclusion of the Murrell case: a suspect who was unable to plead who had committed similar killings. However, when McKenzie later appealed against these convictions the appeals were upheld. In the Court of Appeal it transpired that McKenzie's only crime was that of 'serial confession'. Additionally, McKenzie could not have been the killer, as the sperm found on her body was from a man who had had a vasectomy – and McKenzie had not. After McKenzie's appeal was upheld, the Murrell case was once again an unsolved murder. The police had failed to explore the connections between her death and her involvement with the *Belgrano* affair and opposition to the nuclear reactor at Sizewell.

The strange case of Barrie Peachman – and the private investigation agencies monitoring the Sizewell objectors

Barrie Charles Peachman, despite no police experience or qualifications in investigative work, formed his own company, the Sapphire Investigation Bureau, in 1963. By the 1980s, this was a highly successful company, and Peachman was the president of the Institute of Professional Investigators. By this time he was professionally involved in an undercover operation against anti-nuclear protestors at Sizewell. In January 1983 Peachman had been rung up by a former intelligence officer, Peter Hamilton of Zeus Security Consultants, and specifically asked to list names of the principal objectors to the Sizewell reactor who had met at a public meeting at Snape Maltings in Suffolk – the very meeting that Hilda Murrell would attend.

Peachman in turn called Victor Norris, a freelance investigator who was accustomed to doing 'dirty work' for the Home Office. Norris's colourful past included a six-year prison sentence for sexual offences involving his young daughters, a conviction for carrying an offensive weapon and involvement in a neo-Nazi organisation, the Phoenix Society. By employing Norris, Peachman became the intermediary in a large private investigation including spying, bugging and phone tapping, paid for by Zeus Security Consultants, whose chairman was the right-wing Conservative Peer Lord Chalfont (shortly to become deputy chairman of the Independent Broadcasting Authority).

The crucial unanswered question here is: who was paying Zeus Security to carry out this work? Given the political climate of the time, it seems extremely likely that the responsibility lay with a government department involved in internal security and countering 'subversion' such as MI5.

Gary Murray, in *Enemies Of The State*, cites an unnamed MI5 agent's view that by the 1980s the organisation was having 'serious problems' and was wasting time investigating people and organisations who posed no threat. Murray's source also claimed there were subversive elements within MI5 who were 'a law unto themselves'.

A number of Cornish, Welsh and East Anglian anti-nuclear, environmental and trade union groups and individuals were targeted by Norris in his Sizewell surveillance work. Involvement in this type of work, as well as internal splits within the Institute of Professional Investigators and problems in his private life, were causing Barrie Peachman great stress. He himself believed he was under surveillance. According to his friend Gary Murray, by Christmas 1983 Peachman was 'suicidal'. Twenty-four hours after the death of Hilda Murrell, Peachman was calling Murray and weeping, threatening to kill himself, saying, 'I'm in terrible trouble, something's gone wrong'. Peachman never told Murray the details of what had gone wrong.

Two weeks later, on 17 April 1984, Barrie Peachman blew his brains out with a shotgun. The link between the deaths of Murrell and Peachman was the controversial Sizewell reactor. The *Observer* of 27 January 1985 broke the story that private investigation agencies had been involved in surveillance on opponents to the Sizewell reactor; it was not known on whose behalf this monitoring had been instigated, nor were West Mercia police making any enquiries along these lines.

A week later, on 3 February, Nick Davies wrote in the *Observer* that thirty members of the Institute of Professional Investigators had been identified as currently serving in civilian or military intelligence. The same article claimed that Special Branch used these people to do 'dirty work'.

Why the effort in opposing the opponents of the Sizewell B reactor? Political background

During the 1980s, the Conservative government was a great proponent of nuclear power. One major reason for this was that nuclear power weakened the strength of the coal miners, whom the government confronted during the 1984 miners' strike.

Government hostility towards anti-nuclear power groups was also because of fears that nuclear plants could be invaded by protestors who could then perform terrorist acts. The implementation of the pressurised-water nuclear reactor at Sizewell was seen by the nuclear industry as a task crucial to their future.

What exactly did Commander Rob Green know?

Rob Green, as an intelligence officer in the Royal Navy, had access to classified defence information during the

Falklands War. To work in such a post he was positively vetted on a regular basis by navy security staff, who would also liaise with Special Branch and MI5. Hilda Murrell's anti-nuclear views and activities would have been noted. Green's leaving the navy in December 1982 did not mean that surveillance was at an end: indeed the opposite may well have applied, as Green may have been seen as a disgruntled employee who had 'jumped ship'. In the light of continuing interest in the exact circumstances of the sinking of the *General Belgrano*, what Green could have revealed, either acting by himself or by passing information to his politically active aunt, might have embarrassed or even damaged the government.

Murrell's associates: 'Malcolm' and 'Trina'

For some time before her death, Hilda had been friends with a Shrewsbury couple, who can be identified only as 'Malcolm' and 'Trina'. She was particularly close to Trina, who would assist Hilda in distributing leaflets produced by ECOROPA that were highly critical of nuclear weapons and nuclear power. One leaflet in particular gave precise details of nuclear weapons that had been taken to the South Atlantic for possible deployment during the Falklands War. According to Gerard Morgan-Grenville of ECOROPA, this information had not come from Commander Rob Green. Any security services monitoring these leaflets would have come to a different conclusion, knowing that Hilda was involved in writing and distributing the leaflets and that her nephew was a former signals intelligence officer. In addition, Malcolm's father worked for the MOD in Shrewsbury as a senior signals intelligence officer employed in secret defence work. Again, Malcolm's father would have been subject to the same regular positive vetting as Commander Rob Green, involving questions about his family, friends and acquaintances.

In 1992, Trina made a sixteen-page affidavit which details her friendship with Hilda Murrell, tells of Trina's own experiences of having her phone tapped and her home searched, and most importantly reveals that as a prison visitor she met inmates who claim to know the identities of those responsible for Murrell's murder.

In November 1991, Trina spoke to an ex-prisoner who told her that a prisoner he knew had 'considerable knowledge' of the Murrell case. When she visited this man, he told her that he had been in the same wing as a man serving fifteen years for armed robbery who claimed to have been in charge of a small group responsible for surveillance of Hilda Murrell. According to the inmate, this man had been one of a group of four men and one woman whose duties had involved searching Murrell's house for papers relating to the Falklands and the *Belgrano*. Trina's informant claimed that the leader of this group was 'reporting to the Cabinet Office via an MI5 liaison officer and that the team, in addition to their government work, were also involved in all manner of other illegal activity, including armed robbery, for which they were arrested some time after Hilda's death'.

The informant states that, on the day of her death, Murrell returned home to find three men and a woman searching the house, and one of the men became violent, 'threatened her with a knife, accompanied by obscene sexual acts, including masturbation'. The group then left the house, only to return and abduct Hilda, taking her to a nearby disused military base. Two days later she was taken to the area where her body was eventually found.

Of the members of the 'team' responsible for the death of Murrell, the following is known. The leader is serving his sentence for armed robbery, and refuses to discuss the Murrell case. Another team member is serving sixteen years for armed robbery, and is resident in a secure psychiatric hospital, suffering from depression. Another team member shot himself dead during a police chase. The woman served a two-year prison sentence and then disappeared. The final member, a former police officer, was allegedly the link between the group and MI5.

Enquiry relaunched

In April 2000, West Mercia Police announced that they had received new information from a member of the public regarding the case and were reopening investigations. They would also be applying new DNA techniques to genetically identify the semen left near Hilda Murrell's body.

Former MI5 agent dismisses allegations

In an article in the *Daily Express* on 2 April 2000, a disaffected former MI5 agent, David Shayler, denied claims that MI5 had any involvement in Hilda's murder. He wrote that he had seen the MI5 file on the death of Hilda Murrell and such accusations were 'complete fabrication'.

Conclusion – credibility of claims

Any conclusions that may be reached regarding the death of Hilda Murrell are closely linked to the credibility of the potential witnesses involved. Unfortunately, the most important ones (Trina and Malcolm, the sex counsellor in Shrewsbury who had a curious visit from police and the members of the group that allegedly killed Murrell) have either felt the need for complete anonymity or are unwilling to discuss the Murrell affair in public. Private investigator Barrie Peachman apparently committed suicide, his state of mind possibly disturbed by knowledge he may have had about the murder of Hilda Murrell. The account of the one prisoner willing to talk may well be a fraudulent one, or this may be yet further disinformation.

Certainly, at the time of Murrell's death both the police and the mainly Conservative-supporting British press seemed indecently eager to conclude that her death was the result of a burglary gone wrong and to ridicule claims that she had been murdered by the state. Checkable facts in this case are elusive, precisely because of the lack of witnesses, the number of conflicting accounts, and the apparently contradictory statements of police at the time.

It appears certain that since Commander Rob Green was honest about his aunt's political views from the outset, and revealed these to Royal Navy officers during his positive vetting, Hilda Murrell would have been the subject of an investigation not only by naval security but by MI5 and the local Special Branch. The careful search of Murrell's house had all the hallmarks of an operation by security services or private investigators acting on their behalf; the sexual assault, the brutal wounding and the murder are indicators that those involved were not trained operatives, but people with a criminal and violent past. It seems likely that the death of Murrell was the result of the search of her property being interrupted by her return. In the panic that ensued, Hilda was violently attacked. The lack of progress in the police investigation seems staggering – especially as police kept promoting the idea that the killer was a local man. It has been assumed by many (though without conclusive proof) that the investigation was deliberately inhibited by members of the security services, making any progress impossible.

The coincidences in this case are numerous. According to police, a burglar just happened to break into Murrell's home at the same time as she had completed her paper on Sizewell and had planned to be away for the day. We are also meant to believe it is coincidental that Murrell's nephew was directly involved in naval intelligence regarding the sinking of the *General Belgrano* and that the murder was committed at a time of much government anxiety over what was revealed about the circumstances of its sinking. Unfortunately for the police, too, the two attempts to pin the murder on known criminals both failed. Owing to its complexity and the sinister implications of state involvement, whether the killing was accidental or not, the Murrell case continues to disturb, and crucial questions remain unanswered.

8 PC Keith Blakelock

'This is the Farm. You must be mad. You'll never get out of here alive.'

> *– Anonymous rioter, quoted by the prosecutor,*
> *Roy Amlot, at the trial of the six accused*
> *of the murder of PC Keith Blakelock*

'[Blakelock] had about 40 stab, cut or slash wounds; he had a large gaping wound across the right side of his head ... which fractured and splintered the outer table of his lower jaw and the entire thickness of his jawbone as if to sever his head ...'

> *– Roy Amlot's version of events at Broadwater Farm*

'You ain't got enough evidence. The kids will never go to court. You wait and see ...'

> *– words attributed to Winston Silcott*
> *during his interrogation by police*

Broadwater Farm

The Broadwater Farm estate in Tottenham, north London, was constructed in the late 1960s. It is a typical example of the sort of council housing that was built in inner-city areas in Britain at the time, intended to give people who lived in decaying slums a better environment. The buildings were constructed by the Taylor Woodrow company using prefabricated concrete blocks. The estate, or the 'Farm', as it is known to local residents, is made up of twelve residential blocks of varying size, each several storeys high. With the intention of facilitating ease of movement within the estate, the blocks are joined by walkways. In 1973 the first residents were moved in, mainly from slums elsewhere in Tottenham. Thirty-four flats were allotted to people on the Haringey Council waiting list, whom a local newspaper described as 'the lucky 34 who will be given tenancy of brand new flats in the Broadwater Farm Estate'.

Broadwater Farm is situated off a main road – Lordship Lane – and is very close to local facilities. There are a nursery school, a primary school and two other schools on adjoining streets; a medical centre is nearby. Facilities inside the estate included several shops and a social club.

The flats themselves had large rooms and, due to a communal heating system, were kept warm in the winter. However, within a few years the buildings developed problems such as damp, mould and infestation by cockroaches. The local council had allowed the flats to get into a state of general disrepair. The Farm became known as a 'problem estate' early on, with frequent burglaries, vandalism and graffiti. By the early 1980s the people who had moved there were anxious to get out. As early as 1976 a local newspaper was claiming that the Farm was a violent place; two years later the same paper, the Tottenham *Weekly Herald*, wrote that the estate contained 'a sub-culture of violence'. In letters to the *Herald*, the tenants' reaction to both these stories was to deny that where they lived was violent.

The flats were inhabited by both black and white people. The first negative report on Broadwater Farm, in the *Hornsey Journal* of 11 May 1973, spoke negatively of 'unmarried West Indian mothers' living there. In the context of the tensions and prejudices that existed apparently unchecked in British society at the time, it is not difficult to perceive a racist agenda in the early reporting of life on the Broadwater Farm Estate. Only a few years after the doors of the Farm were opened to residents the negative image of the estate was making people unwilling to live there. A consequence of this was that a major proportion of those moving in were people whose need for accommodation was acute and often desperate – families who had been homeless, or impoverished single parents with children. Many of these people were of Afro-Caribbean descent. An anonymous (black) resident told Lord Gifford's independent inquiry into the 1985 Broadwater Farm disturbances that 'as the black people came in, the whites went out' (Gifford, First Report, p. 22).

The birth of the Youth Association

During the 1970s, despite the racial mix on the estate, the social club remained largely white and members of the black community were not made particularly welcome. Young black people living on the Farm, many of whom were jobless and most of whom were frequently stopped and searched by local police, had nowhere to go. In 1981 these young black people formed the Broadwater Farm Youth Association, with its own premises in a disused shop on the estate. A community leader, Dolly Kiffin, was active in setting up the Association. One of the Association's main activities was providing meals and outings for pensioners on the estate. Later activities extended to selling fruit and vegetables and setting up a launderette and a hair salon. Physical conditions on the Farm were also improving: there was a programme of repair to the buildings, with doors being strengthened to make the flats more secure. The estate was visited by Diana, Princess of Wales, in the spring of 1985, and she was shown around the Farm and its considerably improved environment.

The Youth Association made efforts to improve relations between Broadwater Farm residents and the local police. There was even a football match between the Association and a police team. However, this did little to raise confidence in the police generally; youths were still being habitually arrested and, they felt, picked on, by members of other police units such as the Special Patrol Group.

An escalating climate of violence – rioting in the 1980s

In 1981 across the UK there were many disturbances classified as riots by the press. Media attention focused on violence in Brixton in south London and Toxteth in Liverpool. Both these headline-grabbing disturbances came about as a result of what was perceived as heavy-handed police tactics against young people, particularly those of the Afro-Caribbean community. The Brixton 'riot' was a result of the provocatively named 'Operation Swamp 81', which was intended to curb street crime.

On the afternoon of 4 April 1981, when a youth was arrested by police, crowds gathered to protest and attempted to free him. By the evening the situation escalated out of control, with crowds of black and white youths fighting with police and attacking, burning and looting shops, cars and buildings. On the first weekend of July 1981 violent disturbances broke out in Toxteth. These were followed by what the press dubbed 'copycat riots' in other cities. On 9 September the Lozells Road in Handsworth, Birmingham, was the scene of rioting and mass destruction of property, with buildings burned to the ground. On 28 September 1985 riots broke out in Brixton following the shooting of Cherry Groce by police during a house raid; the weekend's disturbances resulted in 209 arrests.

Policing on the Farm

During the early 1980s the Farm had its own 'home beat officer', PC Brian Stratton, who was respected by many on the estate, black and white alike. In March 1982 a second officer joined him, PC Andy Holland, who was assaulted with a bottle while inside the Youth Association premises. This incident further damaged relations between residents and police. In November of that year several members of the Youth Association were arrested during a lawful demonstration outside Tottenham police station following the arrest of a youth on an unfounded charge of burglary. Tension increased. There were incidents in which beer barrels were thrown on to a police vehicle and PC Stratton was whacked on the head with a billiard cue.

The autumn of 1982 appears to have been a turning point in relations between youths on the estate and the police. The Farm was now continually patrolled by officers; additionally, covert surveillance of residents began, with police installing equipment in empty flats on the estate. In August 1983 a police officer was stabbed, though not fatally, when attempts were made to arrest a female resident.

In the summer of 1985, black youths from outside Broadwater Farm began spending time hanging around the housing blocks; additionally, cocaine and marijuana began to be sold openly on the estate. The people selling the drugs were not residents: they came into the area as a result of police cleaning up other areas in London. People living on the estate, including members of the Youth Association, wanted the drug dealers evicted. Police, however, did nothing to stop them; apparently they were waiting for a go-ahead from Dolly Kiffin.

On the Tuesday before the rioting at Broadwater Farm, there was a massive police operation at the estate, with all black people driving cars in and out of the Farm being stopped and searched. With images of the rioting in Brixton on 28 September still being broadcast on the TV news, there were persistent rumours that Tottenham would have its own riot, taking place in the Wood Green Shopping Centre (a newly built shopping mall located near to the estate), Tottenham High Road or Broadwater Farm itself. Rumours of imminent riots were, however, nothing new, and had been circulating every year since 1981.

By early October 1985, the volatile situation would require only one incident to bring about the full-scale rioting that would ensue during which a police constable, cornered by an angry crowd of youths, would be stabbed to death.

Cynthia Jarrett and the arrest of her son

Jamaican-born Cynthia Jarrett had been a resident of Tottenham for some 25 years. With her husband, she had brought up five children, and at the time of her death had ten grandchildren. She lived at 25 Thorpe Road, near Broadwater Farm.

At lunchtime on Saturday, 5 October 1985, her son, Floyd Jarrett, who was active in the Broadwater Farm Youth Association, was arrested following a police check on his car. PC Christopher Casey noticed that Floyd's tax disc (by law, required to be placed on the front windscreen of all vehicles) had not yet been renewed, and saw a discrepancy of one letter between the car registration plate and the tax disc. Despite having had an acknowledgement via his police radio that Jarrett's car was not stolen, PC Casey told him that he was under arrest on suspicion of car theft. On being told this, Jarrett attempted to run away, only to be chased by Casey and several other policemen.

On being caught, Floyd Jarrett was arrested, charged with an assault on the police and taken to Tottenham police station, where Detective Constable Michael Randall was on duty. Randall made the decision to search Floyd's mother's house in Thorpe Road as their records at St Ann's police station wrongly gave that house as Jarrett's current address (Jarrett himself was now living nearby in Enfield). Following the issue of a search warrant by a local magistrate (although there is some controversy over the exact time of the issue of the warrant, with the issuing magistrate at first claiming to have signed it between 6 and 6.30 p.m. – after the police had entered the Jarrett household), a squad of policemen including DC Randall and PC Casey arrived at Cynthia Jarrett's house. Using Floyd's keys, they entered the property at 5.45 p.m. Mrs Jarrett, her daughter Patricia and two small children were inside, and were shocked and angry to suddenly find police searching the house. (Police lied to Cynthia and Patricia, claiming they had got inside the house because the door had been left open.)

During a search of the dining room, DC Randall allegedly pushed Cynthia Jarrett to the floor; having been knocked down, she was having difficulty breathing. Patricia phoned for an ambulance as her mother's condition visibly worsened; Cynthia's son Michael arrived and told the officers to leave. DC Randall was allowed back in and he attempted to give Cynthia the kiss of life. By the time the ambulance arrived at 6.20 p.m., Mrs Jarrett was already dead.

Judicial findings

The week-long inquest, held at the end of November 1985, established that Mrs Jarrett had severe coronary disease, undiagnosed at the time of her death, and that the fall in her house may well have precipitated her death. The shock of suddenly seeing police inside her house may well have been a contributing factor. The verdict at the inquest was accidental death, which apparently exonerated Randall, as it indicated that his pushing her was not a deliberate act. The coroner stated at the inquest that Cynthia Jarrett's heart condition was so severe that she was 'a candidate for death at any time' (Gifford, First Report, p. 79).

Additionally in December 1985 Floyd Jarrett appeared before magistrates and was acquitted of the charge of assaulting PC Casey. An award of £350 in costs was made against Tottenham police.

Reaction to the death of Cynthia Jarrett

Following Mrs Jarrett's death, members of her family accompanied by friends had gone to Tottenham police station in the early hours of Sunday, 6 October. They met with Chief Superintendent Stainsby, who arranged for them to be shown a copy of the search warrant for Thorpe Road – police were apparently unable to find the original. While they were inside the station stones were thrown at the windows by a small group of protestors.

During the night and later that morning the news spread of the death of Mrs Jarrett. That afternoon a crowd of a hundred people were demonstrating outside the police station. A police officer was badly injured, having been hit by rocks and stones thrown by a group of youths in a street adjoining the Farm. At public meetings held at the local West Indian Centre and at the Youth Association the mood was one of anger against the police.

The rioting starts and escalates

By the early evening large numbers of police equipped with riot gear were arriving at Broadwater Farm, stationing themselves at the four entrances of the estate, apparently to prevent people from leaving. Those outside the Farm were ordered to go inside. Stafford Scott of the Youth Association describes the police as being very hostile at this point: 'There was cries of "wait till we get in there and get you, you coons, you don't come out until we tell you, you bastards, get back in there". So the whole group got pushed back into the estate' (Gifford, First Report, p. 100).

Missiles were thrown at several of the police vans by groups of youths. Those trapped inside the estate had heard rumours that police were about to set dogs on them; at around 7 p.m. police wielding riot shields and truncheons advanced on the assembled youths. A rock was thrown, followed by another, and then further missiles. An anonymous eyewitness described it to David Rose: 'It just went off. I can't describe what happened, the suddenness; the frustration and the bitterness were just all coming out. The riot had begun' (Rose, p. 66 – see bibliography).

The rioters erected barricades of burning cars at each entrance to the Farm; further officers arriving at the scene (including two large coaches containing riot-equipped policemen) now faced a barrage of bricks, rocks and petrol bombs. Paving stones were smashed up and thrown at police. Cars were being siphoned of petrol, which was poured into milk bottles to make makeshift bombs. The shop grocery store on the estate was looted and tins of food were lobbed at police. Their attackers had the advantage of being able to use the walkways around the estate to throw missiles, being passed fresh supplies of the hurriedly made petrol bombs from their friends on the ground. Gunshots were fired at police from the walkways; some thirty rounds of ammunition were fired at police, one bullet hitting an officer in the stomach. A BBC cameraman was also injured by gunfire at around 9.30 p.m.

As rioters regrouped, the violence moved from one area of the estate to another. It soon became obvious that the rioters were gaining the upper hand, as ambulances pulled up outside the entrances of the estate to ferry the injured police officers to hospital. Rose's informant describes the mood thus:

As time went on, it became clear police were taking a ferocious beating. Euphoria is too strong a word, but there was a feeling of wellbeing. The Met was getting fucked over ... People's chests were puffed up. They'd been taking it all these years, and now they were giving some back [Rose, p. 67]

The first national news of the riot was broadcast by the BBC, whose news bulletin at 9 p.m. announced that 'gangs of mainly black youths' were throwing bricks and petrol bombs at police. As radio and television reported news of the riot, people who did not live on Broadwater Farm, including some white youths whom some witnesses described as looking like skinheads, were able to join in the riot as police had failed to seal off the part of the estate that bordered an area of recreation ground directly south of Lordship Lane.

Police used their shields to fend off the missiles; they were shaken by the barrage of bombs, rocks and cans thrown at them. When gunshots were heard the already terrified officers on the ground must have feared that they were about to be fired on. A police firearms unit was summoned to Tottenham at around 8 p.m., armed with plastic bullets and CS gas; these were not deployed. Police marksmen were stationed upstairs in a house in Mount Pleasant Road; they fired no shots.

The killing of PC Blakelock
At around 10 p.m. a group of riot-trained officers, including PC Keith Blakelock – a married man with three sons aged eight, eleven and thirteen, who lived in Muswell Hill, a predominantly white and middle-class district about a mile from Tottenham – accompanied firemen who had earlier been chased off by rioters, to the Tangmere block, where a fire had been started in the looted newsagent's shop. As police helped firemen get hoses and fire-fighting equipment up the stairs of Tangmere, a group of about fifty rioters attacked them.

The police officers and firemen turned to run from their would-be assailants, most of whom were wearing masks and were armed with weapons including knives and machetes. Keith Blakelock slipped and fell to the ground, where he was set upon by the crowd of rioters.

PC Michael Sheppard was quoted in the *Daily Telegraph* of 1 October 1985 as saying, '. . . I saw a group of 40 or 50 people in a circle around something on the ground. I now know that it was Keith Blakelock. They were stabbing and shouting "Kill, kill, kill" . . .'

One of the firemen saw what happened: 'The crowd descended on him. I saw things like machetes, carving knives, a pole with a blade set at right angles to it . . . It was a frenzied attack . . . the people around were striking up and down with their weapons. I saw 8 to 10 machetes being used' (Gifford, Second Report, p. 42).

PC Miles Barton, a friend of Blakelock, described what he saw: 'I saw Blakelock on the ground being stabbed, kicked and punched. His body was lifeless and it moved like a rag doll when it was kicked. The man with the machete attacked the body. There was a youth with a long piece of drainpipe hitting the body with it' (*Daily Telegraph*, 1 October 1985).

Another fireman saw that Blakelock had 'physically disappeared under the weight of people attacking him . . . the last I saw of PC Blakelock was he had his hand up to protect himself' (Gifford, Second Report, pp. 42–3).

Two of Blakelock's colleagues, Sergeant Pengelly and PC Pandya, hit out at the group of youths with their truncheons, but they were turned on by the mob and attacked with rocks. The officers could not prevent what happened next. Between thirty and fifty people were in the crowd of rioters kicking and punching Blakelock; his police helmet was ripped from his head. Then the knives and machetes came out, and the police constable was repeatedly and viciously stabbed. Blakelock had forty wounds to his face, neck, hands and back. He was deeply wounded by a machete blow to his neck; tabloid reports would lay great stress on this and imply that the attackers had intended to behead the policeman.

The attack on Blakelock took a matter of seconds. The mob dispersed, witnessed by police, leaving the limp figure of Keith Blakelock lying on the ground in a pool of blood; a knife handle was clearly visible sticking from the back of the policeman's neck. Other police officers managed to get Blakelock to an ambulance, but he was grievously wounded and was pronounced dead on arrival at the hospital.

After the killing

Following the killing of Blakelock, the rioting died down considerably. Three white youths were seen setting fire to the tobacconist's shop and supermarket on the estate. There was now a danger that this fire would spread, and cause an inferno in the whole of the Tangmere block. Firemen entered the area, having assured the youths present that they would not be accompanied by police. They succeeded in putting the fire out. A police helicopter equipped with a powerful searchlight and, one would assume, photographic apparatus, flew over the area at 11 p.m., causing those still outdoors to hide in order to avoid being identified. Dolly Kiffin informed the youths on the estate that a police officer wounded during the rioting had died.

Broadwater Farm finally became quiet, although there were some incidents and skirmishes with police in the surrounding streets. When rain started pouring down, peace finally fell on Tottenham. However, the spot where PC Blakelock had fallen had not been secured; also, people had been allowed to leave the area unchecked at various times throughout the night.

Blakelock's killers, whose clothing must have been bloodied during the murder, had slipped away into the night or had successfully disposed of the contaminated clothing before police came to their doors; police action leads one to assume that they believed that the murderers were residents of the estate.

At 4.30 that morning police in riot gear arrived at Broadwater Farm and headed for the Youth Association, where they surrounded those inside, assaulting at least three individuals with truncheons as they did so. The policemen, about two hundred of them, then dispersed over the entire estate, where they were to remain the whole of the next day.

What had gone wrong – blunders by police

Once disturbances had broken out, police had difficulty in containing them. A number of factors made a difficult situation worse:

- there was a problem with the police radio system used in the area, which was faulty and allowed communication on only one channel

- the police were armed with plastic bullets but needed the go-ahead from London's Police Commissioner, Sir Kenneth Newman, in order to use them; this was given, but due to the communication problems did not reach officers on the ground until after the murder of PC Blakelock

- although the officers sent to Broadwater Farm were equipped with riot gear, they had no training in riot control

- police were not equipped with bulletproof clothing or body armour that would have protected them from attack by knives.

Media reaction

From the morning following the riots, 7 October, the right-wing tabloid press began ugly, biased and racist coverage of the events on Broadwater Farm. The *Daily Express* called the events 'Britain's most horrific race riot'. The *Daily Mail* reported how white people were suffering daily on the estate. A local councillor, Bernie Grant (later to become a Labour MP), was trashed by the *Sun* for his insensitive but undoubtedly true statement made at a press conference on 7 October that police had had 'a bloody good hiding'. (Bernie Grant never withdrew this remark or expressed any regret for having said it.) On 9 October the paper described Grant as 'peeling a banana and juggling with an orange'.

If black people were to blame for what had happened, these newspapers did not even credit them for having a mind of their own. Another theme was that the riots had been stirred up by left-wing agitators, with the *Express* claiming without any substantiation that 'Street fighting experts trained in Moscow and Libya were behind Britain's worst violence'. The Metropolitan Police Commissioner, Sir Kenneth Newman, claimed at a press conference held on the day after the rioting that 'Trotskyists and anarchists' had orchestrated the disturbances in both Tottenham and Brixton following the death of Cherry Groce.

Tabloids also portrayed Broadwater Farm as being racially divided. The *Mail* on 9 October described white residents as feeling as though they were living in 'an alien and terrifying land'. In these newspapers, which are highly influential in forming popular opinion, there was no analysis of the real causes of the riot, no questioning at all of why police had searched Cynthia Jarrett's house or why the incident had taken place that had formed the genesis of the riot, the stopping of Floyd Jarrett's car for no reason other than that he was young and black.

The police investigation

On the Thursday following the riot, the first arrests were made in connection with the murder of PC Blakelock. A hundred and forty-one arrests of people suspected of involvement in the riots generally were made by the end of November 1985. Two hundred and seventy-one homes on the Farm were searched by police. By May 1986, there were 162 charges. Six people were charged with murder and riot. Of the total arrests, 71 per cent were black, 25 per cent were white. Police conducted hundreds of interviews; police photographers had taken many photographs that night.

Additionally, rioting had been filmed as it happened by professional crews from the BBC and ITN (Independent Television News). There was forensic evidence too: fingerprints on unexploded petrol bombs, weapons found around the Farm, including a number of knives and machetes believed to have been used in the murderous attack on Keith Blakelock. On examination, all the potential murder weapons had been wiped clean of all prints.

An anonymous detective is quoted as saying,

'. . . we should have treated the forensics as if we had been dealing with a terrorist bomb; cordoned off the area, and sifted every particle with a fine-tooth comb. It was dealt with only as the scene of public disorder, not as the scene of many crimes' [Rose, p. 88].

The trial

Six people were charged with the murder of PC Blakelock: Winston Silcott, Mark Braithwaite, Engin Raghip and three juveniles who had been thirteen, fourteen and fifteen at the time of the disturbances. The trial began in February

1987 and lasted for ten weeks. The police could not find eyewitnesses on the Farm who, because they did not trust police, feared incriminating themselves or were worried about the sort of reprisal that might be taken on anyone suspected of being a 'grass'. None of the hundreds of photographs that the police took were found to resemble those of the murder suspects. The police had hoped that the widespread arrests would give them intelligence on who had killed Blakelock. All they could gather was hearsay evidence by unreliable witnesses, most of whom were juveniles.

The view of the Crown, in the words of the prosecution lawyer, Roy Amlot, was that all those involved in the attack on Blakelock 'intended to kill, or do him really serious harm, and are therefore guilty of murder'. Anyone, therefore, known to have been involved in any way in the attack on PC Blakelock could expect to be found to have been responsible for his death.

Winston Silcott

A Broadwater Farm resident, Winston Silcott, aged 27, also known as 'Sticks', was active in the Youth Association. A part-time sound-system disc jockey, Silcott also ran the fruit-and-vegetable shop on the estate. He was well known to local police, who had formed the view that Silcott was dealing in drugs and controlling gangs of muggers. Silcott had a series of brushes with police. He was found guilty of wounding in 1979 following an incident in a club in Southgate. He was accused of the murder of Leonard Mackintosh, following a knife fight between Silcott and another man, kept in prison on remand for a year, and found not guilty by a jury. (There was no forensic evidence that Silcott was responsible for Mackintosh's death, and no witnesses.) On his release, back on the estate police continued to harass Silcott. In

1983 he was fined for possessing a knife that police found in the greengrocer's shop, and arrested and questioned over the stabbing of the policeman that occurred on the estate. Silcott was then in prison again, on remand following a charge of burglary, and then freed without the case coming to court. He was given a further conviction for obstructing the police following a stop-and-search on a vehicle in which Silcott was a passenger.

When Princess Diana visited Broadwater Farm in early 1985 Silcott approached her and made a comment to the effect that she should have brought some jobs for the unemployed with her. This was seen by police as provocative behaviour. In late 1984 Silcott was placed under night and day surveillance by police for several months; from this police could gather no proof of Silcott's involvement in criminal activity. At the time of the riots Silcott was out on bail, having been charged with the murder of a 22-year-old boxer, Anthony Smith, following an altercation in Hackney – the trial would be held in January 1986 and Silcott would be found guilty and sentenced to life imprisonment.

The arrest and trial of Winston Silcott

Following the death of Blakelock, Silcott must have known it would not be long before police came looking for him.

On 12 October 1985 he was arrested, denied a solicitor and interviewed in four sessions over 24 hours. Silcott refused to answer questions until the last interview. Questioned by Detective Chief Superintendent Melvin, Silcott insisted he was not the man in a photograph whom police suspected of being one of the people attacking Blakelock. A crucial exchange allegedly took place:

Melvin: 'I have been told that you played an active part in murdering him.'

Silcott: 'They're only kids. No one is going to believe them. You say they say that. How do I know? I don't go with kids.'

Melvin: 'What makes you think that the people I am referring to that have witnessed your part in the murder are young people?'

Silcott: 'You have only had kids in so far, haven't you?'

Melvin: 'If only one person had told me of your part in this crime I would not be so confident in my belief that you were the ringleader that night. When there is more than one person saying the same thing, the facts become clear.'

Silcott: 'You cunts, you cunts. Jesus, Jesus.'

Melvin: 'Did you murder PC Blakelock?'

Silcott: 'You ain't got enough evidence. Those kids will never go to court. You wait and see. Nobody else will talk to you. You can't keep me away from them.'

Silcott's alleged words would be interpreted by the Crown at the murder trial as being those of a guilty man who was implying he was capable of silencing witnesses by threats he had made.

During the trial for the killing of Keith Blakelock, Silcott was a prisoner, serving his life sentence for the murder of Anthony Smith. The jury in the Blakelock case were not told of Silcott's conviction, which under England's strict sub judice laws had not been reported in the media.

The case against Silcott was based on statements made by the defendant to Detective Superintendent Melvin and on accounts from, among others, two of the three juveniles accused of the murder. These juveniles had allegedly named Silcott, as had several other youths questioned.

Those who named Silcott included:

- Andrew Pyke, aged fifteen. Arrested at a school for children with learning difficulties that he attended, Pyke claimed to have witnessed the attack on Blakelock and named Silcott as being among his attackers. Pyke said he had seen Silcott waving a bloody machete. Pyke did not appear as a witness in the trial. Being illiterate, Pyke had signed a statement he could not possibly have read. But what Pyke had signed was not true. He had appeared at the committal proceedings against Silcott and stated that what he had signed was not true; he had not in fact seen Silcott at Broadwater Farm that night.

- Juvenile B, aged fifteen, a co-defendant at the murder trial. B attended the same school as Pyke. He named ten individuals as having taken part in the murder, including Winston Silcott. His description of what Silcott was wearing was at variance with Pyke's account, and instead of a machete Juvenile B said he had seen Silcott wielding a long knife.

- Howard Kerr, aged seventeen, was questioned by police and made a fifty-page 'confession' naming twenty people involved in the attack on PC Blakelock, Winston Silcott among them, although Kerr was unable to provide police with a description of Silcott. Later it was proved that Kerr had been visiting his girlfriend in Slough, fifty miles away from Tottenham, during the night of the riots.

- Jason Hill, aged thirteen. The only juvenile of the three accused of the murder to be named, Hill was from a white family all of whose members were questioned by police following the riot. When questioned by police, Hill admitted 'looting' – which in his case amounted to his taking some sweets from the shop at the Tangmere block. Further questioned by a PC Cochrane, Hill claimed he had taken part in the attack on Blakelock, stabbing the officer with a knife on the orders of Winston Silcott, who had then told the boy that he was 'cool'. Hill then said that those attacking Blakelock had said they would cut the police constable's head off and put it on a pole. The entire story was fiction. Hill had not taken part in the attack, and had made this false statement because police had told him that if he told them what they wanted to know he could go home. The judge, Justice Hodgson, had to state that Hill's evidence was 'incredible' and that police had acted improperly in their treatment of the boy, and he ruled Hill's evidence inadmissible. Incredibly, however, the jury did not hear this, as they had been moved out of the court when the judge made this ruling. The only direction the judge made to them about Hill was that they should acquit him.

Silcott's own interview with Melvin was presented by the prosecution as indicating that he was guilty. There was much emphasis on Silcott's reply 'You cunts' and his claim to Melvin that police had no evidence against him.

Judge Hodgson indicated to the jury that Winston Silcott could be convicted on the evidence of those few sentences allegedly exchanged with Melvin. (Silcott had also declined to sign the transcript of his interview with Melvin, as he did not consider it to be a true record.) The interviews with Winston Silcott did not take place with a solicitor present and the interview with Melvin was not tape-recorded.

Defending Silcott, Barbara Mills QC (later to become the Director of Public Prosecutions) claimed the police's interpretation of Silcott's answers to Melvin's questions were 'nonsense', particularly their view that 'You cunts, Jesus . . . Jesus' was an admission of guilt. Mills stated that Silcott's words to the police were those of 'a desperate man wrongly accused', which would explain Silcott's words, 'You ain't got no evidence'. Her speech to the jury ended with the reinforcement of the fact that there was no direct evidence: no blood had been found on clothing taken from Silcott's flat, nor did any of the thousand police photographs taken during the night of the riot show that Silcott was even present. Mills advised the jury with these words: 'Unless you can say what Winston Silcott did, you cannot convict'.

The jury found Silcott guilty of the murder of PC Blakelock. The judge handed out a life sentence, with the recommendation that Silcott serve a minimum of thirty years in prison.

The arrest and trial of Engin Raghip

Engin Raghip was nineteen when he was arrested and questioned by police. He was interrogated ten times over a five-day period with no solicitor present.

Having told police that he had left Broadwater Farm before the riots began, on being interrogated for the fourth time Raghip changed his account of what had happened. In this interview he said he had seen the attack on PC Blakelock, in which he said between ten and thirty people were involved, and that he had wanted to attack the police officer but was 'pushed back'. By the eighth session Raghip was claiming that during the attack on Blakelock he was holding a weapon, a broom handle, and that he had wanted to attack the policeman and intended to kick him or hit him if he could get close.

Raghip was later to claim that everything he had said had been forcefully put to him by police, and that he had agreed that what police had said was true after very heavy pressure from his interrogators.

During the trial Raghip agreed that he had signed the transcript of the interrogation as being a true record, but denied that it was accurate; he said he had signed because 'I thought it was normal to sign'. Regarding the broom handle, he said, 'They put it to me and I agreed . . . at first I denied it but they kept on saying it . . . well there was no way out . . . it never happened.'

Raghip was convicted of murder because the police believed he was at the scene of crime with intention of causing harm to Blakelock. He was found guilty of 'aiding and abetting' and sentenced to life imprisonment.

Dr Gisli Gudjonsson, a forensic psychologist who produced a report for the defence team to use in an appeal against the guilty verdict, found that Raghip had a mental age of ten or eleven, with an IQ of 74, and was on the border of being mentally handicapped. He described Raghip as abnormally suggestible and compliant with authority.

Raghip's solicitor, Gareth Pierce, alleged that police 'coerced from him what was later construed as an admission to murder' and that his conviction was 'profoundly unjust' (*Inside Story* – 'Beyond Reasonable Doubt' – BBC Television, 16 May 1990) and that Raghip was 'effectively a juvenile' – if this had been revealed during trial he would have been acquitted.

Raghip was named by a friend, John Bromfield, aged eighteen, who told police that Raghip had been one of those involved in the murder of PC Blakelock. Bromfield included Raghip's name in a whole list of people who had nothing to do with the murder.

Engin's wife, Sharon Raghip, believes that the interrogation process wore down her husband's resistance. She is also convinced that Engin Raghip was not even at Broadwater Farm at the time of Blakelock's murder.

The arrest and trial of Mark Braithwaite

Aged eighteen at the time of the trial, Mark Braithwaite had been arrested in February 1986. He was refused a solicitor until the ninth interview had taken place with police. Again, the only evidence against him was an alleged confession. As in Raghip's interviews with police, the 'confessions' became more and more serious. At the fifth interview, the police claimed, he said he had seen the attack on Blakelock. At the sixth interrogation, also according to the police, he said he had hit Blakelock twice with a metal bar while others were kicking and stabbing him. During the seventh interview he said he had not in fact hit Blakelock with an iron bar, but had attacked another officer who did not resemble Blakelock. As in the case of Raghip, Braithwaite was named by only one person, Bernard Kinghorn. Arrested on suspicion of rioting, nineteen-year-old Kinghorn had included Braithwaite in a long list of names.

Kinghorn has since admitted that he had not seen Mark Braithwaite at the scene of the murder. In fact, he had not witnessed PC Blakelock's murder at all. During the trial Braithwaite said he had admitted to killing Blakelock while under pressure from police, and denied that statements he had signed contained the truth. Braithwaite had not been given anything to eat, suffered from claustrophobia and at the time was desperate to get out of the cell. At his trial he denied he had assaulted any police officer with an iron bar, but thought he might be released and allowed to go home if he confessed. Apparently, Braithwaite kept asking to speak to the police in order that he might be released from his cell temporarily to relieve the claustrophobia. Claustrophobia may well have affected his reasoning during interrogation.

He was found guilty and sentenced to life imprisonment for his part in the murder.

All three convicted

Silcott, Raghip and Braithwaite were convicted only on the basis of what they were alleged to have said to the police. On 19 March 1987 all were given life sentences, with the recommendation that Silcott should serve at least thirty years. Silcott was singled out for particular condemnation by the judge, who told him, 'You are both a very evil and a very dangerous man.'

The three juvenile murder defendants

Thirteen-year-old Jason Hill and Juveniles B and C, aged fifteen and thirteen at the time of the murder, were found by the judge, Justice Hodgson, to have given 'unreliable' statements to the police; on his direction they were all acquitted.

Aftermath of the convictions

The Afro-Caribbean community and the families of the three convicted men have always protested their innocence. On their conviction, the tabloid press portrayed them as savage animals. To these newspapers, Winston Silcott was the personification of all that they feared: a young black man, seemingly with no respect for law and order, who not only was a ringleader of a riot but had been one of the men who, the press and prosecution hinted, had attempted to decapitate a policeman.

PC Keith Blakelock was posthumously awarded the Queen's Medal for Bravery.

In 1988 an application for appeal by the three convicted men was turned down by three judges headed by the Lord Chief Justice, Lord Lane. In May 1990 the BBC broadcast a television programme in the documentary series *Inside Story* entitled 'Beyond Reasonable Doubt'. This exposed the way police had treated the three men during interviews, laying stress on the lack of evidence against them. Raghip's low IQ and gullible nature and Braithwaite's claustrophobia were explored in detail, with appraisals provided by the psychologist Dr Gudjonsson and an expert in claustrophobia, Paul Salkovskis, a psychiatrist.

In 1989 the independent inquiry into the disturbances at Broadwater Farm, chaired by Lord Gifford, published its Second Report, which was heavily critical of the police investigation and the conviction of the three. One chapter of their report was entitled 'The Three Murder Convictions – A Miscarriage of Justice' and went into the details of the questionable elements in each conviction. The inquiry was particularly critical of the absence of solicitors during questioning and the fact that none of the interviews had been tape-recorded.

The acquittal of Silcott, Braithwaite and Raghip

On 26 November 1991 the Court of Appeal cleared Winston Silcott of his conviction for the murder of PC Blakelock. The judges sitting, led by Lord Justice Farquharson, had been shown evidence that two police officers, Detective Chief Superintendent Graham Melvin and Detective Inspector Maxwell Dingle, had fabricated evidence. A new method of forensic examination revealed that the notes made by police during the crucial interview with Silcott had been altered by the detectives. Forensic scientists gave their opinion that some pages had been removed and then replaced. As these notes formed the only evidence against Silcott, the murder conviction was quashed. Simultaneously, appeals by Braithwaite and Raghip were advanced before the court. On the following day the pair were freed from prison; technically they were released into the custody of their solicitors while waiting for the results of their appeal. A week later, their convictions were quashed.

Subsequent events

In 1994, as a consequence of the alleged fabrication of the 'evidence' against Silcott, the police officers involved in the questioning of Silcott – Graham Melvin and Maxwell Dingle – were themselves in the dock of the Old Bailey on a charge of attempting to pervert the course of justice. They were acquitted.

In September 1999 Winston Silcott, still in prison for the Smith murder, was awarded £50,000 compensation for his wrongful conviction for the Blakelock murder. In October 1999 it was reported in the press that the three sons of Keith Blakelock were considering a civil action against Silcott for the killing of their father.

In October 1999 Detective Superintendent David Cox of the Metropolitan Police was put in charge of a reinvestigation of the murder of Blakelock, in which 35 police officers would be involved. Using advanced DNA-testing technology, clothing and weapons seized by police would be re-examined and the 10,000 statements given at the time would be analysed again. In addition a computerised 'virtual-reality' reconstruction of the murder scene would be deployed in an attempt to find the killer. Cox also appealed for any witnesses to the crime to come forward.

9 Rachel Nickell

The tragic murder of Rachel Nickell on Wimbledon Common on 15 July 1992 shocked the nation. A beautiful young woman had been sadistically murdered and sexually assaulted in broad daylight in a public park. Obscenely, the only known witness to the frenzied and bloody attack was Rachel's three-year-old son Alex, who was not physically hurt by the attacker, and was found by passers-by clinging on to his dead mother.

The events that followed her death were extraordinary, with a man whom police regarded as a prime suspect being acquitted after the judge ruled out police evidence gathered during an undercover operation, and the case against the man, Colin Stagg, was withdrawn.

Who was Rachell Nickell?

Rachel Nickell was born in 1968. She grew up in the village of Great Totham, near Colchester. She came from a well-off and comfortable background. Her father Andrew was a former army officer who ran a successful footwear-import business. The family lived in comfort in a large detached home.

Rachel attended Colchester High School for Girls, where she was a high scholastic achiever, with an exceptional talent for dancing and swimming. She was also active in serving the local community, involving herself in organising Christmas parties for senior citizens and devoting her spare time to disabled children. A very attractive blonde, Rachel received offers of modelling work when she was still at school, which she did not take up at the time.

On leaving school she moved to London, where she started studying for a degree in history and English. To support herself she took up part-time work as a model; her ambition was to be a presenter on children's television. In September 1988, while working during her vacation from college as a lifeguard at a swimming pool in Richmond, south London, she met and fell in love with André Handscombe, a professional tennis coach and semiprofessional tennis player. When not earning a living from tennis, Handscombe worked as a motorcycle courier in London.

Rachel became pregnant with their child and moved into André's flat in Balham, where the couple lived happily. Their son, Alexander, also known as Alex, was born in August 1989. Rachel had plans to resume her education and study for a degree with the Open University that would qualify her to teach handicapped children.

During the week, while André was out working in the day, Rachel would look after their son. Rachel loved visiting the parks and wide-open spaces of south London, where she could take Alex and their pet dog Mollie. Tooting Common and Clapham Common were nearer home, but Rachel had had unpleasant experiences of being bothered by lone men while she was out walking in those spots, so preferred to get in her car and drive out to Wimbledon Common, which was further away, but appeared to be a safer place for a young woman to walk with her child. Wimbledon is a prosperous middle-class area of south London; before the murder of Rachel Nickell it was a place best known for the annual Wimbledon tennis championships and for being the habitat of the fictional creatures much loved by British children in the 1970s, the Wombles.

The murder

On the morning of Wednesday, 15 July 1992, Rachel Nickell, accompanied by little Alex and their dog, drove from her home to Wimbledon Common. Having parked her Volvo in the Windmill car park, Rachel, Alex and Mollie started walking across the common. The last person, bar the killer, to see them alive was Roger McKern, an actor who was cycling across the common. Anxious that he was late for a rehearsal at the nearby Wimbledon Theatre, McKern had checked his watch. The time was 10.20 a.m. They walked across the wide expanse of grass into a copse surrounded by trees. Once they were in this part of the park, a place shielded from view by the trees, the killer struck. Rachel was suddenly accosted by a man carrying a sharp knife; he slashed out and stabbed her in the chest twice. The little boy was violently pushed away from his mother; his face was scratched by the attacker as he separated the boy from the injured Rachel. Using the same knife, the attacker slit open Rachel's throat, cutting her vocal cords so she could not scream. The killer repeatedly stabbed Rachel, and a total of 49 stab wounds were found on her body, many of them as deep as the knife would go; impressions of the hilt of the knife were visible at many places where the body had been stabbed. After Rachel had died, the murderer interfered with her clothing, pulling her jeans down and anally raping her.

This vicious assault must have been witnessed by Alex, who was not yet three years old. As his mother lay in a pool of blood, the toddler clung pathetically to her lifeless body.

Discovery of the body

Michael Murray, a retired architect, was walking his dog on the common when he saw what at first looked like a woman sunbathing under a silver birch tree. As he got closer he could see that the lower part of the woman's body was exposed – her jeans and underwear having been pulled down – and that the upper part of her body was violently injured. At the woman's side was a small boy holding on to the body and repeatedly telling her, 'Get up, Mummy.' A small black dog was wandering around in the vicinity of the woman and the child. Seeing that the woman had suffered appalling stab wounds and was not moving, Murray assumed that she was dead.

Prising Alex's hands from gripping the prone figure of Rachel Nickell, Murray gently led the blood-soaked and distressed child away from the dead body. Leaving the child, who was now rendered speechless by what he had witnessed, with some female passers-by, a shocked Murray then informed the local park rangers of what he had seen. A ranger on horseback, Stephen Francis, went up to the body – close enough to see that it was a woman and that her throat had been cut. He then called police. Four police officers arrived in a police car. Other police then arrived on the scene.

Examination of the crime scene

Police arrived and secured the crime area. The officer in charge, Detective Chief Inspector Mike Wickerson, spoke to the media who had gathered on Wimbledon Common. He spoke of the 'horrific' crime that had taken place that day. Rachel's body and the surrounding area were carefully photographed and video recordings made by police photographers. Then the body was examined by police officers and by a forensic pathologist, Dr Richard Shepherd of Guy's Hospital, London.

Examining the body under the tree, Shepherd saw that the ferocious stabbing had caused an enormous amount of blood to be released. Rachel's arms were lifted up over her face and her jeans and underwear were pulled down to her ankles. Dr Shepherd also measured Rachel's body temperature as 76 degrees Fahrenheit. He observed that rigor mortis had not yet set in. Continuing his examination of the body, Shepherd noted that the anus was dilated, as if an object had been forced into it, but that it was not bleeding and it did not appear to have been injured.

The postmortem

After the examination of the crime scene had been completed, Rachel's body was taken to St George's Hospital in nearby Tooting. The stab wounds were counted and the depth, width and the angle of each one were measured. Swabs were taken from various parts of the body, including the anus and vagina. Rachel and her clothing were examined for fibres, bloodstains or anything else that the killer may have left behind in the way of evidence. Nothing of that nature was found. Nothing was found in the anus or vagina that could give police a lead as to who the murderer was. The killing had been very violent, but the murderer had been either very careful or very lucky. Not a trace of foreign DNA was found on the body or clothing of Rachel Nickell; nor did the killer leave any fingerprints.

Dr Shepherd assessed the cause of death as being from multiple stab wounds. The 49 wounds were deep: the knife the killer had used was very sharp and had a depth of nine inches. At the inquest into Rachel's death in February 1993 Dr Shepherd told the Westminster Coroner's Court that the attack appeared 'frenzied'. During the knife attack, which may have lasted only a couple of minutes, Rachel's death occurred from any one of a number of severe wounds to the heart, lungs and liver.

Subsequent events

The traumatised Alex was literally struck dumb by what he had witnessed, and was comforted by his father. The child was seen by therapists, who attempted to get him to talk. A few days after the murder, on the advice of child psychiatrists, André Hanscombe and Alex revisited the murder scene together. It was hoped that their going there together would help the healing process and perhaps enable the boy to express his feelings about what he had witnessed.

Rachel's parents were abroad on a touring holiday in Canada when the murder took place. British police informed their Canadian counterparts, who attempted to trace them and inform them of the terrible events. It took the Mounties four days to find them and the news devastated them.

Police sealed off Wimbledon Common and searched for clues – hoping they might find the murder weapon. Three knives were found; according to police none of them had been used in the murder. On 16 July a local man, whose name has never been publicly released, was detained and questioned by police in connection with the murder, but later released. He was the first of 25 men to be arrested in the six weeks after the murder and then released without charge.

On 22 July, police arranged a re-enactment of Rachel's last movements; a friend of hers named Jane, a little boy and a dog walked along the path to the copse, followed by the press, who took photographs. Police hoped that this reconstruction would jog the memories of local residents.

On 3 August, Rachel Nickell's funeral took place, near to where her parents lived, at St Andrew's Church in Ampthill, Bedfordshire.

Police investigations

Police cast a wide net when interviewing suspects. A known fugitive, Roderick Newell, was tracked by the

Royal Navy on a yacht in the Atlantic. He was arrested on suspicion of the murder of his parents Nicholas and Elizabeth Newell and also questioned about Rachel Nickell. (Roderick Newell and his brother Mark were later tried and found guilty – Roderick of the murder of his parents and Mark of disposing of their bodies.)

The other initial suspects were completely cleared of any involvement, but only after their names and photographs had been splashed on the front pages of the tabloid press. Ben Silcock, a schizophrenic living in Roehampton, who in December 1992 was attacked by a lion at London Zoo when he climbed behind bars to feed it a chicken, had earlier that year been questioned by police, as he was known to visit Wimbledon Common frequently. A photography student named Simon Murrell from Toxteth near Liverpool, hundreds of miles away from Wimbledon, was also questioned by police.

The team at Wimbledon police station were particularly horrified by the Nickell murder and dedicated themselves to finding the killer, with many of them working overtime without extra pay.

Alex

André Handscombe's book, *The Last Thursday in July*, gives a very moving and detailed account of the child's reaction to his mother's murder. The impression the book gives is of a very charming and intelligent child, perplexed by the horror of what happened.

A week and a half after the murder of his mother, Alex was speaking again. Meeting with detectives and therapists, he was encouraged to play with dolls in the hope that the way he positioned them and what type of doll he chose to pick up would give clues to the appearance of the killer. Alex stated that the killer was not a woman, was not black, and was a young man. From these play sessions therapists were able to deduce that Alex thought the killer had been wearing dark-coloured shoes, blue trousers and a white shirt worn with a black belt over it. Alex's phrase for the killer was 'the bad man'. Details emerged slowly from many sessions with police and child therapists – for instance, the man was thin and had short hair. A year after the murder, André Handscombe videotaped a discussion he had with his son in which the child described how the 'bad man' came down from the hillside, pushed him into the bushes and attacked his mother. During this interview Alex also provided the answer to a question that had been puzzling police: why had a piece of paper detailing Rachel's building society PIN been placed on top of her head? What could be the reason for the murderer to have done such a thing? The answer was a simple one: Alex was able to remember that he had put it on her head to comfort her.

Psychological profiling

Although the police had been inundated with information from the public and had questioned several of the initial suspects who were then released, by the end of July 1992 they had drawn a blank as regards forensic evidence.

Their next move was an unusual one for a crime in Britain: they called in a psychologist, Paul Britton, who specialised in analysing the details and circumstances of a murder in order to build up a psychological profile of the killer. In his book on the subject, *The Jigsaw Man*, Britton detailed the rationale behind his assumptions about who killed Rachel Nickell. Britton believed that the murderer did not know Rachel – if he had known her then he would have also attacked and killed Alex. He might also have killed her at home or somewhere he could have lured her that was less public.

Robert Ressler, an American 'offender profiler' who had worked for the FBI, also examined the case. He was flown to the UK by the *Sun* newspaper, in which his analysis was published. Ressler wrote that in his opinion the killer was a misfit who may have had the outward signs of mental illness. The suspect was likely to have above-average intelligence and would more than likely strike again.

The two men's conclusions about the person who had killed Rachel were similar. He was:

- from the local area

- a white man in his twenties

- a loner who lived in a fantasy world

- sexually inadequate.

In addition, Britton drew up a list of likely components of the killer's sexual fantasies. An exciting scenario for the suspect would involve a grown woman being used as a sexual object in a sadistic way, with the likelihood of the man imagining the use of knives, the woman becoming afraid, invasion of body orifices and, ultimately, the killing of the woman.

Witnesses who saw a man acting suspiciously
The police incident room received over 2,500 calls in the month following the murder. Out of these calls there emerged some key witnesses who had been on the common on the morning of the murder. They came forward and gave varying accounts of a suspicious-looking man who had been seen in the vicinity.

Marjorie Piper and Shirley Adam
Both these women were visiting graves in the cemetery adjacent to the common. Both women heard, at around the same time, the sound of someone rushing through the

bushes on the other side of the fence around the cemetery. A vicar who was officiating at funerals there that morning is also reported to have seen a man jumping over the wall into the cemetery, after which he was seen to act suspiciously.

Jane Harriman

Three times that morning, Jane Harriman saw a man wearing a white, long-sleeved shirt and dark-coloured trousers and holding a dark-coloured bag. Between 10.00 and 10.10 a.m. she saw this man walking towards Rachel Nickell.

Amanda Phelan

At 10.40 that morning, Amanda Phelan was out walking on Wimbledon Common. She saw a man apparently washing his hands in a stream over which he was seen crouching. The man was wearing light-blue trousers and a light-coloured sweater.

Crimewatch UK

Police noted the descriptions of the man seen in the vicinity of the common and described by the above witnesses. Jane Harriman had seen the man's face, and from her account police were able to construct a videofit picture of him.

On 17 September BBC television transmitted an edition of *Crimewatch UK* that made further appeals to the public for information. The murder of Rachel Nickell was reconstructed again, this time by actors. The videofit picture was shown, and some details of the conclusions of Paul Britton's psychological profiling of the killer were broadcast. At the end of the programme the telephone number of the police investigation room was given out.

That night, over three hundred calls were made in which viewers offered information on suspects to police. Four calls identified the likeness as being that of a man called Colin Stagg, who lived on the Alton Estate in Roehampton, and who spent a lot of time on Wimbledon Common.

The arrest of Colin Stagg

On the morning after the *Crimewatch UK* broadcast, police arrived at Colin Stagg's maisonette. The first thing they saw was a sign outside the front door that read 'CHRISTIANS KEEP AWAY. A PAGAN DWELLS HERE'.

Having identified Stagg, they proceeded to arrest him on suspicion of the murder of Rachel Nickell. Stagg's reaction was one of shock and amazement, and he immediately denied he had killed her. Detective Inspector Keith Pedder showed Stagg a copy of the *Daily Mirror* in his living room that had published a picture of the videofit and pointed out the resemblance. Stagg's response was again to deny that he had killed her, but said that he had remembered Rachel smiling at him on the common a few years ago. (In his book *Who Really Killed Rachel?*, Stagg admits that in saying this he was mistaken: the woman who had smiled at him had not in fact been Rachel Nickell, as she had not started driving out to Wimbledon Common until early in 1992.)

A search of the rest of the premises revealed a room painted completely black, a pagan altar and other occult artefacts. Police did find two pornographic magazines, but, contrary to the expectations that any psychological profile may have given them, they were of the 'soft' variety available on the top shelf of most newsagents in Britain, a fact glossed over by many newspapers. No murder weapon was found, nor did police manage to find any forensic evidence whatsoever that related to the murder of Rachel Nickell.

About Colin Stagg

One of five children of a working-class family, Colin Stagg grew up on the Alton Estate and attended school locally, where he was the victim of bullying. When Colin's mother decided to leave her husband and family in the mid-1970s it affected the child badly. Colin shared a home with his father Vic until his death in 1986. After that Colin lived by himself. He had no job and existed on social security and welfare payments, earning money from delivering newspapers, a badly paid job usually done by school-children. He was also, at the age of 29, still a virgin.

Witnesses who observed Stagg on the day of the murder

Before and during the police questioning of Stagg, other witnesses appeared, several of whom knew Colin Stagg. The information they supplied police was as follows:

Susan Gale

Susan Gale, a neighbour of Colin Stagg, said she had passed Stagg, who was on his way on to the common, as she was leaving it, having walked her dog, at between 9.25 and 9.30 a.m. She recalls Stagg waving at her in recognition. She describes him as wearing a white T-shirt and blue jeans and having a black bag tied around his waist.

Police were suspicious because Stagg claimed to have been at home at the time Gale recalls seeing him.

Pat Heanan

Pat Heanan, a butcher, was working in his shop when he heard the loud engine of a helicopter flying overhead. At 11.30, according to Heanan, an excited Colin Stagg came through the door and told him that he had been woken up by the noise. Stagg told him that a body had been found on Wimbledon Common. According to police records the helicopter was first flying over the area at 11.14 a.m.

Police were suspicious because they wondered how he could possibly have known about the murder if he had been asleep until 11.14.

Yadnesh Patel

Patel was in his father's newsagent shop when Colin Stagg came in at 11.45 to buy a bar of chocolate. Stagg told him specifically that the body of a young girl had been found on the common.

Police were suspicious because no one had been told that the body was that of a girl. Initial police communications mistakenly referred to the body found as that of an old woman.

Lillian Avid

Another of Stagg's neighbours, elderly Lillian Avid, encountered Stagg on the day of the murder. He came up to her and started talking about the young woman whose body had been found on the common. He told Avid that the woman who was murdered had been out with her child and that he had missed witnessing the murder by ten minutes. Avid, a pensioner, recalls that Stagg was wearing shorts and a white top and looked as though he had just had a shower and washed his hair.

Avid knew only that someone had been injured on the common; wondering how Colin knew any more than she did, she asked him if he had killed the woman, to which he replied that he had not. Avid thought it suspicious that Stagg was wearing very clean clothing and that he appeared freshly scrubbed. She telephoned the police, gave them her details and asked to speak to a detective. According to Avid, the police failed to make contact.

PC Andrew Couch

On the day of the murder PC Couch was one of the officers called in to seal off the common following the discovery of Rachel's body. At 12.30 p.m. that day the officer saw Stagg walking his dog near Putney Cemetery and heading towards Wimbledon Common. PC Couch went up to Stagg and questioned him about the discovery of the body on the common that morning. Stagg volunteered that he had gone for a walk with Brandy on Wimbledon Common between 8.15 and 8.50 that morning. The officer noted down Stagg's full name and address.

Police interview Colin Stagg

While police continued searching his house, Stagg was taken to Wimbledon police station. During the first interview, led by Detective Inspector Pedder, which was recorded, as is customary, on a cassette recorder, Stagg gave his account of his movements that day.

At 6 a.m. he woke up, leaving the house at 6.30 to do his paper round. Having returned home, he later, at around 8 a.m., left with Brandy for a walk on Wimbledon Common. While out, Stagg was struck by a pain in his neck and a migraine, and curtailed the walk, returning home by 9.15. Once home, he turned on the television and began watching a game show, the name of which he could not recall, and during which he fell asleep. (Later, under further questioning, Stagg revealed that the programme was called *Lucky Ladders*. This would appear unlikely, as no programme called *Lucky Ladders* was transmitted that day.) His snooze was interrupted by the sound of a police helicopter; on waking, he went out, and was stopped by a policeman who told him of the murder on Wimbledon Common.

Asked about the occult symbols in his house and the warning to Christians painted outside, Stagg told police he was a devotee of the Wiccan religion. Moreover, claimed Stagg, his beliefs made him incapable of doing harm to any living thing. In Stagg's book on his experiences as the main suspect in the Nickell murder, he explains that this religious belief was a temporary one. Questioned about knives found at his home, Stagg told DI Pedder that he did occasionally take a knife out with him on his walks, but denied he would ever use it to kill anything, even an animal. He admitted being a solitary person who did not have friends, but denied that he was the man seen by witnesses who were out on the common that morning. He denied having had a bath or shower that day, claiming that he bathed only twice a week, on Thursdays and Sundays.

Facing repeated questioning, Colin Stagg firmly denied that he had seen Rachel on the common that day and repeatedly stated that he was not the murderer. After one particularly heated session during which Stagg denied seeing Rachel on the common on the day of her murder six times in succession, his interrogator showed Stagg a gruesome photograph of Rachel's mutilated body lying on the spot where it was found.

However, Stagg did admit that within the ten-day period after the murder of Rachel Nickell he had been sunbathing nude on Wimbledon Common and, seeing a woman walking her dog coming towards him, had covered up his genitals so as not to offend her. The police told Stagg that this woman had complained that she had seen a man wearing sunglasses sunbathing nude on that day who had opened his legs to display an erect penis. On the evidence of what the woman had witnessed, Stagg was charged with indecent exposure. Appearing before magistrates in Wimbledon on Monday, 21 September, Stagg pleaded guilty to the charge and was fined £220.

Released on bail pending further enquiries into the Nickell murder, Stagg was free to go home after his court appearance. The press were taking a great interest in the indecent-exposure case and even greater interest in his status as a suspect in the Nickell slaying. Outside the magistrates' court Stagg told the media that he was an innocent man who wanted to see Rachel's murderer brought to justice as much as anyone else. Following this statement, Stagg ran off, giving the assembled press photographers a two-finger salute.

But Detective Inspector Pedder was not dropping his pursuit of Colin Stagg. Now there was a face to their suspect, police discussed with child psychiatrists how best to find out if Alex would react in any way to a photograph of Stagg. When this was attempted, the result was very surprising. Presented with Stagg's picture among a random selection of photographs of both suspects and people known to little Alex, and asked if he could see the 'bad man' who killed Rachel, the child pointed out not Colin Stagg but the father of a friend of his who was also very close to both André Handscombe and to Rachel. The police thoroughly investigated this man, Andy Abrahams, and concluded that he could not have committed the murder – his whereabouts that morning, confirmed by his wife, firmly rule him out as a suspect. Yet another dead end had been reached in the Rachel Nickell case.

It would be impossible for the Crown Prosecution Service to allow Colin Stagg to be charged with murder on the purely circumstantial evidence that police had gathered so far. A different approach was needed, and by the end of 1992 police began an expensive and time-consuming undercover operation to obtain a murder confession from Colin Stagg.

Julie Pines

In 1992 a woman named Julie Pines, who lived in south London, had placed an advertisement in a lonely-hearts column in *Loot* magazine. Stagg responded. They never met, but exchanged letters – Stagg sending her a total of three. This was cut short when Stagg sent Julie a long and explicit letter in which he described a sexual fantasy involving himself masturbating in the nude on Wimbledon Common and his being interrupted by a woman who then joined him and had consensual sex with him. Julie Pines had remembered the name of Colin Stagg and had kept the letter; when she saw media reports about Stagg, his indecent-exposure charge and the fact that he had been a suspect in the Nickell murder, she immediately contacted the police at Wimbledon.

Pedder's proposal

Police read the letter and contacted the psychological profiler Paul Britton, the man who had given them a checklist of the characteristics of Rachel's killer. Detective Inspector Pedder proposed that a trap be laid for Stagg. A policewoman would act undercover and write to Stagg in the guise of a friend of Julie Pines who wished to correspond with him. Over a series of letters and, eventually, meetings, the policewoman would attempt to get Colin Stagg to reveal violent sexual fantasies which might incriminate him in the murder of Rachel Nickell.

This plan was presented to Paul Britton, who agreed to guide police in what would be a very delicate and potentially risky operation. The plan was approved both by senior officers at Scotland Yard as being a worthwhile operation and by the Crown Prosecution Service as being within the process of law.

Operation Edzell

Operation Edzell, the 'honeytrap' plan to get Stagg to incriminate himself, was launched in late 1992. A very experienced officer was selected to 'play the part' of Stagg's new penpal. Lizzie James (not her real name) had many years of experience as an undercover police officer. She was thoroughly briefed in all aspects of the role she would play and the information she would give Stagg about herself. The plan was for Lizzie to eventually confess to Stagg that since she had been a teenager she had been involved in an occult group that had involved her in ritual abuse, and that as a member of that group she had been involved in the sexual murder of a young woman. His response would be very significant. For several months Lizzie and Paul Britton worked together, discussing every aspect of Lizzie's 'character' and even practising the sort of telephone calls that the policewoman and Stagg might have as their 'relationship' developed. During this time, police hoped, Stagg would begin to feel as if the police had forgotten about him, and would therefore be less likely to be suspicious of the true identity of 'Lizzie James'.

On 19 January 1993, Colin Stagg was sent the first letter from Lizzie James. The letter, like all subsequent ones that she sent, had been concocted by a committee that included Lizzie, Britton and several police officers.

Introducing herself, Lizzie wrote that she was a friend of Julie, who had read one of his letters to her. Lizzie claimed the letter had interested her and made her want to get to know Colin Stagg. She described herself as aged forty, blonde and solitary. Stagg replied quickly, saying he had written back because he felt that Lizzie and he had things in common. He told her of his practice of nude sunbathing in the park and confessed that he was lonely. The sexual content of Stagg's letters increased, not discouraged by Lizzie.

In early February, Stagg sent Lizzie a fantasy he had written about her stripping off in front of him in his back garden while he masturbated, watched by his neighbours. At the end of February, Stagg sent Lizzie a key letter. In it he fantasised about having sex with her from behind in a clearing in a wood near a stream. As the letters progressed, Lizzie suggested to Stagg that she wanted to be 'completely in your power, defenceless and humiliated'. This introduced a new, submissive side of Lizzie. Stagg responded that in the context of a violent sexual episode he would make her scream in agony, abuse her and make her lose her self-esteem. Her letters also began to hint at a history of abusing other people.

In late April the 'relationship' developed further, and for the first time Lizzie and Colin Stagg spoke on the telephone. During that conversation Stagg obliquely referred to the Rachel Nickell murder and the rumours that had been spread about him. The following day, they spoke again and Stagg related a fantasy about Lizzie being assaulted and restrained with a belt while he had sex with her from behind. However, in a subsequent letter to Lizzie, Stagg said he was not a murderer and that he believed in the sacredness of life.

As the telephone conversations became more intimate and the letters more graphic, some featuring crude cartoons of himself and Lizzie having sex and, much to the interest of police, drawings of daggers, it soon became clear that the time had come for Lizzie and Stagg to meet in person.

Their first meeting was on 20 May 1993 in Hyde Park, London. Lizzie was provided with surreptitious recording equipment so any conversation she had with Stagg could be monitored by police. Furthermore, other undercover officers were deployed to watch Stagg's every move. During their hour-long lunchtime meeting, she 'confessed' to taking part in an occult killing. Stagg did not admit anything; in fact he again denied he had killed Rachel Nickell. However, during their meeting, Stagg handed Lizzie a letter that contained a violent sexual fantasy involving himself and another man tying up Lizzie, and the other man tracing a knife blade over her body, then putting his sperm on the blade and forcing Lizzie to lick it off. The story continued with the man cutting himself and dripping blood on to Lizzie's breasts, after which both men would have sex with her while holding her at knifepoint.

In a phone call to Lizzie not long after their first meeting, Stagg confessed that many years ago he and his cousin had killed a girl and hidden her body in the New Forest. This murder was a fictional one, as Stagg was hoping that by thus impressing Lizzie she would consent to sex with him and he would finally lose his virginity.

Finally, Stagg's sexual fantasies began to involve the Nickell murder. Meeting Lizzie again in Hyde Park on 29 June, he told her that he had been walking on Wimbledon Common at the time of the murder and that thinking about her death excited him sexually. He also described the appearance of the dead Rachel Nickell, including details that, according to police, he would not have known from the scene-of-crime picture that he had been shown during his initial questioning. One such detail was the deep incision across Rachel's throat that had almost decapitated her; another was that her vagina or anus had been forced open.

On 21 July 1993, Colin Stagg met Lizzie for the last time in Hyde Park. When Lizzie told Colin that the only way he could satisfy her was to physically abuse her, he felt that their relationship could go no further. He also confessed that his tale about the murder in the New Forest was concocted solely to please her and that it had not in fact happened. Lizzie contacted Stagg again by letter, and suggested they meet again; Stagg turned her down.

With Colin Stagg's revelations of 29 June captured on tape, and with his 'relationship' with Lizzie apparently ended, the Operation Edzell team felt they had enough new evidence to charge him with the murder of Rachel

Nickell. The Crown Prosecution Service considered the evidence and agreed that the case should go to court.

Stagg charged with murder

At 5 a.m. on 17 August 1993, police, led by Detective Inspector Keith Pedder, arrived at Stagg's home and told him that he was being arrested on suspicion of the murder of Rachel Nickell. While a stunned Stagg sat on his sofa, repeatedly denying that he had killed Rachel Nickell, police began a thorough search of the premises and of Stagg's garden. Stagg was taken to Wimbledon police station, where he was formally charged with the murder. A series of interviews with Stagg took place; to many of the police's questions, on the advice of his solicitor, Ian Ryan, Stagg replied with the words 'No comment'. When Stagg was told that Lizzie James was actually an under-cover police officer he was absolutely shocked. When 'Lizzie' interviewed Stagg, she told him that the case against him rested on two assumptions:

- that Stagg, during one of their meetings in Hyde Park, had shown her the exact position of how Rachel's entire body was found at the crime scene – including how her hands were placed; the photograph Stagg had been shown by police *did not include her hands*

- that at another of their meetings Stagg had made a graphic representation, using his fingers, of the shape of Rachel Nickell's assaulted anus; again, the photo Stagg had seen showed no such detail.

Stagg was remanded in custody following an appearance at the magistrates' court at Wimbledon. On the day after his arrest, he was taken to Wandsworth Prison, where he was kept in the hospital wing, apparently for his own safety. Stagg was also given Category A status, which is an indicator that a prisoner is likely to be violent and pose a physical threat to other prisoners and prison staff.

Meanwhile, Stagg's house and garden were being thoroughly searched. Floorboards were pulled up, Stagg's clothing and belongings were scrutinised carefully for any evidence, and his garden was dug up to a depth of two feet and probed with metal detectors. No evidence of any crime was found.

Committal hearing

On 17 February 1994, Colin Stagg appeared again at Wimbledon magistrates' court. The prosecutor, William Boyce, presented witnesses whom he questioned; the defence lawyer, Jim Sturman, would then cross-examine them.

The witnesses included Susan Gale, Jane Harriman, Lillian Avid, Christine Perrior (a neighbour of Stagg's whose only evidence was her account of an inconclusive conversation with him on the day after the murder), and Tina Woodsell, who had not seen Colin Stagg on 15 July but had seen him on many prior occasions walking on Wimbledon Common.

The Home Office pathologist, Dr Richard Shepherd, detailed the injuries to Rachel's body, including the dilation of the anus by an unknown object. He told the court that no DNA evidence whatsover had been found on Rachel's body or clothing. Dr Shepherd described the stages of the attack: the stabbing at the neck, the slitting of Rachel's throat, the moving of her body to under a birch tree where further stab wounds were inflicted, the pulling down of Rachel's jeans and underwear and the violation of her anus by an object. Under later questioning by Jim Sturman, Shepherd told the court that the object could have been an erect penis.

Paul Britton then gave evidence, explaining the nature of the operation involving Lizzie James. Lizzie James, her face hidden behind a screen to prevent her being identified, was also questioned on her evidence. She denied that she had been involved in an attempt to get Stagg to incriminate himself: the rationale behind Operation Edzell had been to find out whether or not Stagg was implicated in the murder.

On the evidence presented, the magistrates' court decided that the case should proceed to the Central Criminal Court. Stagg's application for bail was refused, and he was returned to Wandsworth Prison. At the end of June 1994 he was moved to Winchester Prison, where he awaited the start of his trial in September at the Old Bailey in London.

The precedent of the Hall acquittal

In March 1994 Keith Hall, a man from Leeds, was acquitted of the murder of his wife. The charges against Hall had been put after evidence had been gathered by an undercover policewoman who became acquainted with Hall in a similar operation to that to attempt to get Stagg to incriminate himself. The judge in the Hall case had ruled that the evidence gathered in that way was inadmissible, and therefore the trial could not proceed.

Police in the Nickell case were not concerned about the implications of the Hall acquittal: they believed that Operation Edzell had not, technically, involved the entrapment of Colin Stagg. The prosecuting counsel in the Stagg case, John Nutting QC, took a different view: he raised with police the likelihood of Stagg's trial not proceeding due to the similarity of the circumstances of the Hall case.

The trial

Colin Stagg first appeared in the Number One courtroom at the Old Bailey on 5 September 1994. The swearing in of the jury was postponed; it would now take place after prosecution and defence teams discussed whether the evidence gathered during Operation Edzell would be admissible. Stagg's lawyers, William Clegg QC and Jim Sturman, had objected to the trial proceeding and cited the case of Keith Hall as a precedent. The judge, Justice Ognall, told the court he needed three days to read through Lizzie James's evidence, and proceedings were adjourned.

When proceedings reconvened on 8 September, William Clegg emphasised Lizzie James's hints that she would reward Stagg with sexual experiences if he admitted to certain fantasies and that her replies in her letters had encouraged Stagg to produce such violent fantasies. The prosecution team stated that Operation Edzell was not meant to trick Stagg into confessing anything, but was designed to *allow* Stagg to incriminate himself. The two sides presented their cases as to whether the evidence was admissible; the judge's decision on whether to proceed with a trial would hinge on whether Lizzie James had, in her letters and conversations, attempted to manipulate Colin Stagg into confessing to involvement in things that he had in fact had no connection with.

There was a two-day wait as Judge Ognall retired to decide whether the undercover evidence gathered by Lizzie James would be admissible.

On 14 September, Colin Stagg, the defence and prosecution teams and the jury assembled to hear Judge Ognall deliver his ruling. He described the prosecution's view that Operation Edzell was designed either to allow Stagg to eliminate himself from suspicion or to implicate himself in the murder as 'highly disingenuous'. He accused Paul Britton of 'pulling the strings' regarding the operation against Stagg. Judge Ognall acknowledged that Colin Stagg had at no time confessed to the murder of Rachel Nickell, that Stagg's description to Lizzie James of where

Rachel's body had been found was wrong, and that he had told Lizzie that Rachel had been raped, when she had not in fact been raped. Judge Ognall then cited relevant cases, and then listed examples of manipulative language in the Lizzie James letters, quoting where appropriate. Finally, the judge stated, 'For the reasons I have given, I uphold the defence submissions that the Lizzie James material will not go before a jury.' He then ordered that Colin Stagg be immediately released from custody.

The Nickell family, who were in court to hear the judge's decision, were devastated. In a speech to the assembled members of the press in the street outside the Old Bailey, Andrew Nickell described his disillusionment with the criminal justice system and asked, 'The law has been upheld, but where is the justice?'

Colin Stagg then emerged from the Old Bailey, and again stated his innocence of the Nickell murder, expressing his hope that police would find the real killer and bring him to justice.

Aftermath

Colin Stagg returned to his home, but the press continued to pay him attention. Police carried out a reinvestigation of the Nickell murder, but drew a blank with the new suspects they interviewed, including a serial sex attacker called Robert Napper, who was sent to Broadmoor after confessing to the violent stabbing to death of Samantha Bisset and the murder by suffocation of her young daughter Jazmine in the autumn of 1993.

Police flew to New Zealand to speak to another suspect named John Gallagher; having interviewed him, they were satisfied that he had not been involved in the murder.

In 1995 Colin Stagg appeared in court, charged with threatening a man with an axe on Wimbledon Common. He was given a year's probation for this offence. In the courtroom his solicitor described how difficult life had been for Stagg after his acquittal in the Nickell case.

A report in the *News of the World* in April 1995 that a knife had been found in the garage of an unnamed early suspect led detectives to investigate; there was no evidence that this knife had been used in the stabbing of Rachel Nickell.

In 1997 it was announced that the Nickell incident room at Wimbledon would be closed. The cost of the enquiry had reached £3 million. It was also reported that Rachel's parents were considering a civil suit against Stagg over the death of their daughter.

Colin Stagg has voluntarily undergone two lie-detector tests, both of which failed to indicate that he killed Rachel Nickell.

10 JonBenét Ramsey

'Bad things aren't supposed to happen here, in our white, middle-and-upper-class community. This is Mork-and-Mindy land, and the laws aren't for us, but for the underclass.'

– Attorney Lee Hill, quoted by Stephen Singular in Presumed Guilty.

'One unsolved murder and things just start to unravel'

– Local Boulder activist Evan Ravitz, ibid.

'We are a Christian, God-fearing family. We love our children. We would do anything for our children.'

– Patsy Ramsey interviewed on CNN, January 1997.

For most police forces around the world, when attempting to solve the murder of a child it is a standard procedure to ensure that among the first to be thoroughly questioned are the parents of that child. This is done in order to either eliminate them as suspects or to establish whether they may have been responsible.

The Ramsey family

Christmas 1996. John and Patsy Ramsey lived with their two children, Burke, aged nine, and the unusually named JonBenét, aged six, in a sumptuously equipped, three-storey, Tudor-style mansion at 755 15th Street, Boulder, Colorado. The family had moved there five years earlier from Atlanta, Georgia, when John Ramsey's computer company, Access Graphics, was bought up by the Lockheed Martin Corporation, a company specialising in aeronautics and specifically defence, whose customers included the US government. John Ramsey was retained as a salaried president of the company and moved the company to Boulder, where such businesses were flourishing.

The house, which had been sold to the Ramseys for approximately half a million dollars, had more than the same sum spent on it again in remodelling and extending it to make it approximately double in floor size. Finding the hard cash was no problem for the Ramseys – John had sold his company for an estimated $8 million, and was still earning a high salary as the head of the highly profitable Access Graphics. The house had been extended to provide room for John Ramsey's three children from his previous marriage, in 1980, to Lucinda Lou Pasch.

The Ramseys were quick to become active and accepted members of the upper and richer echelons of Boulder society. Both were Christian believers and members of their local Episcopalian church. Patsy was particularly active in helping out at the elementary school her children attended, but her main interest appears to have been entering JonBenét in local and national children's beauty pageants, where JonBenét, a charismatic and attractive child and apparently a keen contestant, was very successful. Both John and Patsy Ramsey had experienced pain and tragedy in their lives, some of it shared, but their marriage was generally perceived as a successful and solid one.

John Ramsey

John Bennet Ramsey was born in 1943 in Nebraska. His father James had been a distinguished pilot in the US Air Force during World War Two. After the war the family moved to Michigan, where James Ramsey worked in aeronautics.

John Ramsey attended Michigan State University and studied electrical engineering. During his time there he was a successful athlete and was elected president of the Theta Chai fraternity. In 1965 John Ramsey met Lucinda Lou Pasch; the following year they were married. On graduating, John served as a naval pilot, stationed at Subic Bay Training Centre in the Philippines. In 1971 he left the navy and went back to Michigan University, where he gained a further degree – in marketing – in 1971. He got a job in this field in Atlanta, where he and Lucinda started raising a family.

By 1977 John's marriage to Lucinda was over and she was granted custody of their children Elizabeth (born 1969), Melinda (born 1971) and John Andrew (born 1975). John Ramsey then formed his own one-man computer software company, Microsouth. After his divorce John started dating Patsy Paugh, daughter of Don and Nedra Paugh, and a former Miss West Virginia. They were married in Atlanta on 15 November 1980. Patsy, then aged 23, began working for John in his business, whose location was the basement of their home. This company merged with the Advanced Products group, widening its sphere to include computer hardware. Gaining staff, his own premises and riding the crest of the computer boom, in 1988 John Ramsey merged his Advanced Products group with two other companies, forming Access Graphics, specialising in computer systems and services, with offices in both Atlanta and Boulder.

John and Patsy's first child, their son Burke Hamilton Ramsey – according to John the name came to him in a dream – was born on 27 January 1987; their second, a girl, whom they named JonBenét, was born on 6 August 1990. The name JonBenét had been invented by Patsy by contracting and joining together her husband's first and middle names.

On 8 January 1992 an event took place that affected John Ramsey badly. His eldest daughter Elizabeth, known as Beth, died in a car crash in a vehicle driven by her boyfriend, Matthew Derrington. Aged 22 at the time of her death, Beth had been employed as a flight attendant for Delta Airlines. In the accident, which happened during a snowstorm just outside Chicago, her boyfriend's BMW had been hit by a truck and the couple were instantly killed. A quiet and, on the surface, non-emotional man, John Ramsey became even more inward-looking following his daughter's death. His introspection was compounded a few months later when he was told the news of his father James's death. The year 1993 would bring a further tragedy into the Ramseys' lives as Patsy was diagnosed with ovarian cancer. Meanwhile Access Graphics went from strength to strength, and John Ramsey was voted Boulder's 'Entrepreneur of the Year' for 1995.

Patricia 'Patsy' Ramsey

Patsy Ramsey was born Patricia Paugh in Parkersburg, West Virginia, on 29 December 1956. One of three daughters of middle-class parents (her father Don was an engineer), Patsy grew up to be a high-scoring student, and was awarded many prizes for her debating skills. Her mother Nedra encouraged Patsy to enter the beauty-pageant scene at an early age. Having been a runner-up for Miss Teenage West Virginia, Patsy eventually won the title of Miss West Virginia while attending college in 1977. Patsy even attempted to win the Miss America title; unsuccessful, she nevertheless won a $2,000 award for being a runner-up. Her beauty-contest activities had not got in the way of her academic career: Patsy gained her degree in journalism and advertising from the University of West Virginia in 1979. Her younger sister Pam, a dead ringer for Patsy, won the Miss West Virginia title in 1980 – and also went on to become a Miss America finalist.

Patsy Paugh met John Ramsey while she was working at her first job with an advertising company in Atlanta. After their marriage she and John bought a home outside Atlanta. Patsy, always able to integrate socially into a new environment, became active in children's baseball, charity groups and school activities. When the family moved to Boulder, it was Patsy who supervised the extensive building work on the property, the major feature of which was an enormous extension to the rear of the building, and also made decisions about the interior design and furnishings.

When Patsy was diagnosed as having Stage 4 ovarian cancer during the summer of 1993, she was told that her life could be saved only by an immediate hysterectomy. Removal of the cancerous womb and ovaries brought on a premature menopause – 'within five days', according to an interview about her illness Patsy gave to the *Colorado Woman News* later that year. Scans revealed the existence of a tumour and cancer that had spread to her lymph nodes, necessitating gruelling sessions of chemotherapy, the side effects of which included a weakened immune system, nausea and complete hair loss.

During her suffering Patsy began reading religious, mystical and self-help books relating to cancer. Following a prayer session that included a 'laying on of hands' by the Ramseys' Episcopalian pastor, the Reverend Rol Hoverstock, Patsy was scanned for cancerous cells and tumours, and the results showed that there were none. From that day Patsy Ramsey considered herself healed by the power of God and by prayer. But the diagnosis of the disease, and the pain Patsy had been subjected to during its treatment, had undoubtedly changed her outlook on life.

Patsy, JonBenét and the beauty pageants

John and Patsy Ramsey's marriage appeared to involve a sharp divide of interests along traditional lines. John's time and energy went into his business, his employees and managing investments; Patsy took care of the children and the social life of herself and her husband, organising parties and social occasions.

Unusually for a child of such wealthy parents, JonBenét had been active in children's beauty pageants from an early age, as her mother Patsy had been. These pageants, at both local and national levels, are most popular in the Southern United States and most participants are white and working- or lower-middle-class. Pageants are a multimillion-pound business involving not only the competitions themselves but coaches to train the children in how to carry themselves and entertain the judges – usually with song-and-dance routines – costume makers and designers to produce the outfits and photographers to take pictures. Patsy spent thousands of dollars on JonBenét's photographic portfolio.

Many of the parents of the children involved in beauty pageants spend all of their spare time training their offspring in the skills and poise required to win prizes. Competition is fierce, especially when the cash prizes on offer are high. JonBenét's apparel worn for these occasions was extravagant, with some outfits costing hundreds of dollars worn only once. JonBenét, like the other girl contestants, would wear adult make-up, lipstick and high heels. Sometimes the contests would require the little girls to pose and perform in a coy and bizarrely provocative manner for the judges. 'Titles' she had won included 1996 Little Miss Colorado, Colorado State All-Star Kids Cover Girl, America's Royale Little Miss and National Tiny Miss Beauty.

It was Patsy who encouraged JonBenét to enter these contests. John Ramsey thought them to be 'stupid', but realised that this was making Patsy happy, and diverting her mind from the fears she might have about her cancer returning.

26 December 1996

Patsy and John Ramsey awoke early – just after 5 a.m. – on the morning of 26 December. They, along with Burke and JonBenét, were scheduled to catch an early flight that day to Michigan, where they had a vacation home by the lakeside in Charlevoix. The trip was to be an extended Christmas break that would include a celebration of Patsy's fortieth birthday on 29 December.

At 5.52 a.m. on the morning after Christmas Day, 1996, a 911 call was made to the Boulder police by an apparently panicking Patsy Ramsey from the family home on 15th Street. She had gone downstairs to the kitchen to make coffee, having left John in the shower, and had found, left at the foot of the staircase, a ransom note handwritten on lined paper torn from a legal pad using a black felt-tipped pen. The note – misspellings uncorrected – read as follows:

Mr Ramsey,
Listen carefully! We are a group of individuals that represent a small foreign faction. We respect your bussiness but not the country that it serves. At this time we have your daughter in our possession. She is safe and unharmed and if you want her to see 1997, you must follow our instructions to the letter.

You will withdraw $118,000 from your account. $100,000 will be in $100 bills and the remaining $18,000 in $20 bills. Make sure that you bring an adequate size attaché to the bank. When you get home you will put the money in a brown paper bag. I will call you between 8 and 10 am tomorrow to instruct you on delivery. The delivery will be exhausting so I advise you to be rested. If we monitor you getting the money early, we might call you early to arrange an earlier delivery of the money and hence an earlier pickup of your daughter.

Any deviation of my instructions will result in the immediate execution of your daughter. You will also be denied her remains for proper burial. The two gentlemen watching over your daughter do not particularly like you so I advise you not to provoke them. Speaking to anyone about your situation such as Police or F.B.I., etc., will result in your daughter being beheaded. If we catch you talking to a stray dog, she dies. If you alert bank authorities, she dies. If the money is in anyway marked or tampered with, she dies. You will be scanned for electronic devices and if any are found, she dies. You can try to deceive us, but be warned we are familiar with Law enforcement countermeasures and tactics. You stand a 99% chance of killing your daughter if you try to outsmart us. Follow our instructions and you stand a 100% chance of getting her back. You and your family are under constant scrutiny as well as the authorities. Don't try to grow a brain John. You are not the only fat cat around so don't think that killing will be difficult. Don't underestimate us John. Use that good, southern common sense of yours. It's up to you now John!

Victory!

S.B.T.C.

Undoubtedly this was a peculiar and wordy document for a kidnapper to have left at the scene of an abduction.

According to Patsy's statement to police, having read the note, she then ran screaming up the stairs to JonBenét's bedroom on the second floor, to discover that her daughter was indeed missing. She then checked her son Burke in his bedroom on the other side. The first action by John Ramsey, now dressed and downstairs with the police, was to phone one of his closest friends, Fleet White, who lived nearby, and ask him to come over to the Ramsey residence at once. White arrived to find a large number of police, at the house, as well as the Reverend Hoverstock, the family's Episcopalian minister. White was asked by John and Patsy to take Burke over to the Whites' house – having done this, he returned to comfort his friends at 7.45 a.m.

Having read the ransom note, police officers believed this was a genuine kidnapping, and, apparently for this reason, they neither ensured the entire house was forensically secure nor conducted a thorough search of the premises. The note was examined, the Ramseys questioned, but not in any great detail, and traces were put on the phone lines to ensure that the location of any kidnapper calling the house could be tracked down.

At 7.30 a.m. John Ramsey went off to get the ransom cash from a nearby bank. During these events Patsy Ramsey, apparently deeply distressed, was sobbing uncontrollably. As police waited for that phone call that morning, friends of the Ramseys who had been told the news gathered round to give their support. A 'victim assistance advocate' also appeared, alerted by a paged message from police, whose task was to deal with the emotional stress on the victims of a crime. FBI agents, whose job it was to supervise the wiretap, arrived at 10.30 a.m.

Also at this time a warrant for the property was obtained by police, the Ramseys having denied officers permission to search the house. A cursory search of the premises ensued. And still the phone did not ring. Apparently frustrated by the lack of communication with the kidnappers, at 1.05 p.m. John Ramsey and Fleet White took it upon themselves to search the property, unsupervised by police. Heading immediately to the basement, John forced entry (the door was stuck – but not locked) into a small disused cellar room. On entering, the men saw JonBenét's body lying on its back on the floor, covered by a blanket. Her arms were raised above her head. JonBenét was clothed in a shirt, a sweatshirt, white pyjama bottoms and underpants decorated with rosebuds and the word 'Wednesday'. Still wearing a ring, a bracelet and a gold chain, the child had received head injuries; her mouth was gagged with adhesive duct tape and a white cord, attached to a wooden stick, was tied around her neck. Her right wrist was also tied with cord. Seeing the child, Ramsey screamed out loud and, throwing the blanket aside, grabbed the dead child, tore the tape from her mouth and, picking her up, took her upstairs to the ground floor. The crime scene had been disturbed, vital evidence had been tampered with and contaminated; police had been undoubtedly negligent in not accompanying Ramsey and White on their search of the house. On John's entry into the room carrying JonBenét's corpse, Patsy went into a hysterical fit, screaming and praying that her daughter be brought back from the dead, and became so overwrought with emotion that she began vomiting.

Homicide – not kidnapping

On the discovery of the body, police changed tactics: what had been a kidnapping was now a homicide. The Ramseys' friends were ordered to leave the house, and police began a forensic examination of the premises as well as they could, hindered by the fact that the body of JonBenét had been moved from where John Ramsey had apparently discovered it. Within an hour of the discovery of the body, John Ramsey was overheard by detectives to make a phone call requesting that his private pilot fly himself, Patsy and Burke to Atlanta, Georgia, later that day. When police asked that he remain in Boulder, John Ramsey insisted that the questioning could wait another day.

John Ramsey's surviving children from his previous marriage, John Andrew and Melinda, arrived at the house from Denver Airport, having flown in from Minneapolis after their father told them of the kidnapping earlier that day. John Ramsey now had to tell them that JonBenét was dead.

The Ramseys then left the residence and spent the afternoon at the home of their friend John Fernie. They were never to spend a night in their Boulder home again. By 1.50 p.m. police had secured and left the property empty, with JonBenét's body inside, guarded by a coroner's representative and a lone police officer. As the search warrant had not yet arrived, further investigations could not proceed.

Meanwhile, Fleet White contacted John Ramsey's pilot and cancelled that afternoon's flight to Atlanta. White explained that it appeared likely that the Ramseys would need to stay in Boulder to be questioned by police.

That day the FBI questioned Mary and Bob Smartt, the parents of one of JonBenét's schoolfriends, about Jon-Benét. Police questioned Linda Hoffman-Pugh, the Ramseys' housekeeper, and her husband for three hours, asking her to write down the words 'Mr Ramsey', 'attaché', 'beheaded' and '$118,000'. Hoffman-Pugh, shocked by the news of JonBenét's death, was astonished to find that she and her husband now appeared to be prime suspects, and became totally horrified by her own interpretation of what the police were asking her to write – that six-year-old JonBenét had been beheaded.

Preliminary investigations established that there were footprints in snow in the grounds of the house. Also, a footprint made by a hiking boot was found in the dust on the floor of the windowless basement room where the body had been discovered. Also found were marks where someone had attempted to climb out from a basement window, but no footprints outside, as would have been expected if the attempt had been successful. All footprints remain unidentified, despite police enquiries among the Ramseys and some four hundred friends of the family and visitors to the house. Also unidentifiable were a palm print found on the door of the cellar and a pubic hair found on the blanket in which the strangled JonBenét had been wrapped.

The intruder alarm had not been turned on. However, there was no sign that the property had been broken into. A neighbour, Scott Gibbons, reported seeing lights on in the Ramseys' kitchen late that night. Another neighbour, Melody Stanton, recalls hearing screams from the Ramsey house. It further transpired that the Ramseys had given copies of their front-door keys to many of their friends and also to housekeepers and workmen. Police estimated that the house, due to its size, design and number of rooms, would be very difficult for a stranger to find their way around.

The most intriguing piece of evidence so far was the ransom note. Police concluded that the paper it was written on had been removed from a white legal pad found in the kitchen, where the pen it had been written with was also found. The sum of $118,000 was identical to the amount of John Ramsey's Christmas bonus, which his company had paid him for 1996. This, if not a complete coincidence, indicated that the killer (if indeed the killer had written the note) had some inside knowledge of John Ramsey's activities and in particular his finances. And among various interpretations of the initials 'SBTC' with which the writer signed off was that it referred to Subic Bay Training Centre where John Ramsey had done his naval training in the late 1960s.

Autopsy – injuries and the cause of death

The autopsy on JonBenét was performed by Dr John E Meyer on 27 December 1997 – but the report was not released to the public for some time. The injuries to the body were listed as follows:

I. *Ligature strangulation*
    A. *Circumferential ligature with associated ligature furrow of neck*
    B. *Abrasions and petechial hemorrhages, neck*
    C. *Petechial hemorrhages, conjunctival surfaces of eyes and skin of face*

II. *Craniocerebral injuries*
    A. *Scalp contusion*
    B. *Linear, comminuted fracture of right side of skull*
    C. *Linear pattern of contusions of right cerebral hemisphere*
    D. *Subarachnoid and subdural hemorrhage*
    E. *Small contusions, tips of temporal lobes*

III. *Abrasion of right cheek*

IV. *Abrasion/contusion, posterior right shoulder*

V. *Abrasions of left lower back and posterior left lower leg*

VI. *Abrasion and vascular congestion of vaginal mucosa*

VII. *Ligature of right wrist*

In addition, no drugs or alcohol were found in JonBenét's blood. Cause of death was given as 'asphyxia by strangulation associated with craniocerebral trauma', i.e. that JonBenét had received damaging injuries to the skull and brain and had subsequently been strangled. JonBenét had been wearing both long pyjamas and panties; these were stained with urine and red staining. What Dr Meyer describes as 'a deep ligature furrow' on the child's neck (one injury in a long list of places of haemorrhage on the body) appears to have been critical in causing her death.

The anal and genital area was examined. Dried blood was found along the perineum, and there was hyperemia and abrasion to the hymen, which was intact. Vaginal tissue was discoloured but showed no sign of haemorrhage. Head injuries included extensive haemorrhaging and a skull fracture. An area of purple contusion was visible on the brain.

The autopsy revealed that JonBenét was alive when her head was injured, as there had been subsequent bleeding. After many damaging blows to her head, the most brutal of which had succeeded in dislodging part of the skull, she had been strangled with the cord. The attack had undoubtedly been savage and merciless. The coroner's ruling was that JonBenét's death was a homicide.

Time of death

According to her parents, JonBenét was last seen when she went to bed at around 10 p.m. on Christmas Day. Just after 1 p.m. the following day, when John Ramsey picked up the body and removed it from the basement, it showed signs of rigor mortis, which takes between six and twelve hours to take place. The temperature of the corpse may have indicated a more precise time of death; however there is no record that this was taken at the time it was discovered. According to police, the body smelled as if it was decomposing, which would indicate that death had taken place possibly before midnight on 25 December.

A sexually motivated attack and/or a history of abuse?

A forensic pathologist, Dr Cyril Wecht, in his book *Who Killed JonBenét Ramsey?* focuses on elements of the autopsy results that led to the conclusion that the child had been sexually assaulted during an attack before being strangled. He also theorises that the girl had been a victim of sexual abuse for a long time before 25 December 1996. The Ramseys' paediatrician, Dr Francisco Beuf, has denied that JonBenét had ever shown any sign of emotional or physical abuse – although the child did have genital infections and was still, at the age of six, wetting her bed, which might indicate some emotional disturbance. In his fascinating study of the sexual and political cultural implications of the life and death of JonBenét, Dr Stephen Singular – despite his extensive interviews, research and time spent on the Internet attempting to find a link between child pornography and the pageant scene – failed to find any evidence or even rumours of any sexual abuse. (In fact, the only negative rumour of a sexual nature about John Ramsey – that he had an affair with a woman named Kim Baller during the time of Patsy's illness – turned out to be a completely fraudulent one.)

However, the full autopsy report does reveal a series of indicators that JonBenét had been sexually interfered with prior to her death. The 'reddish hyperemia' of the vagina mentioned in the report indicates some type of trauma or assault. The vagina also showed 'epithelial erosion with underlying capillary congestion' and the presence of red blood cells, indicating that some foreign object had been inside her. During the autopsy Meyer told detectives that the child had received an injury that indicated vaginal penetration. Also, traces of a substance were found on her upper thigh that appeared to be dried semen, and blood smears on the child's labia were dried in such a way that the coroner believed that the area had been wiped with a cloth. No such cloth was found on the Ramsey premises or elsewhere.

Additionally, Meyer noted the presence of partially digested pineapple in the child's stomach. Her parents denied she had eaten pineapple before she went to sleep. A bowl of pineapple pieces was found in the living room; had JonBenét got up in the night and eaten pineapple? And, if she had, what else had happened to her after she had had her snack?

Police errors from day one?

Even at this early stage in the investigation, the death of JonBenét raised many questions. Was the ransom note completely fraudulent, designed to delay police and the Ramseys from searching the house for the body? Why had someone apparently attempted to make a cold-blooded murder initially appear to be a kidnapping? Or had someone acted in haste to desperately cover up a deliberate murder? And why had the sum of $118,000 been demanded? Was it in any way coincidental that this was the sum of money that had just been paid to John Ramsey as an annual bonus? And if so was the killer an employee or former employee of Access Graphics? Or did the writer of the note have some inside knowledge and want it to appear that a co-worker of John Ramsey had committed this crime?

The behaviour of police on 26 December may also be questioned. Critically, why did the police have no suspicions about the authenticity of the ransom note? If they had, a more thorough search of the premises would have been undertaken immediately – and JonBenét's body would have been found hours earlier. Even a brief reading of the ransom note would have raised doubts in a trained police officer.

As police arrived at the Ramseys' home, so did several of their friends, who were in no way monitored and had access to all rooms in the house. It is extraordinary that John Ramsey and Fleet White then searched the house without being accompanied by police, and bizarre that

John Ramsey was able to get into the 'wine cellar' in the basement when police, during their brief search some seven hours earlier, had found the door jammed shut. John Ramsey initially refused to let police search his house and insisted that a search warrant be issued, and he seemed eager to leave Boulder for Atlanta on the very day his daughter had been found dead – both actions indicating an unwillingness to help police, which does appear suspicious.

It is usual procedure to interview the parents of a murdered child before widening the field to include others who may have been close to the child or had access to the family property; for whatever reason this did not take place.

Questions also may be raised about Burke Ramsey. According to Patsy, Burke was still asleep when she rang police early on 26 December. However, on playback of her emergency 911 call, Burke's voice is allegedly audible in the background. Why were the Ramsey parents so eager to have Burke removed from their home and taken to the Whites' house – at 7 a.m.?

After JonBenét's death – the investigation

For whatever reasons – the Ramseys' social stature in Boulder, or an unwillingness to subject the apparently already traumatised couple to the additional stress of police questioning – John and Patsy Ramsey were not questioned by police on 26 December.

The story hit the local news media, and shocked Colorado. On 27 December the Boulder *Daily Camera*'s headlines announced 'MISSING GIRL FOUND DEAD' and revealed that the case was a homicide and that police had no suspects. At a press conference given by police that day it was revealed that JonBenét's death had been by asphyxiation. It was admitted by a senior Boulder detective, John Eller, that the parents had not yet been interviewed.

Also on that day John Ramsey's friend Fleet White was interviewed by detectives, and went over the events of the previous morning. Also interviewed were Pam Griffin, the local seamstress who made JonBenét's sometimes extravagant pageant costumes, and her daughter Kristine. Both denied there had been any abusive elements in relations between JonBenét and her parents.

As the first results of the autopsy were discussed by detectives, Police Commander John Eller, who was in charge of the investigation, decided that the Ramseys were prime suspects, and that the presence of what appeared to be semen on JonBenét's body would make John Ramsey a possible suspect. A search of the premises and computer files at Access Graphics was ordered, and at 9.30 p.m. that day detectives visited the Fernies' house with the intention of interviewing JonBenét's parents, but were unable to proceed. Although Patsy was in a state of deep sedation she was nonetheless requested to copy out parts of the ransom note – which led to her becoming hysterical. For his part John was in no condition to answer detailed questioning.

As the story spread and was reported on national news media, the TV networks installed themselves, their reporters, technicians and equipment in hotels and motels in Boulder, and the Ramseys' neighbours found themselves under siege, constantly badgered by eager reporters.

On Saturday, 28 December, the Ramseys told police that they would not be interviewed without their own attorney present, and that they were unwilling to share privileged information with investigators. On hearing this, Police Commander Eller asked the coroner to withhold JonBenét's body from burial until interviews had been conducted with her parents. Meyer declined to do this.

Meanwhile, the Boulder County District Attorney Alex Hunter, holidaying in Hawaii, was told via a phone call about the murder, but did not yet return to Colorado. John Andrew and Melinda Ramsey were also interviewed, and questioned on their whereabouts on 25 and 26 December. Although claiming to have remained in Marietta, Georgia, during that time frame, John Andrew had several hours he could not account for – long enough for him to have taken a return flight to Boulder. Only after airline and private-plane checks were made would he be eliminated as a suspect.

On Sunday, 29 December, police videotaped the mourners at JonBenét's memorial service at the Ramseys' church, St John's, hoping that by his or her body language or behaviour a suspect might give him- or herself away. No evidence of any usable kind emerged from this. Following the service, the body was flown that day to Atlanta, where the funeral was scheduled to take place. Meanwhile, Fleet White was interviewed by police and maintained that in his view an intruder had been responsible for the murder.

JonBenét's open-casket funeral took place at the Peachtree Presbyterian Church in Marietta, Georgia. She was buried next to her half-sister Beth. After the funeral, mourners, friends of the family and relatives went to Patsy's parents' house in Roswell, Atlanta. There it was noticed that a furious quarrel was taking place between John Ramsey and Fleet White. In the portion of the argument that was overheard, White was urging Ramsey to talk to police in Boulder, and criticising him for having arranged for himself and Patsy to take part in a televised interview on CNN the following day. This disagreement was a crucial one, and after that day Fleet White and John Ramsey, who had been the closest of friends in Boulder, would never speak again.

Meanwhile, in six days the story had become a news priority in the national and international media, with the finger of suspicion pointing firmly at the Ramsey parents.

Now in death JonBenét Ramsey had achieved what Patsy had hoped she would do in life – to become known throughout the world.

The Ramseys appear on CNN

On 1 January 1997 John and Patsy Ramsey were interviewed live by Brian Cabell, a reporter on CNN. The broadcast came about at the request of John Ramsey, who wanted to explain to the public why he had made no public statement so far, and also must have been alarmed by the accusations against him now appearing daily in newspapers and magazines and on radio and TV.

During the interview John explained that in hiring attorneys for himself and Patsy he was only following legal advice. He also claimed his family had been a loving and gentle one. He offered a $50,000 reward for information leading to the conviction of the killer. They both went over the now familiar events of 26 December: finding the ransom note, checking JonBenét's and Burke's bedrooms and the discovery of the body in the basement. It was revealed that both John and Patsy had given hair and blood samples to the police. Patsy alarmed parents and children in Boulder by declaring that there was a killer on the loose, and in particular by warning, 'Keep your babies close to you – there's someone out there.' They also told Cabell that they were employing their own investigators. During the final part of the programme John Ramsey described the accusations against him and Patsy as 'nauseating beyond belief'.

Investigations continue

The day after the CNN interview, a tabloid revealed that JonBenét had been the victim of a sexual assault, and the Mayor of Boulder, Leslie Durgin, responding to the fears that Patsy's remarks had caused the town's parents, denied that there was any 'killer on the loose'.

On 3 January the Ramseys returned to Boulder, where they stayed at the homes of various friends. The DA, Alex

Hunter, returned from his holiday in Hawaii on 4 January, the day that police finished searching the Ramsey home in Boulder and began a search of their holiday home in Charlevoix, Michigan. Much evidence from the Boulder mansion had not yet been examined: for example, computers and computer disks were removed, as were the Ramseys' large videotape collection. Among other items found in a basement room with windows was a suitcase with a blanket inside it – that blanket had traces of John Andrew's semen on it. John Andrew and Melinda were interviewed by police again, this time in Atlanta.

Meanwhile, Patsy and John had acquired a press representative, Pat Korten, whose first piece of media manipulation involved the distraught-looking Ramseys' attendance at St John's Church on Sunday, 5 January, which was widely covered by TV news. Investigations continued, with Burke Ramsey finally being interviewed by a child psychologist on 8 January. Carefully phrased questions intended to reveal any sexual abuse within the family were met with apparently honest answers; according to Burke there had been none. Police watching the taped interview could not tell if Burke was covering up for anyone.

Also on that day, the Ramseys handed over to police their written replies to questions. Access Graphics employees and ex-employees were systematically quizzed, with detectives hoping to find someone with a grudge. Computers at Access were also examined. By the second week of 1997 America's tabloid newspapers were boldly announcing exclusives indicating that John Ramsey had killed JonBenét. It was now widely known that John and Patsy had still not submitted themselves to a thorough interview by Boulder police. And there were still no arrests.

The enquiry was now extended to Georgia, where family and friends were systematically interviewed. Media interest was now sustained and, for the Ramseys' friends, family and neighbours, inescapable. The *Globe* newspaper published leaked or stolen photographs of the autopsy and the crime scene on 14 January, causing widespread boycotting of the paper and a lawsuit from the coroner's office. On 22 January it was widely reported that the Ramseys were refusing to subject themselves to polygraph lie-detector tests. Investigations continued throughout January and into February; many lines of enquiry were followed up, including identifying the handwriting on the ransom note and establishing where the duct tape and cord used to strangle JonBenét had been bought. However, still there were no arrests, but many tabloid-fuelled rumours about the guilt of Patsy and John (either as a couple or with one partner covering up for the other), Burke, John Andrew and various others, including a man who acted as the Ramsey family's Santa Claus for the past three Christmases, Bill McReynolds. A former University of Colorado teacher, McReynolds, an eccentric-looking man with a long white beard, was recovering from recent open-heart surgery. It emerged that not only had Bill's daughter Jill herself survived a kidnapping at the age of nine in 1974, but his wife Janet had written a play, *Hey Rube*, about the killing, in the basement of a house, of a young girl.

May 1997 – an interesting interview

Reporters in Boulder were granted access to John and Patsy Ramsey, and permitted to ask questions that had been previously approved by the Ramseys' lawyers. During the questioning John Ramsey stated categorically, 'I did not kill my daughter JonBenét. There have also been innuendoes that she had been or was sexually molested. I can tell you that those were the most hurtful innuendoes to us as a family. They are totally false.'

Patsy echoed his words: 'I did not kill JonBenét and did not have anything to do with this.' She went on to announce that the reward for finding the murderer was now upped to $100,000. She continued with this extra-ordinary statement: 'We feel like there are at least two people on the face of this earth that know who did this. That is the killer and someone that the person may have confided in.'

Both John and Patsy went on to warn the killer or killers that they would be found, with Patsy warning them, 'God knows who you are.'

www.ramseyfamily.com – the Ramseys go on-line

Inevitably, the Internet became a public forum for dissemination of news and views about the Ramsey case. The Ramseys set up a website, www.ramseyfamily.com, via which they and their media advisers issued information to the press.

In January the Ramseys used the site to chastise the proprietors of the *Globe* for insinuating there was a link between JonBenét's appearance in beauty pageants and child abuse, and then to threaten them with legal action over the publication of the autopsy and scene-of-crime photos. On 14 February the site issued a denial of the abuse allegations, including the transcript of an in-depth TV inteview with JonBenét's paediatrician, Dr Franceco Beuf.

On 2 March the Ramseys published a detailed account of John Andrew Ramsey's whereabouts during the Christmas holiday of 1996, emphasising that he was not a suspect, and that he had not been in Boulder on the night of 25–26 December. Both John Andrew and Melinda were declared no longer to be suspects on 6 March, the same day that rumours were denied that the Ramseys had hired private detectives to investigate members of the Boulder police department. On 19 March the Ramseys stated that neither Patsy nor John wrote the ransom note, and, moreover, handwriting experts in their employ could confirm this.

April 1997 saw much activity on the website, with eleven postings. The briefest – 'John and Patsy are enormously frustrated' – was issued on the 3rd and referred to the fact that one hundred days after the murder there had been no arrests. The issue of formal interviews with detectives was still under discussion – a further posting informed the media that the Ramseys had made an offer to do this to the Boulder police, and that they were, as always, willing to co-operate. On 23 April a long statement was issued, the major part of which was a letter to the DA, Alex Hunter. In it, the Ramseys' attorney expressed dismay that the Boulder police were unwilling to accept the 'format' of interview that the Ramseys had requested. The police were accused of portraying the Ramseys as 'unwilling to grant police interviews'. There then followed a long list of examples of the Ramseys' co-operating with the Boulder police. Police were accused of mounting a 'smear campaign' against the Ramseys.

June was a quiet month. The Ramseys were travelling with Burke, and the police had been granted permission to conduct a further search of the Boulder residence. On 10 July it was announced that the Ramseys had moved to Atlanta. On 24 July John Ramsey issued a personal statement urging that someone step forward and name the killer; included in the statement were a list of possible signs, including increased drink and drug consumption and other changes in behaviour, that might indicate that someone was the murderer.

On 13 August the Ramseys responded to the release of details of the autopsy results by stating that the murder was 'well planned'. On 13 September a *Vanity Fair* article was condemned as 'tabloid trash'. The year 1997 ended with an emotional 'Christmas Message from the Ramsey Family': JonBenét had been missed 'every day', but 'Had there been no birth of Christ, there would be no hope of eternal life, and, hence, no hope of ever being with our loved ones again'.

The existence of the website, and the use of paid, full-time public-relations experts acting as press officers for the Ramseys, is yet another extraordinary aspect of this case.

Suspects and scenarios

Burke Ramsey – Theory that Burke did it and his parents covered up

It is one theory that Burke may well have had hostile feelings towards JonBenét, who appears to have been Patsy's favourite. As a beauty pageant contestant she ensured that much of the family's time and attention was focused on his sister. JonBenét was strangled with a cord tied to a stick; an adult would surely have been able to strangle her with his or her bare hands. The putative scenario that labels Burke as the killer involves the nine-year-old boy, late at night on Christmas Day, using a paintbrush in a game of 'doctors and nurses' during which JonBenét was intimately examined in a way that hurt her. When JonBenét complained about this game and said that she was going to tell their parents, Burke's reaction may have been a violent one involving a blow or blows to JonBenét's head – possibly not intending to kill his sister but accidentally resulting in her death. This theoretical scenario would subsequently involve the cords and garrotte being added after JonBenét's death by adults present, in an attempt to draw attention away from the real cause of death. The ransom note may also have been part of this cover-up. This particular scenario would also involve a cover-up involving John Ramsey and his connections within the higher echelons of power in Boulder. The consequence would be a decision by politicians or police that as Burke was below the age of criminal liability and no crime therefore had been committed, that it was better that this crime never be solved.

This above scenario seems unlikely if one takes into account the response by the District Attorney's office to a series of two hour interviews Burke gave to a police officer with degrees in psychology and counselling who interviewed Burke for 6 hours between 10 June and 12 June 1998. As a result of these interviews neither DA Alex Hunter nor the Boulder police considered the child to be a suspect.

However if this scenario were true, the reason for John and Patsy refusing to take FBI polygraph tests would be revealed: if the lie detector showed that the Ramsey parents were telling the truth that they had not killed JonBenét, suspicion would then fall on Burke. Likewise, if, during the polygraph test, the Ramseys were asked if they knew who did kill JonBenét and the test revealed that their answer – that they did not – was a lie, that would also implicate Burke. If it were true it might also shed light on the Ramseys' unwillingness – repeatedly denied by them in TV interviews and on their website – to co-operate with police by submitting themselves to an interview where they did not know the questions they would be asked in advance.

Patsy Ramsey and the 'clues' in the ransom note

Theory that Patsy wrote the ransom note
Patsy Ramsey's handwriting has certain similarities with that found in the ransom note; one analyst, Sheila Lowe, found her handwriting 'very similar'. The ransom note

was undoubtedly bogus: JonBenét had not been kidnapped or abducted and the 'kidnappers' never made any contact requesting the $118,000.

The content of the note is bizarre: it goes into unnecessary detail and sometimes uses ambiguous language. The sum of $118,000 is identical to John Ramsey's bonus – an indication that whoever wrote the ransom note had personal knowledge of the family. The number 118 is also significant for other reasons. Patsy Ramsey, at the time of the murder, had a very strong Christian faith. Psalm 118 in the Old Testament reads:

> The Lord is our God. Who has shown and given us light, Decorate the festival with leafy boughs and bind the sacrifices to be offered with thick cords to the horns of the altar.

In an analysis of the ransom note commissioned by Boulder police in 1997, a psychological investigator, Dale Yeager, cited the above verse as crucial to understanding the death of JonBenét. It refers to making a blood sacrifice as atonement to God. In 1998 the police commissioned Yeager and his colleage Denise Knoke to write a psychological profile of Patsy. They affirmed that Patsy was influenced by fundamentalist theology, and listed as relevant the following elements in the case:

- The cords mentioned in Psalm 118 – JonBenét was tied with a cord, presumably before being strangled and then bludgeoned.

- 'S.B.T.C.' appears in the ransom note – used in fundamentalist circles to stand for 'Saved By The Cross'.

- Sacrifice – the possibility that JonBenét was 'sacrificed' by Patsy as an atonement for sins. Yeager and Knoke labelled Patsy 'a delusional sociopath' who was so far out of touch with reality that since the killing, or covering up for the killing, she 'convinced herself of her own innocence'.

The choice of words in the ransom note may always be telling: as someone traumatised by cancer and the very unpleasant medical treatment she had undergone to survive it, the theory throws up the scenario of Patsy, in writing the note, leaving some very obvious clues. Phrases or words such as 'small foreign faction', 'if we monitor you', 'scanned', '99% chance of killing' and 'under constant scrutiny' are analysed in depth in Andrew G Hodge's *A Mother Gone Bad – The Hidden Confessions of JonBenét's Killer*. The analysis is that the language used in the ransom note reveals that the writer has cancer and has suffered deeply and to an extent that she cannot avoid using metaphors for and unconscious references to the illness.

There are further clues in the note that indicate that Patsy may have written it: the word 'attaché' in the note has an acute accent on the e, as does JonBenét's name. Also, there is a correction to the note: the word 'not' is inserted into a sentence using a symbol used by proof-readers – and Patsy had majored in journalism and had experience of proofreading.

Theory that Patsy wrote the ransom note but did not kill JonBenét
If either Burke or John Ramsey killed JonBenét, Patsy may still have written the ransom note. In the case of Burke's being the murderer (see above) this would have been as part of the cover-up to protect him and make it appear that the killer was, if not an intruder, someone from outside of the immediate family. If John killed the child, especially during a sex game that went wrong, Patsy might have feared the calamitous effects of this being made

public, and therefore the misleading ransom note may have been a deliberate means of diverting attention from John Ramsey.

Theory that Patsy both wrote the ransom note and killed JonBenét

If the report of Yeager and Knoke is to be believed, Patsy was suffering from a mental illness that led them to label her a 'delusional sociopath'. That factor, combined with fundamentalist religious mania, may have caused her to kill JonBenét as a sacrifice to God, perhaps as an offering of thanks for Patsy's own delivery from death from ovarian cancer. If she had done this in a moment of 'madness', John Ramsey may have taken control of the situation and asked Patsy to write the ransom note. In this case, John may well have made phone calls to politicians and police (see above) and lied that it was Burke who had killed the child.

John Ramsey

John Ramsey is in many people's minds still the most likely suspect. The theory is that he was involved in sexual abuse with JonBenét, either by himself or with others, and that during a bondage or torture 'game' an accident took place and JonBenét was strangled. This view is supported by evidence in the autopsy report of damage to the child's vagina – although experts diverge on whether the damage was superficial or was evidence of repeated sexual assault – and semen being found on the body. The view that John Ramsey is guilty is given much credence by the pathologist Cyril Wecht in his analysis of the case, *Who Killed JonBenét Ramsey?*. The Ramseys' paediatrician has always denied any abuse took place; thorough investigations into John Ramsey have all proved negative – and such enquiries included whether he had molested his daughters by his first marriage. It is believed that most paedophiles and child abusers seek out and hoard child pornography; a thorough search of John Ramsey's home and offices, computer files and videotapes found absolutely no evidence of this.

Fleet White
John Ramsey's former friend Fleet White was initially a prime suspect and was interviewed several times. The precise details of the quarrel with John Ramsey are not known – but the disagreement was so deep that the two families, once very close, have not made contact with each other since the day the two men argued.

Revenge of a pageant runner-up
Examining the evidence, this seems unlikely – a far-fetched motive for such a bizarre murder. Whoever killed Jon-Benét undoubtedly had prior knowledge of the layout of the enormous Boulder house, its staircases and which corridors led to which rooms – which seems unlikely in the case of a rival pageant contestant's family. The lack of footprints in the snow leading away from the house is a major indication that the killing was done by one or more members of the Ramsey family.

Too many questions
There are enormous grey areas in the Ramsey case, too many unanswered questions, some of them of as much labyrinthine complexity as the theories as to who was responsible for the murder of JonBenét. From the moment John Ramsey brought the body upstairs the evidence could be considered tainted; police seemed unwilling to make arrests; a vital piece of evidence – the semen stain on the girl's body – was sent to Cellmark Laboratories (the lab responsible for the DNA testing in the OJ Simpson case), who reported that what had been sent was not semen.

Additionally there was tension between police, who wanted to bring charges, particularly against John Ramsey, and the District Attorney, Alex Hunter, who failed to bring those charges. The officer in charge of the case, Steve Thomas, resigned from the police in August 1998, complaining that Hunter had not given his department enough support and that the DA was too co-operative with Ramsey's lawyers. In a contradictory situation another investigator employed by Hunter, Lou Smit, resigned because he believed the Ramseys were innocent but that Hunter was determined to prosecute them anyway.

The Grand Jury issue no indictments
For thirteen months a Grand Jury sat and considered the evidence in the Ramsey case. Thirty thousand items of evidence were submitted for their examination and they listened to many days of testimony from Ramsey associates and forensic experts. Following their secret deliberations they were discharged, and on 13 October 1999 the Boulder County DA, Alex Hunter announced, 'We do not have sufficient evidence to warrant the filing of charges against anyone who has been investigated at this time.' The Ramseys were quoted as being 'relieved' at this outcome.

The Ramseys make further public statements
In March 2000 John and Patsy Ramsey published their book, *The Death of Innocence*. Appearing on an ABC Television network interview with Barbara Walters, they made a plea for investigators to find out who killed JonBenét. John Ramsey said that this was the only way the couple's innocence could be proved. Hinting that they believe that the child was killed by an intruder who was also a friend of the family, Patsy stated, 'Someone killed

our daughter, so we have to start looking. We start at the inner circle and keep moving out.' And John gave his analysis that the killer was 'male . . . a paedophile'.

The Ramseys went on to criticise Boulder police's handling of the murder. Once again, Patsy denied having written the ransom note.

The Death of Innocence and *JonBenét: Inside the Murder Investigation* published

The Ramseys' book was then published. It summarised their own theories about who the killer might be. A paedophile somehow got into the house while its occupants were elsewhere, hid there, and in a bungled kidnap attempt ended up killing JonBenét. The Ramseys itemised some forensic evidence that they believed could lead police to the killer – these included unidentified hand and palm prints and a human hair found on JonBenét's bed.

Only days later, Detective Steve Thomas published his book on the Ramsey case. In *JonBenét: Inside The Ramsey Murder Investigation*, he concluded that Patsy had committed the murder, that the fatal injury to JonBenét may well have been accidental and that John Ramsey had acted to cover this fact up. Thomas also claimed that Patsy wrote the ransom note and since writing it has deliberately altered her handwriting. The Ramseys' attorney, L Lin Wood, called Thomas's accusations 'fiction and utter nonsense'.

Polygraph tests

On 25 May 2000 the Ramseys released the results of lie-detector tests which were widely reported in the news media as being arranged and paid for privately, by them or those close to them. The tests measured their responses when they were asked if they were involved in the murder of JonBenét or if they knew who killed her. Polygraph expert Edward Gelb, who tested the Ramseys, stated that they answered truthfully when they responded in the negative to both questions. Police in Boulder reacted to this by stating that the only polygraph tests results that they would find credible would have to be administered by the FBI. The Ramseys have, so far, declined to take an FBI polygraph test. It is also a matter of public record that John and Patsy Ramsey did not allow themselves to be questioned by police until many months after their daughter's death during which the couple had been willing to be interviewed on television and by newspapers many times.

There is no statute of limitations on the crime of murder in Colorado.

John, Patsy and Burke Ramsey now live in Atlanta, Georgia.

11 Tupac Shakur and Biggie Smalls

'When I die I want to be a living legend'

> – *Tupac Shakur, 'No More Pain'*, All Eyez On Me
> *(Death Row/Interscope Records, 1996)*

Who was Tupac Shakur?

On 16 June 1971, Tupac Amaru Shakur was born in New York City. His mother, Afeni Shakur, born Alice Faye Williams some 24 years previously, had recently been released from the Women's House of Detention in New York following her acquittal of 156 counts relating to her revolutionary activities. Afeni Shakur had joined the Black Panther Party in 1968, and the following year had been arrested and charged along with twenty others – the so-called 'Panther 21' – with conspiracy to bomb banks and department stores. She had been pregnant while in prison. Tupac was not told until he was much older that his father was Billy Garland, a fellow Black Panther.

Afeni had changed her name when she married Mutulu Shakur, a Black Panther and Muslim. He was with Afeni for long enough to have a child with her, Tupac's half-sister Sekyikwa Shakur. In 1986 Mutulu Shakur was convicted for his part in a 1981 robbery in which two police officers and a Brinks security guard were killed. He is currently serving a sixty-year sentence.

In naming herself and her child, Afeni showed an awareness of both Muslim and ancient South American traditions: the name Shakur is Arabic for 'Thankful to God'; Tupac Amaru is the name of an Inca warrior and translates as 'shining serpent'. However, there is some confusion as to Tupac's own legal name: the name given out in police statements following Shakur's death is 'Lesane Parish Crooks, a.k.a. Tupac Shakur'. It is not known from where the name Crooks originated and this may well have been an error by police.

Tupac was born in the era of vocal black nationalism in the US, and in the midst of campaigns to free the Black Panther leader Huey Newton, the activist Angela Davis and Geronimo Pratt, a leading Black Panther activist – Pratt was Tupac's godfather, and had been handed a life sentence for murdering a white woman in Los Angeles. The early 1970s were also a highly creative and exciting period in African-American popular music, whose lyrics now reflected the genuine black experience of inner-city America. This too would have an influence on Tupac Shakur, both politically and artistically.

Tupac was raised by his mother in what can only be described as poverty, moving in and out of whatever accommodation could be found in Harlem and the Bronx, even living in shelters for the homeless from time to time. His mother used to take Tupac and his sister to the House of the Lord Church in Brooklyn, where the ten-year-old boy would tell the pastor there, the Rev. Herbert Daughtry, that when he grew up he wanted to be a revolutionary. Daughtry, an activist preacher, encouraged the young Tupac in his ideals and in particular in his interest in drama; Tupac expressed himself by writing plays. At the age of twelve Tupac joined a Harlem theatre group, the 127th Street Ensemble, where he played the role of an alienated young boy named Travis in *A Raisin in the Sun*. That same year a figure on the New York drugs scene known as 'Legs' – whom Tupac eagerly accepted as a father figure – had come to live with the Shakur family. Legs introduced Afeni to the smoking of crack cocaine.

In 1985 the family – minus Legs, who had been arrested for credit-card fraud – moved to Baltimore. Shortly after their arrival Legs died of a heart attack after a crack-pipe session.

Settled in Baltimore and attending junior high school there, Tupac started listening to and imitating the rap music that was an integral part of 1980s hip-hop culture. In 1986 Tupac began studying ballet and acting at the Baltimore School for the Arts. His rap skills were still being developed; his pride in his Bronx and Harlem background reflected in his renaming himself MC New York.

Tupac never graduated from school in Baltimore. In 1988 his mother, by this time addicted to crack and also wary of the street crime and gun violence that was becoming more prevelant in the black sections of Baltimore, moved herself and her children again, this time to Marin City in Northern California. Marin City turned out to be a crime-ridden ghetto area despite its close proximity to Marin County, which, per capita, has the wealthiest residents in the entire United States.

Tupac was badly affected by leaving the School for the Arts, and once in Marin he left home and began selling crack on the streets. He also became a part of the Marin City rap scene, joining groups such as Strictly Dope and the One Nation Emcees. He developed his own rapping style of lyrical directness, with subject matter the hardships faced by young blacks on the street. In 1990, having gained a manager, Leila Steinberg, he joined the black pop-rap outfit Digital Underground on tour, first as a road-crew member, then as a dancer and rapper. He appeared on their album *Sons of the P*.

With subsequent royalties and money earned on the tour he bought himself a car and several firearms. He was offered a part in Ernest Dickerson's movie *Juice*, which he accepted and played the part of Bishop, a violent and tough street kid. The film director John Singleton told *Vibe* magazine how impressed he was by Tupac in *Juice*, calling him 'an actor who could portray the ultimate crazy nigga'. On the strength of this, Singleton subsequently directed Tupac in *Poetic Justice*. But, according to friends of Tupac, some of the character of Bishop rubbed off on the aspiring actor and rapper, and he became a harder, tougher individual. Tupac had his 'Thug Life' tattoo done at the time of filming *Juice*.

By 1991 he had his first recording deal with the Time-Warner subsidiary Interscope Records, and the following year released the album *2Pacalypse Now*. The record – an angry statement in the mould of NWA's *Straight Outta Compton* or Public Enemy's *Fear of a Black Planet* – would draw on the same violent, anti-police and firearms-oriented lyrics employed by those artists. Vice-President Dan Quayle publicly attacked the lyrics for their violence and mysogyny. In the track 'I Don't Give a Fuck' Tupac envisaged black alienation, unrelenting gun culture and even – not for the last time – a violent death for himself.

His first serious criminal charges also date from this period – he was accused of battery for hitting a woman who demanded his autograph. He also pleaded guilty to misdemeanour assault charges following the use of a baseball bat against another performer at a show at Michigan State University.

Tupac's film career started around this time with the release of *Juice*. Other films he appeared in included *Gridlock'd* and the ironically titled *Bulletin* and *Gang Related*. The gold-selling album *Thug Life Vol. 1* was released in 1993.

That same year he served ten days in jail for assaulting a member of his audience during a performance, and was arrested, though not charged, for shooting two men in Atlanta, Georgia. While driving to his hotel during a stay in Atlanta, Tupac had intervened in an argument in which he saw two white men reach into the window of a car in front of him – believing the man in the car to be a black victim of an assault. As Tupac challenged the two men, the car sped off, leaving the pair, brothers and off-duty police officers, Scott and Mark Whitwell, facing Tupac and several cars behind him containing Tupac's friends. Fearing trouble, Mark Whitwell reached for his gun, to which Tupac responded by shooting at the brothers. One was shot in the stomach and the other in his posterior. Both survived. Tupac was later charged with assault, but these charges were later dropped.

That same year he was also briefly jailed for assault and battery on Albert and Allen Hughes, the directors of *Menace II Society*, who had fired Tupac from the cast of that movie. In November of that year Tupac and three others were accused of raping, sodomising and sexually abusing nineteen-year-old Ayanna Jackson in an incident in Tupac's Manhattan hotel room.

In early 1994 he released his second (and eventually platinum-selling) album, *Strictly 4 My N.I.G.G.A.Z.* In March 1994 the film *Above the Rim* was released, in which Tupac played the role of a drug dealer. In November of that year, Tupac's trial began for the charges arising from the alleged sex attack on Ayanna Jackson. On the day that the jury at his trial were considering their verdict, he was shot five times, including once in the genitals, and robbed at a recording studio in Times Square. This, Tupac believed, was a deliberate attack by rivals in the music business (see below). On 1 December 1994 Shakur was found not guilty of sodomy and weapons charges, but guilty of sexual abuse. In January 1995 he started serving his four-and-a-half-year sentence, of which he actually served a total of eleven months.

While he was in the Clinton Correctional Facility in New York, to which he had been moved from Riker's Island, his new album, *Me Against the World*, was released. In October 1995 Tupac was released from jail and signed with Death Row Records, whose boss, Marion 'Suge' Knight, had paid the $1.4 million bond required to free the rapper. Tupac rapidly recorded the double album *All Eyez On Me*, which was released in February 1996 – within two and a half months, this achieved five-times-platinum sales. By this time Shakur was the most popular rap artist in the world, an instantly recognisable icon whose body was etched with dramatic tattoos – most famously the words 'Thug Life' spelled out on his stomach below a semiautomatic machine gun, 'Fuck The World' across his shoulder blades and 'Laugh Now, Cry Later' on his back. He wore a huge gold cruficix and enormous diamond and gold rings on each hand. His lyrics featured his boast that he was a powerful 'player' capable of devastating violence, but also repeatedly and in detail predicted a violent death by the gun for himself.

30 November 1994 – Tupac shot in Times Square

Tupac was in New York, awaiting the verdict of the jury in the weapons and sex charges. Always willing to appear on other people's records for cash in hand, Tupac had been contacted by a man named Booker, who wanted him to go to the studio with a New York rapper called Little Shawn. The fee for the recording session was agreed at $7,000, and then Booker and Tupac had an argument over the telephone when Booker said he didn't have the money; after Tupac insisted on being paid, Booker gave in and said that Little Shawn's record company, Uptown Entertainment, would definitely front him the money. Partly due to this heated disagreement, Tupac was nervous about dealing with Booker, but he badly needed the money.

Having stopped en route to buy some 'chronic', Tupac arrived at Quad Recording Studios at twenty minutes past midnight. As he walked into the foyer, accompanied by his sister, her boyfriend and two other friends, two black men dressed in army fatigues approached Tupac, pointing pistols in his direction. He was told to get down on the floor and to hand over his cash and jewellery. Shakur immediately reached for his own gun – the two men responded by shooting him in the genitals. He was then punched and kicked and his jewellery was forcibly removed. The men shot him another four times in his chest, head, arm and leg. According to his own account of the events in *Vibe* magazine, Tupac feigned unconsciousness during the attack. When the gunmen fled, Tupac's friends – none of whom had been hurt by the gunmen – came to his aid. Seeing police outside, they didn't leave the foyer, but instead went towards the studio in the building, where the rapper Biggie Smalls was recording at the time. An ambulance was called and Tupac was taken to hospital. He had been shot five times. One bullet had gone through his head and caused him to black out. After surgery to remove bullets and also one of his testicles, Tupac horrified hospital staff by checking himself out of the hospital because he feared that the gunmen would try to find him there and finish the job. (Radio bulletins referring to the shooting were sampled at the start of Tupac's album *Me Against the World*, which was released while he was in jail on Riker's Island serving time on the sex charges.)

Attempts by police to investigate this attack were hampered by Tupac's unwillingness to co-operate with enquiries. No suspect emerged until almost a year after Tupac's death, when one Walter Johnson, whose alias was 'King Tut' – a person unconnected with the music business or gangs, who had been a sixteen-year-old known criminal at the time of the attack in the studio foyer – told an unnamed police informant that he had shot Shakur because the rapper wasn't a real gangster.

Tupac came to suspect that Biggie Smalls and Sean 'Puffy' Combs had set up the shooting. Smalls and Combs were to the East Coast what Shakur and Suge Knight were to the West Coast – a gifted rap artist and the highly entrepreneurial producer and owner of a record label. During the eleven months Tupac spent in jail for the sexual charges his mind dwelled on the shooting and he convinced himself that his East Coast rivals were responsible for setting him up. In an interview from prison with Kevin Powell, published in *Vibe* magazine in April 1995, Tupac maintained his innocence on the rape charge and spoke in detail about the Times Square shooting, accusing Puffy and Biggy of being behind the incident. In the August edition of *Vibe*, Puffy and Biggy replied to Shakur's accusations. Combs claimed he would never try to hurt anyone, and of Tupac he said, 'I ain't never had no beef with that man . . . I pray for him.'

Biggie claimed that Tupac's accusations were 'shit' but 'he always gonna be my man.'

In January 1996 Tupac's single 'California Love' was released; it reached No. 1 in the US charts. Seeing Tupac's video on MTV, Suge Knight realised that Tupac could be made into a megastar, and contacted him in prison, anxious to sign him up for a three-album deal with Death Row. Knight provided the bail money to get Tupac out of Riker's Island – $1.4 million – while an appeal against his conviction was being heard. Following his release Shakur became an incredibly prolific artist for Death Row, recording some two hundred songs in the year before he was fatally shot.

Crips, Bloods and Death Row Records

Black gangs have been active in the downtown Los Angeles area since the 1920s, when black people started moving south from central LA, eventually displacing the white population, which moved out in response to the new influx of racial minorities. Districts such as Compton and

Watts are nowadays between 90 and 95 per cent non-white. The first black gangs in the 1920s and 1930s were based upon criminal activities such as prostitution and robbery. During the 1940s, further gangs evolved, the best known being the Purple Hearts and the 31st Street and 28th Street gangs, who specialised in protection rackets.

By the 1950s new gangs with names such as Low Riders, Road Devils and Coasters appeared, whose members' activities were based on the cars they drove. These gangs, like their predecessors, were highly territorial. Disputes took place between members of gangs who had strayed into each other's 'hoods' (neighbourhoods), but, unlike the gangs of today, they settled scores with fists, baseball bats, chains and knives. During the 1960s some black gangsters became involved in the Black Panther movement; it was during this time that the use of firearms became more prevalent.

At the end of that decade a high school gang was started named the Avenue Cribs or Baby Avenues; somewhere along the line the name became Crips, and gangs calling themselves by that name spread to the East and West sides of the 110 Harbor Freeway (East and West Side Crips) and to Compton. Existing gangs renamed themselves as Crips; early gangs included the Main St Crips, 5 Deuce Crips and Rolling 20 Crips. As the Crip gangs multiplied during the 1970s, a rival set of gangs was born – the Bloods. Crip gangs wore blue clothing – 'colors' that made gang members instantly recognisable.

Although he was born in New York, by the time of his death Tupac's allegiances were with the West rather than the East coast. And the record label he was contracted to, Death Row, owned by Suge Knight, had connections with and was staffed largely by members and former members of the Bloods gang. When Tupac signed with Death Row, the label's biggest success to date was Dr Dre's *The Chronic* album, released in 1992, an album that explicitly celebrated the joys of smoking strong marijuana, the machismo of the 'gangsta' life, the denigration of 'hoes' and 'bitches' and even the LA Rodney King riots. Death Row followed this with Snoop Doggy Dogg's *Doggystyle*, another huge success for the label, with the dreadlocked rapper (real name Calvin Broadus, who shortly before the album's release had faced a murder charge on which he was acquitted) performing raps on similar themes.

In the 1980s Snoop had been a member of the Rolling 20 Crips in Long Beach; by the time he was recording for Death Row he had served time, mainly for drugs offences. Tupac's first album for Death Row was influenced both by Dre and Snoop. On the cover of *All Eyez On Me* he appears giving the Westside gang hand signal.

Once taken on by Death Row, Tupac became fiercely loyal to Suge Knight, who after all had got him out of jail and was now showering him with money. Death Row records was staffed by gang members, for the most part Bloods who were friends of Suge Knight. Many of them carried guns, as did members of the rival Crips gang, some of whom also worked or hung out at Death Row. Violence and intimidation were daily occurrences in the Death Row offices.

About Biggie Smalls

BIG, also known as Biggie Smalls (real name Christopher Wallace), was a former crack cocaine dealer. He was a large man, over six feet tall and weighing three hundred pounds, and his rap demo tape had been played to the producer and record company boss Sean 'Puffy' Combs, who had signed him to Uptown Records, where he was head of artist development. Sacked from his job at Uptown in 1993, Combs re-signed BIG, this time to his own Bad Boy label. Combs had formed the company as an East Coast version of Death Row. In a *Rolling Stone* interview Combs said, 'Bad Boy was kinda modelled after Death Row because Death Row had become a movement.' Notorious BIG's *Ready To Die* was released in 1995. It was a platinum album, selling more than a million copies in the USA.

During the previous year, before the Times Square shooting, BIG had been a friend of Tupac's in New York and the two had hung out together, smoking 'chronic' and discussing their music and Tupac's imminent rape trial. However, increasing rivalry between Death Row and Bad Boy came between them, as both companies became more and more successful, and a series of events escalated this rivalry into a fully fledged feud.

The feud

The first sign of tension between Bad Boy and Death Row came at the awards ceremony run by the hip-hop magazine *Source* in August 1995. Suge Knight went up to Puffy and insulted him publicly over a dispute he was having with a disabled former Crips gang member named Mike Concepcion. According to Ronin Ro, Suge states that he said to Combs, 'How you let a motherfucker in a wheelchair whup you ass?' Combs then presented Snoop Doggy Dogg with an award for Artist of the Year, after which he made a speech asking for unity between the East and West coasts. Later on Daz, a member of Tha Dogg Pound (signed to Death Row), went on stage and addressed the audience, telling them, 'Y'all can eat this dick.'

On 24 September 1995, Suge Knight and Puffy Combs were to meet again. At a party in Atlanta, Jake Robles, a close friend of Suge Knight, was shot by an unknown gunman. He was hospitalised and died a week later. The press accused one of Combs's cousins of being the killer, but Puffy denied that this was the case. Suge was of the opinion that the bullets that had ended Robles's life had been intended for him and that Robles had died protecting Suge from the gunman.

With a perceived threat on his life, as far as Suge was concerned this was now a serious feud. Also by now there would be no doubt Suge had his own opinions on who had been responsible for the 1994 Times Square attack on Tupac. Puffy spoke again about the shooting, claiming that Tupac knew who was responsible, but that he was unwilling to say who they were – Combs stated that Tupac 'knows he's not gonna get away with that shit. To me, that's some real sucker shit'.

Towards the end of 1995, as news of the feud hit the national press, Suge, possibly only half joking, suggested a boxing match between Puffy and Tupac. In private, his rage against Combs and Bad Boy was increasing. Knight became angry with a *Vibe* reporter who was asking questions about the death of Jake Robles. When Death Row released *All Eyez On Me* in February 1996, the record included barbs aimed at Biggie Smalls, and in the track 'Heartz of Men' hinted at revenge – 'Y'all gotta be careful who you fuck with'. Despite this, in an interview with *Vibe* in February 1996, Tupac denied any feud, echoing Combs's words in the same publication some six months earlier by saying, 'I don't got no beef with nobody, man.' In the same interview he went on to claim that Biggie Smalls had become successful by borrowing Tupac's rap style and given it a New York slant.

The personal animosity between the two rappers intensified. Tupac went on to claim he had slept with Faith Evans, a performer and songwriter whom Biggie had married and was now separated from, performing a song in which he proclaimed, 'I fucked your bitch, you fat motherfucker'. In his song 'Who Shot Ya?', written after Tupac had accused Smalls and Combs of being behind the 1994 shooting, Biggie taunted Tupac by rapping, 'You'll die slow but calm . . . front-page nigga'. Tupac responded with 'Hit 'Em Up' by directly attacking his perceived enemies with the words 'Fuck Biggie, Fuck Bad Boy . . . die slow, motherfucker'.

At the *Soul Train* awards in 1996 there was a confrontation between Tupac and Biggie. Insults were exchanged between both entourages, and someone, allegedly in Tupac's crew, drew a gun.

Whatever incidents happened, and whatever insults were exchanged on record, when talking to the press in 1996 both rappers downplayed the animosity between them, with Tupac maintaining that Biggie, despite their differences of opinion, was still a brother.

Las Vegas – Saturday, 7 September 1996

The hotels, motels and casinos on the famous Strip of downtown Las Vegas were filled with boxing fans from all over the US and the world. That evening 'Iron Mike' Tyson was to fight Bruce Seldon in a heavyweight bout at the MGM Grand. Among the 16,000 people packed into the arena was the rap star Tupac Shakur, the Death Row record company boss Marion 'Suge' Knight and their entourage of friends and bodyguards, mainly from Compton, South Los Angeles. Typically, Tupac had been the centre of some attention during his entry into the hotel and the arena, with fans taking photographs and asking for autographs, despite the heavy security with which he surrounded himself.

The fight lasted exactly 109 seconds, and, to the surprise of no one, was a victory for Tyson, who managed in such a short time to get in fifty punches at his opponent. Some spectators, more disappointed at the brevity of the fight than its outcome, started booing the boxers.

As they left the Grand via the backstage area, there was a violent altercation between members of Tupac's entourage and one Orlando Anderson from Compton, Los

Angeles. Travon Lane, a friend of Suge Knight's and a member of the LA Bloods (a gang fraternity identified by their wearing red colours), recognised Anderson as one of seven members of the rival Crips gang (their colour was blue) who, the previous July, had forcibly snatched a gold chain with the Death Row emblem from his neck. Security video footage taken of the Las Vegas incident shows Tupac, Suge Knight and others beating and kicking Anderson. Anderson was quite seriously beaten – 'stomped' in the words of one participant. When security at the hotel came to Anderson's aid, Tupac, Suge and co. fled. When questioned, Anderson stated that he did not wish to press any charges, and he too went on his way.

Tupac Shakur returned to his room at the Luxor hotel, where he was staying with his girlfriend Kidada Jones (daughter of the record producer Quincy Jones) and changed his clothes. He had left his bulletproof vest behind in Los Angeles, not believing he was in any serious danger in Las Vegas. Tupac and his friends then left the Luxor in an assortment of luxury cars, driving to Suge Knight's residence before making their way to a benefit party – $75 admission to members of the public – which Mike Tyson would be attending at Club 662, a nightclub some two miles away, run by Suge Knight. The number 662 had not been chosen for any innocent reason – 662 as a phone-dialling code spells out MOB, which it is alleged stood for 'Members of Blood', Suge Knight's favoured LA gang.

Tupac's and Suge's bodyguards were not armed, as they did not expect gang-related violence to occur outside of Los Angeles. Also, both private security and the Las Vegas Metropolitan Police were much in evidence at the MGM Grand, and also outside Suge's house and Club 662 – Suge Knight had requested specifically African-American off-duty police officers, and these were duly dispatched, the cost being billed to Death Row Records.

Having left the Luxor Hotel's car park, the entourage of between six and fifteen cars, among them Suge driving his black BMW with Tupac in the passenger seat, headed east towards Club 662. The top of the car was down and loud rap music was blaring out when Suge stopped at a red light by the Maxim Hotel, on the edge of the Strip. The area at the time was full of pedestrians. To the right of the BMW there pulled up a white Cadillac, one of whose four passengers – all black men – started firing bullets from a high-calibre gun, aiming at Tupac and Suge. Tupac attempted to hide in the back seat of the car, and while doing so was shot twice in the chest as well as in the arm and leg. The incident was over in seconds. Even so, according to some eyewitnesses, members of Tupac's entourage in other cars fired several rounds at the Cadillac.

Two of Suge's car tyres were blown out before the white Cadillac drove rapidly away from the scene, pursued by at least six cars from Tupac's convoy, the others remaining to assist Suge and Tupac. The car with the gunman, however, managed to leave Las Vegas. Meanwhile, drivers and pedestrians stopped and stared at the BMW riddled with bullets and with its occupants covered in blood and glass.

Thirteen bullets had been fired, five of them going right through the passenger door. Suge, amazingly unharmed but for bullet fragments to the head, asked Tupac if he had been shot. 'I'm hit,' he replied from the back seat. Despite the blown-out tyres, Suge succeeded in driving the car away with the intention of getting Tupac, now lying in the back seat in a pool of blood but apparently fully conscious and able to maintain a conversation with Suge, to a doctor.

Police, who had heard gunshots, arrived – on mountain bicycles – and failed to secure the crime scene for a good twenty minutes. The justification for this was that they felt it more important to go after Suge's crippled BMW and the convoy of vehicles. Evidence that may have given police some clue as to the identity of the gunmen may well have been lost as pedestrians and cars were allowed to enter the road at the spot where the shooting had taken place.

Suge's speeding BMW had gone down the Strip, through a red light and down Las Vegas Boulevard. At about a mile from the scene of the shooting the vehicle – by now with all of its tyres flat – and its pursuing entourage came to a halt in the middle of the road. At this point police and Highway Patrol cars, ambulances and fire department trucks converged in a cacophony of sirens. Cops ordered everyone out of their vehicles and forced them to lie on the ground with their hands behind their heads. Even the badly bleeding Suge Knight was subjected to this treatment. Paramedics on the scene assessed Tupac's condition and called for emergency response teams, who took the still conscious Tupac, who was now having breathing difficulties, to the Las Vegas University Medical Center, where he was admitted to the intensive-care department and prepared for emergency surgery. In the operating theatre, Tupac underwent an investigative operation and those bullets that could be found were removed. Following this surgery, a hospital spokesman told reporters that Shakur was back in his hospital room and that his condition was 'critical'. Tupac was on a life-support ventilator and respirator, and in a virtual coma due to painkilling and sedative drugs. He was visited by his mother, his aunt and others, including Suge Knight, Mike Tyson, Kidada Jones and the Reverend Jesse Jackson, who had been in town for the big fight.

The news of the shooting had now spread via news media to the whole of the US and beyond. Crowds gathered outside the hospital, some holding photographs of Tupac. On 8 September Las Vegas Metropolitan Police Department issued a statement giving details of the attack on the BMW and asking for information. Apparently members of the Death Row entourage had not been able to provide the police with much in the way of further details. Sergeant Kevin Manning of the LVMPD commented, 'They were not quite candid.'

Suge Knight, having said he was too busy being visited in his hospital bed to talk to police, was able to leave for his Las Vegas home by midday on the day following the shooting. On 9 September, security in the trauma unit in the University Medical Center was increased, as gang violence became a theory for the attack. Back in the operating theatre, Tupac's right lung, badly injured by a bullet, was removed.

The following day media speculation turned on the public rivalry between West Coast-based Death Row Records and the New York-based Bad Boy Entertainment. On 11 September, a man connected with the Southside Crip gang was shot dead in his vehicle. Word on the street was that this had been done in retaliation for the attack on Tupac. And Suge Knight finally brought himself to the Las Vegas Police Department for interview, while investigators watched the security video taken at the MGM Grand in which Orlando Anderson was attacked.

The following day Tupac's condition worsened. A statement from a trauma centre doctor spoke of 'a very fatal injury' and gave the shot rapper a one-in-five chance of survival. At 4.03 p.m. on 13 September, Tupac died of his injuries. Cause of death was given as respiratory failure and cardiopulmonary arrest. Crowds gathered outside the hospital. Visitors arrived, including, briefly, Suge Knight.

His death was a turning point in African-American culture – rap music would never be the same again. 'Gangsta' fantasies and paranoia had become reality – and, if rumours were to be believed, the slaying of Tupac would be avenged by other deaths.

Aftermath of the shooting – the downfall of Suge Knight

The year 1996 had not been a good one for Suge Knight. True, he had signed Tupac to Death Row, but now his star artist was dead. In February, bowing to government and shareholder pressure over the violent content of the label's output, Death Row had been dropped by its distributors Time-Warner. The label was picked up by Universal for the sum of $200 million, but Death Row now faced certain conditions – Universal could refuse to issue material that it considered offensive. Also that year Dr Dre left the label, not liking the violent culture he felt it engendered.

But worse was to come. The shit was starting to hit the fan. Death Row was being sued for $1.7 million by American Express – debts that had been run up on platinum credit cards and left unpaid. After Tupac's death his mother Afeni filed a suit claiming $17 million in royalties from Death Row that she claimed Suge Knight had been withholding. He was facing criminal charges, having failed to appear for a mandatory drugs test on two occasions and therefore having violated probation conditions for an earlier offence. On 22 October 1996 Suge appeared in court in Los Angeles, from which he was taken into custody. Additonally, the videotape footage of the fight with Orlando Anderson at the MGM Grand on the night of the Tyson fight and the shooting of Tupac had surfaced, and Knight would face charges for his part in that as well as for his probation violations.

At the trial, the judge ruled that Knight had been an active participant in the beating of Anderson, and that he now faced a long sentence. Strangely, none of the others involved in the beating of Anderson, all of whom were clearly identifiable in the security video, were ever charged. Nor did the Las Vegas police file a crime report

– so technically the assault on Anderson was never reported as a crime.

The Justice Department was also now in the process of investigating Knight's links to street gangs and the Mafia and Death Row's involvement in tax evasion, money laundering and drug dealing. Knight denied all the allegations, and claimed he was a victim of racism. In an interview with the *Los Angeles Times* he answered his own question – 'A black brother from Compton creates a company that helps people in the ghetto, so what does the government do? They try to bring him down.'

On 28 February 1997 Suge Knight was sentenced to nine years in prison. After a brief spell in North Kern State Prison in Bakersfield, California, Knight was moved to a medium-to-high-security jail, the California Men's Colony East near San Luis Obispo.

The police investigation

Three Las Vegas Metropolitan Police Department homicide detectives – Sergeant Kevin Manning, Detective Brent Becker and Detective Mike Franks – arrived at the scene of the shooting about an hour and a half after the shots were fired. Many witnesses, including people travelling in the cars accompanying Tupac, were interviewed. Not one of them could describe the men with guns, and many of them denied having seen anything or even having been there. Mistrust of the police and fear of being labelled as a police informant ran deep.

Suge Knight was asked on an ABC-TV news programme if he would tell the police who had killed Tupac if he knew their identity, and he replied that he would not: 'I don't get paid to solve homicides. I don't get paid to tell on people.'

The nearest police got to a description was that the Cadillac the assailants were driving was light in colour, possibly white. Police were astonished that not even Tupac's professional, trained bodyguards could recall any detail of the gunmen. No aerial photos were taken following the shooting, no helicopter was used by police to try to track down the light-coloured car and no closed-circuit TV camera footage could be found that would shed any light on the attackers.

Police succeeded in securing the scene where Suge and Tupac's car had stopped, and took detailed photographs. A dog team was brought in to search for the gun used to shoot Tupac, as someone had told police they saw a gun being thrown out of the Cadillac as it sped off. However, as we have seen, the actual scene of the shooting was secured only some twenty minutes after police arrived at Suge's wrecked BMW. Witnesses at that spot would have disappeared by now, and any forensic evidence left at the site could have been disturbed.

What police did know was that apparently there were four men, all African-Americans, in the Cadillac and that shots were fired from inside the vehicle, most likely from the back seat. Police also had shell casings and bullets taken from Suge's car.

There was one witness who was willing to talk. Yafeu Fula, a young rapper, had been in the Lexus car behind Suge and Tupac, and claimed he had seen the gunman. After the shooting, the LVMPD failed to question Fula in any detail. They later attempted to rectify this, by which time Fula had obviously reconsidered his willingness to testify and could be contacted only through a Death Row attorney. Two months after the Las Vegas shooting, on 13 November 1996, Fula was fatally shot in the hallway of his girlfriend's apartment in Irvington, New Jersey. The two juveniles charged with his murder were said to have no connection with gangs and Fula's death was in no way related to what he may have known about Tupac's killer. The only witness willing to talk to police was now dead.

Who killed Tupac?

What was the motive for killing Tupac? The three most likely ones are:

- the tension between Death Row and Bad Boy that reflected rivalry between the West and East Coast rap scenes

- the long-standing conflict between the Mob Pirus, a Blood faction from Compton to whom Shakur and Suge Knight were affiliated, and the Crips; possibly escalated by the contretemps with Orlando Anderson (allegedly a member of the Southside Crips) shortly before the shooting

- Tupac was killed by conspiring record company bosses; his death would be a quick way of selling more records.

Rumours spread rapidly after Tupac's death; and Sean 'Puffy' Combs and Biggie Smalls figured largely in those rumours. Puffy and Biggie have always denied any involement in Tupac's death.

More realistic speculation centred on whether the killing of Tupac was gang-related, and specifically whether the bullets that killed him were intended for Suge Knight. There may well have been reasons why eyewitnesses claimed that they had not seen the faces of the man or men who shot Tupac – if the killers had been enemies of Knight from Los Angeles, then some sort of revenge killing would have taken place.

If the killing of Tupac was not not gang-related, the violence that resulted in Los Angeles in the days after his death certainly was. There were three fatalities and many shooting incidents as the Bloods, seeking revenge for the death of Shakur, attacked the Southside Crips.

An alternative scenario is that the men in the Cadillac were members of a Las Vegas-based gang that had Crip connections. Yet another theory is that the killers were driving around Las Vegas and chanced upon Tupac Shakur heading a convoy of expensive cars; they had guns, and could not resist firing them.

Suge Knight has always regarded the idea that he plotted Tupac's death as ridiculous; it does seem far-fetched, particularly as Knight himself was injured during the shooting and was sitting in the same line of fire as the wounded rapper. However, Knight was under suspicion for the murder, as he had taken out an insurance policy, said to be worth some $4 million, on Tupac's life.

Was Orlando Anderson the killer – or did the assault on him trigger off a revenge attack?

Orlando Anderson did make a statement to police after Tupac was shot, but the LVMPD have never revealed what he said. On 2 October 1996, Los Angeles police arrested Anderson at his girlfriend's apartment in connection with a local murder. They were accompanied by Las Vegas cops, who were there to question him further about Tupac. Neither police force was able to bring charges. In an interview with *Vibe* magazine in December 1997, 22-year-old Anderson discussed the events of 7 September the previous year. Proclaiming his innocence of the murder of Tupac, he claimed the fight outside the MGM Grand was started by Tupac, denied that he was a Crip gang member, said he had received numerous threats as a result of media speculation. William Shaw, in his excellent book on the rap culture of Southcentral Los Angeles, describes how a confidential informant told the Compton police, on the day before Tupac died, that local Pirus had heard that Travon Lane, a gang member who was with Tupac during the assault on Anderson, had said that the man who shot Tupac was the same man who had been beaten up outside the MGM Grand. It is surprising that with such circumstantial evidence the LAPD were able to obtain a warrant for Anderson's arrest.

Anderson's life after the death of Tupac seems to have been one dogged by fear. In public, he would be pointed at as 'the man that shot Tupac'.

On the afternoon of 29 May 1998, Orlando and his friend Michael Dorrough got into an argument with Michael Stone, a Corner Pocket Crip, and Stone's cousin Jerry. The dispute was apparently over a debt. A gun battle broke out between them. Only Dorrough survived. Orlando Anderson had lived to the age of 24.

The death of Biggie Smalls

On 9 March 1997 Biggie Smalls attended a party to mark the annual Soul Train Music Awards. The function was held at the Petersen Automotive Museum in Los Angeles. Biggie was celebrating: he had won the award for best lyricist. The party was ended when fire department inspectors declared that there were too many people inside the building. At 12.35 a.m., Biggie got into the front seat of his car next to his bodyguard and driver D-Rock. In the back was Biggie's friend, the vocalist Li'l Caesar. Biggie's car drove off behind another vehicle carrying Sean 'Puffy' Combs; following close behind was a third vehicle, a Chevy Blazer, in which were Biggie's and Puffy's security guards. When the cars stopped at the junction between Wilshire Boulevard and Fairfax Avenue, a car pulled up alongside Biggie. Aiming a nine-millimetre pistol at Biggie, a gunman in the car let out a fusillade of shots. Biggie received seven bullets. The dark car that the gunman had been driven in escaped at speed. Puffy got out of his car and attended to the unconscious and heavily bleeding rapper; Biggie's driver, accompanied by Combs, then drove the seriously injured Biggie to the Cedars-Sinai Hospital, where he was pronounced dead on arrival.

Twenty police were assigned to find Biggie's murderer. The witnesses in the car with Biggie were able to give a description of the gunman, an African-American in his early twenties. Investigators had no doubt the killing was gang-related. The LAPD were hopeful of making an early arrest of the suspected killer, but, as the weeks and then months went by, they realised that, as in the murder of Tupac Shakur, people were just not willing to talk openly.

Biggie's second album, *Life After Death*, was released a few weeks after he was murdered. The cover artwork included a hearse with the registration plate BIG, and the final track, whose lyrics made reference to Tupac Shakur, was entitled 'You're Nobody (Til Somebody Kills You)'.

Who shot Biggie?

On 20 April 1999, LAPD investigators headed for Death Row's offices in Beverly Hills, to search for evidence linking the record company to the death of Biggie Smalls. Warrants were served on four premises with links to Suge Knight. Police stated that their investigations had now led them to conclude that the shooting had been well planned and had been accomplished by a professional hit man, which led them to believe that the imprisoned Suge Knight was a key suspect. It was implied that he may have hired a gunman to shoot Biggie dead as retaliation for the death of Tupac. Sean Combs was interviewed, as were various LA gang members.

It is not known what Suge Knight may have said to the LAPD when they questioned him in jail. To date there have been no arrests for the murder of Biggie Smalls, and police appear no nearer to solving the crime.

Public fascination with Tupac and Biggie has not ceased, and their posthumous record releases have all sold well. Suge Knight is alive, but in jail. Sean 'Puffy' Combs, renaming himself Puff Daddy, is one of the most successful writer/producer/rappers in the USA.

12 Further Unsolved Murders: Marilyn Sheppard, Janice Weston and Caroline Dickinson

The Murder of Marilyn Sheppard

After midnight on Saturday 3 July 1954, a wealthy osteopath, Dr Sam Sheppard, and his wife Marilyn, who was four months pregnant, had said goodbye to their neighbours, Don and Nancy Ahern, whom they had entertained at their home in the Bay Village district of Cleveland. Their seven-year-old son, Sam Reese Sheppard, who was nicknamed Chip, was asleep in his room, when Marilyn went upstairs to go to bed, while her thirty-year-old husband stayed downstairs and watched television. He dozed off, and woke up some hours later, having thought he heard Marilyn shouting downstairs for him.

Disoriented and groggy with sleep, he went upstairs and in his wife's bedroom he could see the dim outline of two people struggling in the half-light. Then he was knocked out by a violent blow from behind. Recovering, he found himself prostrate on the bedroom floor and saw the bloody form of Marilyn. He examined her and found that she had no pulse. Anxious about what might have happened to his son, he went into the boy's bedroom, where he was sleeping peacefully. Hearing the sound of an intruder downstairs, he went down and looked out of the back door, where he saw a man running away from the house. The vanishing figure was that of a tall man, with dark bushy hair, who was wearing a white shirt. Dr Sheppard sprinted towards the man and managed to grab him. A struggle ensued, in which Sheppard found himself being choked, and he then fell out of consciousness. When he came to, he ran back into the house and entered the bedroom where Marilyn lay. It was 4.50 in the morning when Sam Sheppard telephoned a neighbour named Spencer Houk who was the Mayor of Bay Village. Houk and his wife drove over to the Sheppard residence and were met by the shaken Dr Sheppard, who in the past few hours had twice been made unconscious by acts of violence. Sheppard showed Spencer Houk the body of Marilyn in the bedroom; Houk immediately called police.

Police and detectives investigate

At 6.02 a local police officer arrived, Fred Drenkhan. The officer went up to see the scene of the crime and was horrified at the bloody sight that met him. Detectives Gareau and Schottke of the Cleveland police department were summoned to the Sheppard house. Examining the property, they found no suspicious fingerprints and no sign that the house had been broken into. Meanwhile, Sheppard had been taken to the local hospital to have his injuries attended to. They included damage to his upper spine and neck, bruising to his face and damage to his mouth and teeth. By seven in the morning the area outside the house was crowded with reporters and neighbours. The house and the scene of the crime were not secured, and neighbours, reporters and police were able to come and go freely. The house was sealed off by police at 3 p.m. that day.

The press were briefed by the coroner, Samuel Gerber, who examined the body. He gave the the reporters a few details of what he had seen. Mrs Sheppard's head had been wounded in 35 places; her watch had stopped at 3.15, which was likely to have been the time that she was murdered.

Dr Sheppard, sedated and on painkillers, was not left in peace at the Bay Village hospital. The Cleveland detectives paid him a visit and asked him probing questions about his relationship with Marilyn. Questions about the events of the early hours of that morning were met with Sheppard's answer that as he was asleep or unconscious for much of that time, he simply did not know what had happened. The session ended with Detective Schottke telling Sheppard that he suspected that he had killed his wife. Police were keen to question Sheppard further, but his brother Steve, who was a doctor of medicine, told them that he was too ill to talk. The detectives did manage to question Dr Sheppard in his hospital bed during a nine-hour session.

Meanwhile, the Cleveland newspapers were filled with speculation about the murder of Marilyn Sheppard. Marilyn Sheppard's funeral took place on 7 July, after which pressure from newspapers intensified even further, with their headlines announcing fictitious stories including Dr Sheppard's refusal to take a polygraph test.

Inquest findings

The three-day inquest into the death of Marilyn Sheppard began on 22 July. Presided over by Coroner Gerber, it was held in the auditorium of a local elementary school in order to accommodate the maximum number of newspaper, television and radio reporters.

The Sheppards' dinner guests, Mayor Houk and his wife and Officer Drenkhan all gave evidence. Sam Sheppard was interrogated by Gerber on the events of the night of his wife's murder. Questions were also asked about the state of the Sheppards' marriage, with Sheppard denying he had had a sexual relationship with a nurse, Susan Hayes. At the end of the proceedings on 25 July, when Sheppard's attorney William Corrigan attempted to make a statement and introduce his evidence, he was physically removed from the auditorium. That afternoon the newspapers appeared with pictures of Susan Hayes, accounts of the times that she and Dr Sheppard secretly met and the revelation that, according to Susan, the doctor had promised her that they would get married.

Sheppard arrested

At 10 a.m. on 30 July, after the appearance of newspaper headlines containing lurid accusations, Dr Sheppard was arrested at his father's house and taken, in handcuffs, to the City Hall, where the police displayed him to the reporters and television cameras who had been summoned there. Once he was in the county jail, pressure was relentless, with detectives taking shifts to interrogate Sheppard in twelve-hour stretches.

Bizarrely, Mayor Spencer Houk was arrested and questioned over the Marilyn Sheppard murder. After questioning, he was released.

The media frenzy over the murder of Marilyn Sheppard increased to fever pitch, with daily headlines, rumours and speculations about who was responsible. Almost all the newspapers were convinced of Dr Sheppard's guilt.

The trial

Following his indictment for murder on 17 August, the selection of jurors began on 18 October 1954. William Corrigan asked that the trial be postponed because of the unfavourable publicity the defendant had suffered; this request was turned down by the judge, Edward Blythin. The jurors were chosen; each one had their name, address and photograph reproduced in the press. The trial was to last for six weeks.

Witnesses appeared, including the Aherns, the Sheppards' dinner guests, who said that Marilyn had told them that the couple were considering a divorce, and that Marilyn also knew of Dr Sheppard's relationship with Susan Hayes. Spencer Houk and his wife Esther told similar tales of marital disharmony. The coroner, Dr Gerber, went over the interviews he had conducted with Dr Sheppard and stated that on examining the pillowcase covered in Marilyn's blood he had seen an impression that could only have been made by a surgical implement. The final prosecution witness was Susan Hayes, who spoke about her relationship with Dr Sheppard. She had met with him in secret, had once spent the night in bed with him. He had also discussed whether he should divorce his wife.

Witnesses for the defence, Sam Sheppard's brother, Dr Steve Sheppard, and his wife, described the Sheppards' marriage as a happy one. Medical experts described the extent of Sam Sheppard's injuries, with the aim of convincing the jury that these could not have been self-inflicted.

Sam Sheppard was then questioned. He denied that he had ever considered divorcing Marilyn. He admitted that he had slept with Susan Hayes and some minor intimacies with women other than Marilyn. Firmly and emphatically, he denied that he had killed his wife and deliberately injured himself to make it appear that he had been attacked. In closing statements the prosecution asked why, if there had been an intruder whom Dr Sheppard had witnessed, the intruder had not murdered Dr Sheppard as well in order to silence him. William Corrigan attacked the biased coverage in the newspapers. The jury went off to deliberate.

Dr Sheppard found guilty

On 21 December 1954 the jury returned. Their verdict was that Dr Sam Sheppard was guilty of second-degree murder. The defendant made a plea to the court that he was not guilty. Judge Blythin pronounced sentence: life imprisonment.

Appeals – and the case of Richard Eberling

The guilty verdict devastated Sam Sheppard's parents. In January 1955 his mother blew her brains out with a shotgun and his father died from internal bleeding due to advanced stomach cancer.

Sheppard's attorney, Corrigan, initiated a series of appeals against the conviction, arguing that there had been mistakes made by Judge Blythin and media publicity that was highly detrimental to the defence case and the defendant's reputation.

Five years after the guilty verdict on Dr Sheppard, a window washer, Richard Eberling, was charged with theft from houses during the course of his work. Stolen items were found in his apartment; they included a ring worn by Marilyn Sheppard. When police questioned him on this, he said he had stolen the ring from Marilyn Sheppard's sister-in-law – which was later confirmed as true. He added that he had been cleaning the windows of the Sheppard house a few days before the murder, during the course of which he had cut himself and spilled his blood down the Sheppards' staircase.

F Lee Bailey gets the conviction overturned

The Sheppard family asked an attorney, F Lee Bailey, if he could help them in the fight to free Dr Sheppard. In April 1963 Bailey went to the federal court and asked that Sheppard be freed, as his trial had been unfair because he had been denied constitutional rights. He raised, as William Corrigan had done, the matter of the pre-trial publicity and the way the jury had not been cut off from the influence of the media once the trial had started. Hearings began in 1964 and concluded on 16 July of that year when the federal district court judge, Carl Weinman, ordered that Dr Sheppard be released from jail immediately.

Conviction reinstated

In May 1965 Sheppard's case went to a federal appeals court, where the 1964 decision to overturn the conviction was reversed. Dr Sheppard was to remain free, but would appeal to the US Supreme Court as to whether the conviction should stand. In effect, this would be a retrial. On 6 June 1966 the Supreme Court ruled that Dr Sheppard had not received a fair trial due to the publicity surrounding his case. It was found that the jurors had not been sequestered properly and had themselves been the subject of the media to an excessive extent. The Supreme Court statement ended with the ruling that Sheppard be freed 'unless the State puts to him its charges again within a reasonable time'.

The second trial

The state *did* put to him its charges again. On 1 November 1966 the second trial of Dr Sheppard for the murder of his wife started. This time the media were not allowed anywhere within the court building and the jury's phone calls and exposure to news stories were controlled so as to eliminate their access to reports on the trial. The witnesses from the first trial reappeared: Spencer and Esther Houk, Officer Drenkhan, Detective Schottke, the Aherns and Dr Gerber for the prosecution; Jack Krakan – a bread-delivery man who had once seen Marilyn giving a strange man a door key and telling him not to let Sam see the key – and a criminal expert, Paul Kirk, for the defence. On 16 November Dr Sam Sheppard was found not guilty of murdering his wife.

Subsequent events

Dr Sheppard remarried and worked as a doctor briefly before he was served with a malpractice suit, after which he retired from medicine and earned a living as a wrestler. He became a heavy drinker and died of liver failure in April 1970. He was 46 years old.

Since the death of Dr Sheppard his son, Sam Reese Sheppard, had made attempts to find out who killed his mother. Dr Sheppard's body was exhumed in 1997 and DNA samples were taken, which concluded that blood found at the murder scene was not his. In 1998 the Ohio Supreme Court ruled that Sam Reese Sheppard could sue the State of Ohio for the wrongful imprisonment of Dr Sheppard. In 2000 a civil trial took place that lasted for ten weeks, in which new forensic evidence was presented following the exhumation of Marilyn Sheppard for DNA and other tests. The jury's verdict was that they did not find Dr Sheppard innocent; therefore the State of Ohio was not liable to pay Sam Reese Sheppard damages.

Suspects

If Sam Sheppard didn't kill Marilyn, then who did?

Those who fall under suspicion are:

Spencer Houk

The Mayor of Bay Village was initially suspected by police and was questioned by them at length. The bread-delivery man, Jack Krakan, told F Lee Bailey that one morning he had seen Marilyn and Spencer Houk kissing, but Bailey did not produce this as evidence in court. Bailey also knew that Sam Sheppard had been hypnotised in order to glean any further information about the murder; under hypnosis he recalled lying injured on the ground, having been assaulted, and seeing a foot walk away that had a limp. Spencer Houk had a limp.

Richard Eberling

Richard Eberling, the window cleaner who was found in possession of Marilyn Sheppard's stolen ring, died in prison in 1998, where he had been serving a life sentence for another murder. Before he died he confessed to fellow prisoners that he had raped and murdered Marilyn Sheppard.

Suspicious deaths litter the life of Richard Eberling. Born Richard Lenardic, he was adopted by the Eberling family. In 1946, when he was sixteen, he had an argument with his foster father about whether he could change his surname to that of his new family. Shortly after, Mr Eberling died, apparently from taking the wrong dosage of his medicine.

In 1956 Eberling was in a car crash in which his female passenger was killed.

In 1962 the sister of a woman that Eberling would later be convicted of killing was violently murdered.

In 1984 Eberling was found guilty of aggravated murder after the death of Ethel May Durkin after she fell down in her home (Durkin's sister was murdered in 1962). DNA samples from Eberling's body could solve this mystery once and for all.

The Murder of Janice Weston

Janice Weston, who was known by the maiden name of Janice Wright at work, was 36 at the time of her murder, had studied law at Manchester University and then been employed by Herbert Oppenheimer, Nathan and Vandyck, where she specialised in company law, advising businesses on takeovers and investments.

While working for that company she had formed a close relationship with one of their clients, Heinz Isner, who was in his late sixties when they met, and was an executive at the Mettoy company, which manufactured toy cars. When Isner's wife died in 1975 he courted Janice, even proposing marriage to her, which she declined. On Isner's death in 1977 Janice was left antiques and shares worth £140,000.

In 1981 Janice Weston became a partner in the prestigious firm Charles Russell & Co. In June 1982 she married Tony Weston, a wealthy property developer and another Oppenheimer client. They bought a large manor house in Cambridgeshire with the intention that Tony would turn it into flats, one of which would be for their own use. The couple lived in a flat in Addison Avenue in Holland Park, an exclusive area of west London.

Saturday, 10 September 1983

On Saturday, 10 September 1983, Janice went into the office. Tony Weston was in France over that weekend, concluding the purchase of a château for himself and Janice to use as a holiday home. Returning to the flat in Holland Park, Janice appears to have eaten a meal and then left the flat at around 4 p.m. Unusually, she did not take her handbag. She had driven off in the bad weather – it was very rainy that day – in her silver Alfa Romeo and headed up the A1. It is possible that she was going to stay in the manor house, but unlikely as it had not yet been furnished or decorated and there were no beds to sleep in. Perhaps Janice had been called out by someone, possibly a client, at short notice. Police have speculated as to why she drove out to that place at that time, but have failed to come up with any answers. At some point she had either stopped her car for some purpose – possibly to change a tyre – or been forced off the road. She had then been violently attacked and bludgeoned about the head with a car jack, which police found in a field near the layby.

Discovery of the body

At 9 a.m. on Sunday, 11 September 1983, a cyclist who was out riding on the A1 at Huntingdon, Cambridgeshire, stopped at a layby and walked down into a ditch in order to empty his bladder. He was stopped in his tracks by what he saw: the grievously battered body of a woman, still wearing an expensive gold watch (the watch had stopped at 1.29) and wedding ring, lying in the open air as if she had been thrown down there – no attempt had been made to conceal the body. Police were called and arrived on the scene accompanied by a Home Office pathologist, Dr Ian Hill, who examined the body and estimated the time of death as between 9 p.m. on the Saturday and 2 a.m. that day. The body was not identified as being that of Janice Weston until Monday, when she failed to turn up for work and her sister had been contacted to find out where she might be. Also on Monday, Tony Weston returned to London. The next day the Alfa Romeo, its seats and dashboard covered in bloodstains, was found in Redhill Street, Camden Town, London. Janice's purse, containing £35 in cash, was found intact in the vehicle. Also in the car was an overnight bag containing clothing.

Possible murder scenarios

Police investigating appealed for anyone who had had sightings of the Alfa Romeo at any time or any persons seen on the layby to come forward. The officer in charge of the murder enquiry, Detective Chief Superintendent Len

Bradley of Cambridgeshire CID, said the attack on Janice had been savage and that the injuries would indicate that the killer 'went berserk'. Janice Weston had not been sexually assaulted, nor did it appear that she had been robbed. It is likely that she put up a struggle – as she had a black belt in judo, she may well have injured her attacker.

Police were puzzled as to why she had driven out there, and established that her journey was an act that was out of character – she never visited the manor house alone, never drank alcohol and drove (she had drunk some wine at home before she drove off), and that it was unheard of for her to leave home without her handbag.

Possible scenarios developed:

- Janice Weston had been forced to leave her flat by her killer, possibly as a plan to kidnap her and hold her to ransom; he then drove with her on the A1 and murdered her

- Janice's car was stopped somewhere on her journey and a man forcibly entered it

- Janice stopped the vehicle to change a tyre, and, while doing this herself or having asked a passer-by for assistance, she was then attacked

- Janice stopped and gave a hitchhiker a lift; he forced her to stop at the layby and then killed her.

Other facts emerged that raised further questions. The spare tyre from the Alfa Romeo was missing – where had it gone and who had taken it? More bizarrely, mid-morning on the Sunday when the body was found a man went to a garage in Royston, Cambridgeshire, about twenty miles from where Janice's body was found, and bought a set of car registration plates with the identical number to the Alfa Romeo – KMR 769X. He paid in cash and left as if in a hurry, without collecting his change. The man has never been traced.

Sightings were reported of a man seen standing by the silver Alfa Romeo at the layby at around a quarter to midnight while the bonnet and boot of the car were open. The description of this man – between five foot nine and six foot tall, with brown hair and in his late thirties or early forties – match that of the man who bought the number plates. Efforts to trace this man proved fruitless.

Police investigate

Other factors emerged. Janice Weston's work involved her in legal matters concerning industrial espionage. At the time of her murder she was working on a book on data protection and security. Police researching whether there were any links between this work and the murder were unable to draw any firm conclusions.

Tony Weston was held by police in December 1983 and interviewed about the murder. He was able to prove that he had been in France for the entire weekend and was completely eliminated as a suspect. The relatives of Heinz Isner were questioned, as his step-granddaughter had, in the High Court, legally contested the will and the legacy that had been left to Janice Weston. They had absolutely no connection with the murder, either.

At the inquest in April 1984, the pathologist Dr Hill provided further details of his findings, including a more accurate estimate of the time of death as being around midnight. The jury at that inquest returned a verdict of unlawful killing.

Further developments

In 1990 it was reported that the murder enquiry had been reopened following information received from a convicted killer, Robert Delgado. Delgado claimed that a London criminal called Charles Fowler (police had no record of his ever existing) had kidnapped Janice Weston and had then beaten her to death. Delgado also claimed to have killed Fowler and dumped his body in a reservoir. Police investigated but could not confirm Delgado's claims.

In 1994 there was further speculation that Weston may have been killed by Alan Conner, a suspected serial murderer who committed suicide by hanging himself in Brampton, Cambridgeshire, close to where Janice's body was found. Conner is believed to have raped and murdered at least five other women. DNA evidence that he left on his other victims was not found on Janice's body or in the Alfa Romeo.

The case remains unsolved.

The Murder of Caroline Dickinson

The rape and murder of a British schoolgirl called Caroline Dickinson in the dormitory of an *auberge de jeunesse*, or youth hostel, in the picturesque village of Pleine-Fougeres in Breton, France, shocked parents throughout Britain and France. The thirteen-year-old girl from Launceston, Cornwall, was one of forty students accompanied by five teachers who were on an end-of-term school trip in 1996.

Caroline had been sharing a dormitory on the first floor with four other girls; because she wanted to share a room with her friends, a mattress was put on the floor for her. The other girls slept on two bunk beds. Of the four girls sharing the room with Caroline, three had been asleep during the vicious attack, and one had heard the sound of Caroline's feet banging on the floor beside the mattress on which she had been sleeping, but thought that her friend had been having a nightmare.

Caroline's body, clad in the pyjamas that she had gone to sleep in, was found when one of the girls reached out to wake her up at 8 a.m. on Thursday, 18 July, and found that her body was lifeless and cold. Police and ambulance staff arrived and it was ascertained that Caroline was dead. There had been no sign of any break-in at the hostel, and a security guard was employed at the front door to ensure the safety of visitors staying there.

After the murder, French police sealed off the village and went door-to-door with an identikit picture of a curly-haired man aged about forty. This picture was withdrawn after a few days and it is not known who it was intended to portray. Detectives accompanied by translators began systematically interviewing Caroline's schoolmates – five boys and 34 girls – and the teachers who had accompanied them.

The French judicial system

In the United Kingdom it is the police and in the USA the police, District Attorney and FBI who are responsible for investigating crime. France has a different system: the police act on the orders of a local magistrate known as the *juge d'instruction*. This person conducts the investigation along the lines that he or she thinks best, and if the case comes to trial will be the judge presiding over it.

Patrice Pade

On Saturday, 20 July, police arrested a French vagrant, a former abbatoir worker named Patrice Pade. The tattooed forty-year-old tramp had been seen in Pleine-Fougeres a few days before Caroline's murder and since then had been seen begging in a neighbouring village. Pade had a criminal record that included rape, sexual assault on a teenage girl and indecent exposure. While Pade was in custody, it was confirmed that on the night of 17 July both the doors of the hostel had been left unlocked and therefore it would not have been difficult for an intruder to enter and leave the building unnoticed.

Pade was interrogated for several days about the Dickinson murder, and was then taken to the hostel to stage a reconstruction of events. He then confessed that he had raped and murdered Caroline Dickinson. As they believed they had a confession, police immediately ordered that the manhunt be discontinued. Gerard Zaug, the examining magistrate in charge of the Dickinson enquiry, addressed a press conference and told the media of the arrest of Pade and of the subsequent confession. He told the gathered reporters, 'With this kind of individual, from the moment he spotted his prey, nothing could stop him. Once he got this crime into his mind, it was inevitable.'

It turned out that Zaug was completely mistaken about the mindset and guilt of Patrice Pade. Specimens taken from Pade showed that his DNA did not match that found in the semen left inside Caroline's body. Pade, therefore, was not guilty and his confession had been false.

On 6 August this startling news was released to the public. Zaug then ordered the DNA samples to be retested; police on the case told the press that an accomplice of Pade may have raped her, after which Pade suffocated her. Incredibly, they had suggested that *two* men had been involved. In an attempt to prove this theory a known associate of Pade was arrested on 14 August and his DNA tested. The results were negative.

Residents of Pleine-Fougeres and surrounding villages were angry at police and felt that they had bungled the investigation, allowing the murderer to remain on the loose. The fact that the investigators had got it wrong was very distressing for Caroline's parents, John and Sue Dickinson, and for Caroline's schoolmates in Launceton. On 16 August a five-strong team of French detectives arrived in Launceton to question members of the school party that had stayed in the hostel. It was also revealed that the two male teachers in the party as well as the coach drivers had given DNA samples to police and had been eliminated as suspects. However, none of the five schoolboys in the party had been tested, and Devon and Cornwall Police now requested that they be so.

The modern means of testing DNA is by swabbing inside the mouth for saliva and cells containing the genetic component. The schoolboys' samples were duly taken and then flown to a forensic laboratory in Rennes, France, where tests on them proved negative. Superintendent Stephen Pearce of the Devon and Cornwall Police urged that French police systematically test the DNA of the male residents of Pleine-Fougeres, adding that this was a matter for them to decide.

On 23 August it was reported that a man from St Malo in Brittany had been arrested on suspicion of raping three women in the town in June and August 1996. Furthermore, the suspect had confessed to these crimes. A sample of his DNA was taken and compared with that of the semen left at the scene of Caroline's murder. Results were negative. For a second time, the French authorities had identified a suspect in the murder of Caroline Dickinson, only to have DNA tests refute their original statement. Whoever had raped and murdered Caroline Dickinson was still free.

Subsequent events

Over a year after Caroline's murder, Gerard Zaug was removed from the case and replaced by Renaud van Ruymbeke. For a year a fifteen-man squad of police had worked on the case and interviewed over three hundred people. The court in the nearby town of Rennes, who had requested Zaug's dismissal, ordered police to test the DNA of all males between the ages of 15 and 35 in Pleine-Fougeres. This mass DNA testing had been urged by

Caroline's parents and by the police in Cornwall; Zaug had for some reason been unwilling to do this. The mass testing went ahead, with four residents of the village refusing to give samples.

Further pieces of information emerged long after the event. In January 1998 Nick Ward, one of the teachers on the school trip, revealed that he had seen a man who may have been an intruder outside Caroline's dormitory door on the night of the murder. He had been too frightened to admit this at the time, and had felt considerable guilt ever since. Ward helped French police construct a Photofit of this man, who had a similar appearance to a man that Caroline's school friends had seen in the vicinity of the hostel before her murder.

By August 1998 the new investigator in charge, Jean-Pierre Michel, said he had a short list of 21 suspects and was certain that Caroline's killer was one of them. He promised a conviction within six months.

In October of that year a man from Frome, Somerset, was arrested as a suspect. The 41-year-old businessman apparently was similar in appearance to the Photofit based on Nick Ward's description of him. DNA samples were taken from him and he was eliminated.

By December 1998 the man in the Photofit was identified by a woman who had been raped in Nancy, France, in May 1993 as being the man who had attacked her. This man resembled a caveman and drove a Harley-Davidson motorcycle. A man answering this description was arrested in Marseilles in December 1998 and tested for DNA, but, the test proving negative, he was released from custody.

In September 1999 Yves Godard, a doctor from Brittany, and his wife and young children disappeared under mysterious circumstances. Dr Godard resembled the Photofit; samples of his DNA were found and tested, and proved negative.

The Dickinson investigation has proved to be a cycle of expectation that a newly arrested suspect is the killer, only to be followed by those expectations being dashed by the result of a DNA test.

The murder enquiry team in France was disbanded on the fourth anniversary of the murder – 18 July 2000. The *juge d'instruction*, Francis Debons, said the case remained open, but that the best they could hope for was 'a stroke of luck'. Caroline's parents have not given up their hope of seeing the murderer brought to justice.

Bibliography

1 Elizabeth Short – 'The Black Dahlia'

Ellroy, James, *The Black Dahlia* (Century, 1988)

Gilmore, John, *Severed: The True Story of the Black Dahlia Murder* (Amok, 1998)

Knowlton, Janice, and Newton, Michael, *Daddy Was the Black Dahlia Killer* (Pocket Books, 1995)

Webb, Jack, *The Badge* (Prentice-Hall, 1958)

2 Mary Pinchot Meyer

Burleigh, Nina, *A Very Private Woman – The Life And Unsolved Murder of Presidential Mistress Mary Meyer* (Bantam, 1998)

Leary, Timothy, *Flashbacks: A Personal & Cultural History of an Era* (GP Putnam's Sons, 1983)

Mangold, Tom, *Cold Warrior – James Jesus Angleton* (Simon & Schuster, 1991)

Reeves, Richard, *President Kennedy – Profile of Power* (Simon & Schuster, 1993)

Rosenbaum, Ron, *Travels With Dr. Death* (Viking Penguin, 1991)

3 The Bible John Murders

Crow, Alan and Samson, Peter, *Bible John – Hunt for a Killer* (First Press, 1996)

Forbes, George, *Bible John and Such Bad Company* (Lang Syne, 1982)

Stoddart, Charles, *Bible John – Search for a Sadist* (Paul Harris, 1980)

4   The Zodiac Killer

Davis, Howard, *The Manson/Zodiac Connection* (Pen Power Publications, 1998)

Graysmith, Robert, *Zodiac* (St Martins Press, 1976)

Penn, Gareth, *Times Seventeen* (Foxglove Press, 1987)

5   Helen Smith

Arnot, Richard, *Arabian Nightmare* (Allen & Unwin, 1999)

Foot, Paul, *The Helen Smith Story* (Fontana, 1983)

Robertson, Geoffrey, *The Justice Game* (Chatto & Windus, 1998)

Wilson, Gordon, and Harrison, Dave, *Inquest: Helen Smith – The Whole Truth?* (Methuen, 1983)

6   Karen Silkwood

Kohn, Howard, *Who Killed Karen Silkwood?* (Summit Books, 1981)

Rashke, Richard, *The Killing of Karen Silkwood* (Houghton Mifflin, 1981)

7   Hilda Murrell

Anonymous. *Hilda Murrell: A Death in the Private Sector* (*Lobster*, Issue 16, 1988)

Cook, Judith, *Who Killed Hilda Murrell?* (New English Library, 1985)

Murray, Gary, *Enemies of the State* (Simon & Schuster, 1993)

Smith, Graham, *Death of a Rosegrower* (Cecil Woolf, 1985)

8   PC Keith Blakelock

Gifford, Anthony (Lord Gifford QC) (Chair of Inquiry), *The Broadwater Farm Inquiry* (First Report) (Broadwater Farm Inquiry, 1986)

Gifford, Anthony (Lord Gifford QC) (Chair of Inquiry), *Broadwater Farm Inquiry* (Second Report) (Karia Press, 1989)

Rose, David, *A Climate of Fear* (Bloomsbury, 1992)

9   Rachel Nickell

Britton, Paul, *The Jigsaw Man* (Transworld, 1997)

Fielder, Mike, *The Murder of Rachel Nickell* (Blake, 2000)
Handscombe, André, *The Last Thursday in July* (Arrow, 1997)
Stagg, Colin, and Kessler, David, *Who Really Killed Rachel?* (Aspire, 1999)

10   JonBenét Ramsey

Hodges, Andrew G, *A Mother Gone Bad* (Village House, 1998)
McLean, Linda Edison, *JonBenét's Mother: The Tragedy and The Truth* (McClain, 1998)
Ramsey, John and Patsy, *The Death of Innocence* (Thomas Nelson, 2000)
Schiller, Laurence, *Perfect Town: JonBenét and the City of Boulder* (HarperCollins, 1999)
Singular, Stephen, *Presumed Guilty* (New Millennium Press, 1999)
Smith, Carlton, *Death of a Little Princess* (St Martin's, 1997)
Stobie, Jane Gray, *JonBenét's Gift* (Blue Balloon Press, 1999)
Thomas, Steve, *JonBenét: Inside the Ramsey Murder Investigation* (St Martin's, 2000)
Von Duyke, Eleanor, *A Little Girl's Dream – A JonBenét Ramsey Story* (Windsor House, 1998)
Wecht, Cyril, *Who Killed JonBenét Ramsey?* (Onyx, 1998)

11   Tupac Shakur and Biggie Smalls

Alexander, Frank, and Cuda, Heidi Siegmund, *Got Your Back – The Life of a Bodyguard in the Hardcore World of Gangsta Rap* (St Martin's Press 1998)
Lee, Malik Jr, with Williams, Frank, *Chosen By Fate – My Life Inside Death Row Records* (Dove Books, 1997)
Ro, Ronin, *Have Gun Will Travel – The Spectacular Rise & Violent Fall of Death Row Records* (Q, 1998)
Scott, Kathy, *The Killing of Tupac Shakur* (Huntington Press, 1997)
Shaw, William, *Westsiders – Stories of Boys in the Hood* (Bloomsbury, 1999)
Vibe (Editors of), *Tupac Shakur* (Plexus, 1997)
White, Armand, *Rebel for the Hell of it – The Life of Tupac Shakur* (Q, 1997)

Virgin

Look out for other true crime titles from Virgin Publishing

THE LAST VICTIM
by Jason Moss

As part of a college assignment, ambitious student Jason Moss set himself the challenge of exploring the minds of the most depraved men in the American prison system – men named Dahmer, Manson and Gacy. Moss's reasearch led him to pose as the perfect victim, writing letters to the infamous killers, with the focus on his growing relationship with the fascinating 'killer clown', John Wayne Gacy. Initial letters progress to weekly telephone calls and result ultimately in an invitation to Gacy's prison domain, recalled in nightmarish detail. The secure middle-class world from which Jason originated slips away, as he is dragged into the underworld inhabited by Death Row convicts.

£5.99   ISBN 0 7535 0398 0

CROSSING TO KILL
by Simon Whitechapel

'Juarez is the ideal place to kill a woman, because you're certain to get away with it. The failure to solve these killings is turning the city into a Mecca for homicidal maniacs' (founder, Citizens Committee Against Violence). Since 1993 over 180 women have been killed in Ciudad Juarez, a Mexican border town notorious for its pollution and overcrowding. The police continue to arrest suspects, but the killing won't stop. Authorities suspect that killers are coming from all over Mexico – and the USA – to kill with impunity. This is the first detailed portrait of these astonishing unsolved crimes.

£6.99   ISBN 0 7535 0496 0

ADDICTED TO MURDER
by Mikaela Sitford

It was one of the most sensational murder trials of modern times. Could Dr Harold Shipman, a well-loved Tameside GP, have murdered fifteen women in his care? Had the people of Hyde been treated by Britain's biggest ever serial killer? And how many more did he kill? This gripping, horrifying read covers the whole story, from his birth to his eventual conviction: how Dr Shipman was able to get away with the crimes for so long; the events in his background that led to cold-blooded murder; and the inside account – in a world exclusive – of an earlier police investigation that failed to bring Shipman to justice. By the journalist who broke the story.

£5.99   ISBN 0 7535 0445 6

LONE WOLF
by Pan Pantziarka

In 1996 Thomas Hamilton calmly drives to Dunblane Primary School, makes his way into the gym and proceeds to murder 16 children before turning the gun on himself. In Chicago 1999 a gunman goes on a 36-hour rampage, attacking Jews, blacks and other minorities in a hate-filled spree which ends in his own death. Other cases occur with frightening regularity over the summer of 1999, signs of a chilling new trend of brutal and indiscriminate killing. Mass murderers. Spree killers. Mad men. Who are these lone killers who maim and murder at random? What drives them to turn on friends, family and perfect strangers? Is there any way to stop this epidemic of violence that devastates entire communities?

£6.99   ISBN 0 7535 0437 5

KILLERS ON THE LOOSE
by Antonio Mendoza

According to an FBI Behavioural Unit study, serial killing has climbed to an 'almost epidemic proportion'. In the UK there are up to four unidentified predators, with many more travelling around Continental Europe. Authorities estimate that there are between 35 and 50 serial killers on the loose in the USA – and new reports of suspected killers are constantly surfacing all over the globe. This is the first look at serial killers at large, from one of the world's foremost authorities. Antonio Mendoza runs the Internet Crime Archives www.mayhem.net

£6.99   ISBN 0 7535 0442 1

The best in true crime from Virgin Publishing:

Please send me the books I have ticked above.

Name ....

Address ....

....

....

.... Post code......................

Send to: Cash Sales, Virgin Publishing, Thames Wharf Studios, Rainville Road, London W6 9HA

US customers: for prices and details of how to order books for delivery by mail, call 1-800-805-1083.

Please enclose a cheque or postal order, made payable to **Virgin Publishing**, to the value of the books you have ordered plus postage and packing costs as follows:

UK and BFPO – £1.00 for the first book, 50p for the second book and 30p for each subsequent book to a maximum of £3.00;

Overseas (including Republic of Ireland) – £2.00 for the first book, £1.00 for the second book and 50p for each subsequent book.

We accept all major credit cards, including VISA, ACCESS/MASTERCARD, AMEX, DINERS CLUB, SWITCH, SOLO, and DELTA. Please write your card number and expiry date here:

....

Please allow up to 28 days for delivery.

Signature ....